Crossings

Crossings

THE GREAT TRANSATLANTIC
MIGRATIONS, 1870 – 1914

Walter Nugent

BLOOMINGTON   *Indiana*
University   INDIANAPOLIS
Press

© 1992 by Walter Nugent

All rights reserved

The paper used in this publication meets the minimum requirements of American
National Standard for Information Sciences—Permanence of Paper for Printed
Library Materials, ANSI Z39.48-1984.
$\otimes^{TM}$

Manufactured in the United States of America

Library of Congress Cataloging-in-Publication Data
Nugent, Walter T. K.
    Crossings : the great transatlantic migrations, 1870–1914 / Walter
Nugent.
        p.   cm.
    Includes bibliographical references and index.
    ISBN 0-253-34140-X (cloth)
    1. United States—Emigration and immigration.   2. Europe—
Emigration and immigration.   3. Emigration and immigration.
I. Title.
JV6465.N84   1992   92-7156
304.8′094—dc20

1 2 3 4 5   96 95 94 93 92

For Suellen

CONTENTS

CONTENTS

LIST OF MAPS

LIST OF TABLES

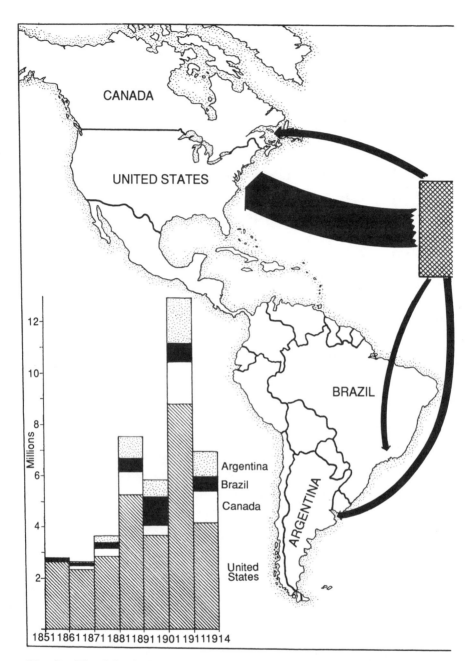

Map 1. The Atlantic Region and Its Migrations, 1871–1914 (*Map by Norman Pounds*)

Arrows indicate the relative size of migration from and to the various donor and receiver countries ("Width of migration lines," bottom center, indicates numbers of migrants). The bar graph at bottom left indicates the share of immigrants absorbed by the four major receivers, by decade, 1851–1914. The bar graph at bottom right indicates the share of out-migrants who left the major European countries, 1871–1914.

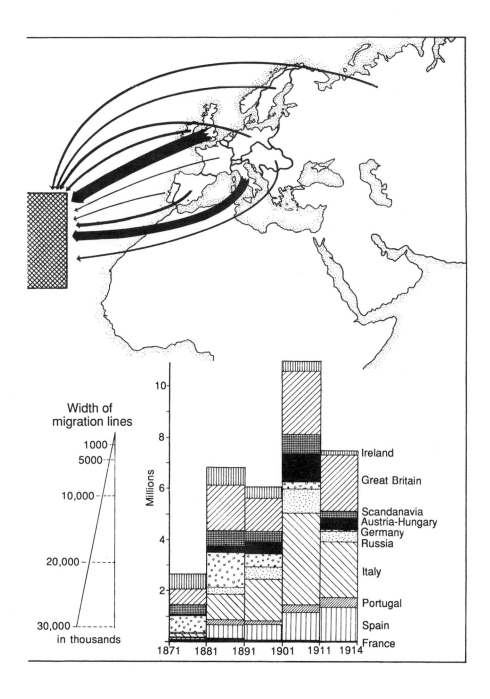

Width of
migration lines

1000
5000
10,000
20,000
30,000
in thousands

Millions

10
8
6
4
2

1871 1881 1891 1901 1911 1914

Ireland
Great Britain
Scandanavia
Austria-Hungary
Germany
Russia
Italy
Portugal
Spain
France

PREFACE

Sometime in the mid-1970s I read Fernand Braudel's *The Mediterranean and the Mediterranean World in the Age of Philip II* and was appropriately stunned.[1] I compare the encounter to my first hearing of Mahler's First Symphony, by the Chicago Symphony under Bruno Walter in 1959, and to turning a corner at the Museum of Modern Art in New York in 1952 and suddenly confronting Picasso's *Guernica*. Encountering Braudel, however, takes days rather than moments; and, moreover, his art is in prose, which I can work in. The idea dawned on me, as someone who had written about the late nineteenth century, that if, as Braudel demonstrated, the Mediterranean was the brilliant center of the late sixteenth-century world, surely the Atlantic was the center of the late nineteenth, and the Atlantic in the 1880s the most remarkable time and place of all. Why not, then, a book in the Braudelian mode on the transatlantic world of the 1880s? Why not a book that treated Europe, North America, South America, and Africa as a regional unity, sharing demographic characteristics, an unprecedentedly large migration, domestic and public architecture and city planning, nineteenth-century liberal ideas about political economy, immense frontiers of settlement and exploitation, and hubristic imperialism?

Alas, the 1980s have come and gone, and my book on the rich world of the 1880s remains unwritten, and will remain so. What would have been the final section, on why Europeans and their descendants successfully settled New World frontiers yet ultimately lost the empires they were so busy building in the 1880s, is glimpsed at in a recently published essay.[2] What would have been the first two chapters, on "natural demography" (fertility and mortality) and on migration in the Atlantic region, have become this book. Suggestions, but only that, of the economic side of the rich world of the 1880s are included; they remain to be explored, and in terms more definite and clear than simply "modernization." Here, at any rate, is the demographic mosaic of the transatlantic region from 1870 to 1914. My apologies to the spirit of Braudel for not accomplishing more.

My many debts to people and institutions who helped me now stretch out over ten years. I thank the staffs of many libraries, including the Library of Congress, the National Archives, the British Library, the University of California at Berkeley (the main library and the Bancroft Library), the University of California at Los Angeles, the University of Washington's Suzzallo Library, the University of Iowa, the University of Wisconsin, the Latter Day Saints' Genealogical Society of Utah in Salt Lake City, and most especially Indiana University and the University of Notre Dame, with particular thanks to the latter's Interlibrary Loan service. Three extended stays at the Henry E. Huntington Library in

San Marino, California, twice as a fellowship recipient, enriched me and this work greatly. Hamburg University granted me scholar-in-residence status in 1980 and 1982, which allowed me to work in its libraries and also in the excellent Hamburg Staatsarchiv; I am especially indebted to Professor Dr. Günter Moltmann and Dr. Hans-Jürgen Grabbe.

For a wide range of references, photocopies, offprints, encouragement, and tips without which this book would have taken even longer, I thank Willi Paul Adams, Klaus Bade, Sam Baily, Dino Cinel, Charlotte Erickson, Paula Fass, Donna Gabaccia, Jim Gregory, Dirk Hoerder, Romuald Kudlinski, John V. Lombardi, Frederick C. Luebke, Fred Pike, Bruno Ramirez, Martin Ridge, Dorothy Ross, Michael Rozbicki, Ingrid Winther Scobie, the late James R. Scobie, Wlodzimierz Siwinski, Eleanor Turk, Rudy Vecoli, and Birgit Wetzel. For opportunities to speak on this topic I thank the Huntington Library Seminar (October 1985), the Israel Association for American Studies (January 1986), the Organization of American Historians (April 1986), the UC-Berkeley History Department Colloquium (March 1987), and the Kenneth B. Keating Lectureship at Tel Aviv University (October 1987). Attentive listeners on those occasions forced me to think more clearly on many points.

Professor Norman J. G. Pounds, my friend and former colleague, cartographer as well as historian-geographer, prepared the maps. I am especially fortunate to have benefited from his skill and knowledge.

Several people read earlier versions and graciously commented: Charlotte Erickson, Dirk Hoerder, Walter Kamphoefner, Peter Marschalck, James C. Riley, Robert Swierenga, and Linda Pritchard. I, not they, am of course responsible for the style and content of this book. Of enormous help were my research assistants at Notre Dame: Bruce Smith, Bradley Young, and Drew Buscareno.

Most of all I thank Suellen Hoy, my editor of the first resort, counselor, and sustainer.

Part I

The Atlantic Region and Its Population

1

WHAT THIS BOOK IS ABOUT

The primary purpose of this book is to pull together in one place the main contours of population change in the Atlantic region during the 1870–1914 period. That region, for present purposes, includes Europe, North America, South America, and to a slight degree Africa. All of the societies of the region experienced natural demographic growth, that is, more births than deaths, but at widely varying rates. They also experienced change through migration, some as donors of people, others as receivers, and a few as both.

The forty-five years between 1870 and the outbreak of World War I were the preeminent age of international, especially transatlantic, migration. During that period a unique set of factors operated to promote migration: steam-powered transportation, an absence (compared with periods before and since) of legal and political restraints, potential agricultural development on several New World frontiers, and industrialization, hence a demand for non-farm workers both in Europe and in North America—all of which helped extend long-standing European migration patterns to transatlantic distances. Migration had taken place before 1870 within Europe and from Europe to other parts of the world but, thanks to railroads and steamships, the scale of the post-1870 period expanded into something altogether larger. Migration continued after 1914, but it became much reduced because of World War I, the restrictive laws passed by several countries in the 1920s, and the economic depression of the 1930s. Between 1870 and 1914, tens of millions of Europeans and others crossed and recrossed international borders and sailed the North and South Atlantic, often many times. The cumulative picture of movement is one of a swarming or churning of people back and forth across the Atlantic highway, fed by growing railroad networks on either side of it.

Library shelves have groaned for years with the weight of writings on transatlantic migration, and one may well ask why even a slim volume such as this need be added to the collection. The answer is that much of that collection consists of writing about a single migrating group rather than about many or all of them. Much of the writing done by Europeans concerns the European background, often in a single country; much of what Americans (North and South) have written concerns the American destination. Immigration historians are familiar with the injunction made in 1960 by the English historian, Frank This-tlethwaite, to tear down the "salt-water curtain," which separated the European and American sides of the subject. "The best hope of a new advance," he wrote, "is to take a new look at the subject *as a whole* . . . we should try to think neither of emigrants nor immigrants, but of migrants, and to treat the process of migra-tion as a complete sequence of experiences whereby the individual moves from one social identity to another."[1]

In the ensuing thirty years, enough scholars have heeded Thistlethwaite to make it no longer satisfactory for a monograph to leave out one side or the other. Most studies published in the 1970s and 1980s, either in Europe or in America, consider both sides. But the curtain has yet to be torn down com-pletely. Only recently have immigration historians attempted to connect migra-tion within a country to migration within Europe across national boundaries and then to transatlantic migration.[2] Latin America, which was a major destina-tion for many south Europeans, seldom gets considered as part of the region because North American and North European scholars have given most of their attention to traffic between their own subregions. This book tries to integrate Latin America—especially Brazil and Argentina, its major receiving countries— into the regional picture.

In the United States, not surprisingly, most discussions of migration during the pre–World War I period have been about migration to the United States itself. Such myopia has inhibited an understanding of how migration to the United States differed from and resembled migration elsewhere in the region. This book does not wholly avoid a focus on the United States, implicitly and often explicitly. In fact the study began with the United States as, in a sense, the dependent variable in the regional story, and the book retains that focus. Hence this is not comparative history of the purest kind. Each migrant group, source, or destination does not get equal time. But the study does, at least, place the American story in the context of the entire Atlantic region, looking at it along with a dozen or more other countries in terms of their natural demographic increase and their respective roles within the Atlantic migration pool.

Even so, the inclusion of Europe and both North and South America does not tell the entire world story. Migration also took place from Europe to Australia, New Zealand, and South Africa, and much less successfully (because less mas-sively) to European colonies in Africa and Asia. Besides that, some migration of Chinese, Japanese, and other Asian peoples to North America also occurred. I hope I will be forgiven for not including those migrations in order to focus on the Atlantic region as a whole and by itself, especially since the numbers of migrants crossing that ocean were far greater than those crossing the Pacific or the Indian.[3]

At the same time, however, the opportunity arises to take a look at two sets of ideas for which the demographic description can provide empirical proof or disproof. Examining them is my secondary purpose. The first is the notion or conviction that American history has been exceptional, that is, substantially and even morally different from the histories of other national societies either in Europe or elsewhere in the New World. Although demographic arguments will probably never change anyone's moral stance, they do force a reexamination of exceptionalism in a new way. This book, from that standpoint, is a demographic test of American exceptionalism. The result, put most briefly, is that nothing was ever really exceptional but an abundance of accessible farmland (the frontiers of settlement), and even that had disappeared by 1915.

The second set of ideas is modernization theory, the rather amorphous body of thought that says that societies proceed from traditional to modern forms to arrive at high material and cultural levels such as now exist in Western Europe, North America, and most recently Japan. It also argues that "Less Developed Countries" (LDCs) are undergoing the modernizing process right now. While modernization theory is difficult to confirm or deny for many reasons, it does have a demographic corollary—the theory of demographic transition. That too has been expressed in different ways, but the central idea is that societies proceed from high levels of both fertility and mortality (traditional) to low levels of fertility and mortality (modern). In that blunt sense, transition did happen. But did it take place in the sequence that many of its proponents have claimed? Comparative population history provides a generally negative answer. To focus the discussion, however, some definitions are in order, after which the story of transatlantic migration from 1870 to 1914 can proceed.

America an Exception?

Several important forms of American exceptionalism have reverberated through American culture in the past, and still do. They share, most basically, the belief that the United States is and always has been not only different from other societies but also unique, "better," and exempt from others' corruptions and mundane concerns.[4] Besides this main theme, exceptionalism has also been related to class structure and to the United States' stance toward the rest of the world. The principal theme of uniqueness and special national character is deeply embedded in American culture. Its roots go back to the Puritans' idea of a "City on a Hill" as well as to their missionary "Errand into the Wilderness," the sense of having made a compact directly with God, or of having been singularly chosen by God. As the writer Frances FitzGerald put it: "Americans see history as a straight line and themselves standing at the cutting edge of it as representatives for all mankind." In a similar vein, the historian David W. Noble wrote: "From the Puritans through the writings of Charles Beard, American historians have interpreted their culture as if it were standing apart, independent and unique from the experience of other nations."[5]

Nationalist rhetoric from the Revolution and the War of 1812, reiterated by the Populists of the 1890s, celebrated the exempt status of American yeomen and mechanics from the sordid tyrannies of Europe. George Bancroft wrote that American history was the visible working-out of "the Will of Providence." Frederick Jackson Turner explained to Progressive Era Americans (and he spoke most directly to historians then and since) that America was no European transplant; rather, it was a unique product of the confrontation between the North American wilderness and peoples of European stock, whose great achievement was to transform savagery into civilization and, in the process, create their own unique national character. Most historians have retreated from pure Turnerism, but the frontier myth persists throughout American popular culture, from the Marlboro man to "the last frontier of space" and other presidential clichés.[6]

A more specialized meaning of "exceptionalism" has concerned scholars writing in the Marxian tradition or in criticism of it. Here the focus is on the idea that American uniqueness has rested in the avoidance of the "vice and misery"—and class conflict—which Malthus predicted would afflict societies whose populations almost inevitably outran their food supplies. America is exceptional, thought Jefferson and Madison, because widespread property ownership among yeomen and artisans would prevent those dire results. (Tocqueville later agreed.)[7] Toward the close of the nineteenth century, Marx and Engels, and then the German economist Werner Sombart, raised the same idea in a different, implicitly critical way: why was there no class consciousness in America? Why no socialism? why was the United States, despite being perhaps the most advanced capitalist nation, so devoid of the working-class manifestations present in capitalist Europe? From this perspective, exceptionalism means that "without a widespread and sustained working-class socialist presence . . . America is somehow exceptional, deviant (some would say deficient), awash in liberal ideas [instead of the preferred radical ones], and bereft of class consciousness."[8]

Perhaps the premise is faulty. Perhaps the United States, around the turn of the century, was more like Britain and France in those respects, while Germany with its active Social Democracy was the exception. Or perhaps the United States, with its lack of socialism, was the leader, not the laggard that Sombart maintained.[9] Others have recently criticized the notion of an exceptional American response to industrialization and related processes, or for that matter any nation's exceptionalism, including *Der deutsche Sonderweg,* the German "special way."[10] As Dirk Hoerder has written, "it is time to debunk notions of exceptionalism [including the *Sonderweg*] and admit that the way to industrialization and its societal consequences was unique in each country, that no country's uniqueness stands out in such a special way as to set it off . . . compared to all others."[11]

Whatever the assent or dissent, however, "exceptionalism" refers in this context to "lack of class consciousness." This meaning of exceptionalism is a restricted case of the general idea of uniqueness. America is exceptional because it has escaped mass poverty and class conflict through widespread property ownership—so said Jefferson, Madison, and Tocqueville. It is exceptional because of its moral superiority and covenant with God, said the Puritans; because it lacked class consciousness for various material reasons, said Engels and Sombart; and because of the frontier, said Turner.

Another aspect of exceptionalism that demands at least brief attention is its traditional connection with a "sense of mission." Here uniqueness becomes, paradoxically, outward-thrusting and didactic, even assertive. Again, this notion can be traced to the Puritans, but it gripped Americans most powerfully from the 1820s to the Civil War—the era of Jacksonian Democracy (and Indian removal) and of Manifest Destiny (and the annexation of northern Mexico). Robert Johannsen, the biographer of Stephen A. Douglas, quotes an 1837 editorial which claimed that the United States must " 'carry forward the noble mission entrusted to her of going before the nations of the world as the representative of the democratic principle and as the constant living exemplar of its results.' "[12] This sense of uniqueness should have meant that American institutions were not for export, and certainly were not to be forced on other people. It should also have meant opportunity and liberty rather than expansionism; so it meant to the historian Ray Allen Billington, the biographer and explicator of Turner.[13] Unfortunately the idea of mission could sour into racism and imperialism, as it did in the 1840s and the 1970s and other times. A returning foreign correspondent recently wrote: "After 21 years . . . I returned home [in 1987] to a country bristling with astonishing problems, most left untended. Many Americans persist in believing that their country has a divine mission on Earth as a model for all others. Yet ignorance about the world seems total."[14]

One could multiply examples of "good" exceptionalism and "bad" or bullying exceptionalism. The sense of uniqueness, whether applied to class dynamics or to foreign involvements, or even if it remained benignly at rest, has been a powerful and long-lasting idea in American culture. (So have similar ideas in France, Germany, Britain, Japan, and many other countries; the sense of uniqueness itself is not unique.) Arnold Toynbee and Paul Kennedy, the authors of two quite different world histories, both of whom doubted the validity of "mission" or that American history was uniquely different from other histories, have taken their lumps from nationalist critics.[15] This "national myth," despite hard knocks from the assassinations of the 1960s, Vietnam, Watergate, and other punctures of national self-esteem, lives on.[16] While the following demographic discussion will surely not scotch it, it does say something about its underpinnings.

A Note on Modernization and Demographic Transition Theory

Modernization, as stated above, is the idea that societies and individuals develop from a "traditional" condition to a "modern" one.[17] "Traditional" societies are rural, illiterate, agrarian, undifferentiated economically, often tribal or familial, fatalistic, and unchanging; and so are the people within them. "Modern," on the other hand, means urbanized, literate, and media-affected, having skilled and educated work forces, organized into strong nation-states, progress-oriented, and developing. The "modernized" personality has a "heightened sense of personal efficacy," in one formulation.[18] The concept of modernization has an immediate appeal. Most people will conjure up ideas about typical "medieval" or "peasant" societies in the past, or tribal ones today in Africa and the Middle East, and contrast them with the present advanced industrial societies of Europe, North America, Japan, and the former British dominions. Surely massive changes have been—and are—taking place historically.

But problems arise as soon as one tries to define "traditional" and "modern" carefully and relate them to concrete situations, past or present.[19] "Traditional societies" differ so greatly from one time and place to another as to make that key starting point almost impossible to locate. Close examination usually shows that they are much more dynamic than the theory admits. Besides problems of definition, the theory seldom specifies just when and how the process of moving from traditional to modern actually operates. Proponents have disagreed about what makes the process happen and therefore where to spend money—such as "foreign aid"—to make it happen: on education? factories? roads and sanitation? medicine? something else?).

Another problem is irreversibility. The concept of modernization, centrally about progress from traditional to modern, does not allow for reversals; yet Iran since 1979 has certainly "de-modernized," and there are other cases. Here modernization encounters the same problem as Marxism-Leninism does when confronted with strikes or dissidence: such acts must be defined as "counterrevolutionary" or the theory fails. (In fact modernization was grasped by U.S. policy makers in the 1950s and 1960s as a liberal-capitalist development theory that could stand in opposition to the missionary Marxism of the Soviet Union, Cuba, and China and which could thereby help save the Third World for the West.)[20]

A final and critical problem with modernization theory is its proponents' impatience with, and tenuous grasp of, history. Any development theory must simplify and draw patterns, but if one simplifies too much, one reduces history to a mere sketch. This is often true of Marxism-Leninism as well as modernization theory, and the recently popular center-periphery theory.[21] In the case of modernization, unlike Marxism and core-periphery theory, reference is seldom made to historical examples, and never in detail. Yet history is essential.

The advanced industrial societies of the present First World would have to be the prime, indeed the only, cases, by definition, of modernization. If the theory has any universality, those societies must once have been traditional. And if the progression from traditional to modern did take place, much of it had to happen in the 1870–1914 period and in the Atlantic region. If it does not appear then and there, the theory falls.

The key terms involved in "traditional" and "modern" are so broad and vague that they have never been fully grounded historically, and certainly will not be in this book. In the restricted area of demography, however, modernization has a corollary whose terms are sufficiently concrete to permit a test for the 1870–1914 period. That corollary is the theory of demographic transition. As with modernization, the transition process has been stated in various ways. A very common one, in fact the prevailing version until recently, adopts the traditional-modern shift and attempts to specify the stages through which societies progress from one to the other. This may be called the sequential version of transition theory.

The sequential version begins with a traditional situation where birth and death rates are high by modern standards. Since both are high, however, the net change in population size is small. Then death rates fall, for some reason or set of reasons. (Industrialization? health improvements? education? a combination of these? Surprisingly there is no consensus on exactly why this crucial change occurs.) The result, with high birth rates continuing alongside falling death rates, is unprecedented growth of the society's population. Only gradually (and for even less well specified reasons) does the next stage happen—a fall in birth rates, the ultimate result of which is slow growth once more, even stable or declining population size.

The sequence from traditional high vital rates but slow growth, through mortality decline, hence population explosion, to fertility decline, hence slow growth again, has been central in the thinking of many demographers and policy makers in recent decades. The theory has been thought of sometimes as predictive, sometimes as descriptive, but always as a general model of human behavior. As a predictive theory it says: if that is how populations have behaved, then that is how they will behave. Thus if population explosions are to be avoided, measures (usually state policy) will have to intervene to slow down fertility much closer to the point at which mortality starts to decline. As a descriptive theory it says, more humbly: now-developed societies have followed the sequence in the past, though at varying rates and for reasons not entirely clear. Again, the Atlantic region in the 1870–1914 period is a sufficiently broad historical testing ground to see whether the sequential version of transition theory did take place.

The sequential version has had its critics. An early warning shot came from Etienne van de Walle and John Knodel in 1967, when they wrote: "If conventional statements of transition theory are inappropriate for the European experience, on which they profess to be based, they are even less likely to be useful in predicting or explaining future transitions."[22] Despite this warning and further work by Knodel and others connected with the Princeton European Fertility Project, some scholars and policy makers were still clinging to sequential transition theory years later with little qualification.[23] Yet the Princeton demographers, while still retaining the terminology, have disclaimed the content:

Given the rough coincidence of modernization and the demographic transition, and the persuasiveness of the stories that were told to explain their relation, it is surprising that, in country after country, the tests of the hypotheses embedded in [sequential] demographic transition theory produced no certain confirmation of the theory.[24]

As we will see, the theory is undercut by several counterexamples. The United States (exceptional, or just one of several such nonfitting cases?) is an important one. It is a society where fertility started falling well before the onset of industrialization began and still longer before mortality began to fall, contrary to the theory either as prediction or as description. Recent and more chastened statements of transition theory simply state that (most) societies once had high birth and death rates, and the developed ones now have low rates. The observation is sound enough, but the explanation is more elusive than ever. Demographers, mindful of history, should and no doubt will continue to search for explanations. I hope they do, and suggest they look to historical diversity to bring forth a more refined transition theory. The Atlantic region and its constituent societies underwent, in fact, far richer and more varied changes in fertility, mortality, and migration than the customary versions of modernization and transition have let on. Mass migration in the transatlantic region will be, however, the principal concern of what follows.

2

THE ATLANTIC REGION IN THE
LATE NINETEENTH CENTURY

Europeans had approached, explored, and colonized North and South America for about four centuries by the time of World War I. But never, before the closing decades of the nineteenth century, had they approached it in such numbers, with such ease, and with so many designs in mind. Between the imperial and industrial nations of Europe and the frontier and industrial nations of the New World flowed a set of interactions which changed all of them and much of the rest of the world as well. The interchange of people, goods, and ideas was manifest in many areas—domestic and commercial architecture, the fine arts, investment and economic development, technology diffusion, the building of empires and penetration of frontiers, and the migration of tens of millions of people across borders and seas.

Migration was an old story in both Europe and the Americas. Its magnitude in the late nineteenth century, however, was unprecedented, thanks to steamship and steam railway networks after 1870, and most dramatically in the 1880s. It then began reaching into remote corners of eastern and southern Europe, the western interiors of the United States and Canada, and the inner reaches of several provinces of Brazil and Argentina. (The newly available transportation options are discussed in chapter 4.)

The economic impetus, and payoffs, on both sides of the Atlantic appeared on the broadest macroeconomic level as output from manufacturing, mining, and agriculture circulated on regional and world markets. It also appeared on the most personal levels as men and women decided to improve their lives in one way or another by migrating. By no means were their motivations wholly economic. For Mennonites and East European Jews migration was closely connected to religion; for some others it meant improved social status; and for a great many it satisfied psychological needs and desires which have only begun to be measured and described. Much of the migration was, however, economically motivated. Economic improvement explains, or at the very least coincides with, more of the migrations than does any other evident explanation. The flow of migration within Europe and across the Atlantic weakened and strengthened over time, but in general it responded to economic activity on both sides of the Atlantic. The 1870s and 1890s, each decade containing several years of depression in Europe and North America, brought lower migration flows than did the generally prosperous 1880s and 1897–1914 period. Yet even in the 1870s and 1890s, at least wherever steam transportation had become available on land or sea, it surpassed previous migrations.[1]

Migration also began expanding from intra-European to transatlantic in the late 1870s (see table 1). And in every European country, the number of transatlantic migrants in the decade of the 1880s at least doubled compared with the average of the 1850s, 1860s, and 1870s. The number of overseas migrants from the British Isles rose from 1.6 million in each decade from 1851 to 1880 to over 3.2 million in 1881–1890; the number of German migrants rose from 692,000 per decade in 1851–1880, to 1,342,000 in 1881–1890. In other countries, where migration had been more local or no more than intra-European, 1880

TABLE 1

Gross Migration (Intra-European and Transatlantic) from Selected European Countries (000 Omitted)

	1871–80	1881–90	1891–1900	1901–10	1911–20	1871–1914[a]
Aust.-Hung.	46	248	440	1,111	418	2,263
Britain	734	1,788	1,310	2,496	2,219	7,902
France	66	119	51	53	32	321
Germany	626	1,342	527	274	91	2,856
Ireland	624	771	433	346	151	2,285
Italy	168	992	1,580	3,615	2,194	7,318
Portugal	131	185	266	324	402	1,134
Russia	58	288	481	911	420	2,158
Scand'ia[b]	227	622	410	747	267	2,137
Spain	13	572	791	1,091	1,306	3,567

B. R. Mitchell, *European Historical Statistics 1750–1970* (New York: Columbia University Press, 1976), 135, table B8. The figures for Britain (England-Wales and Scotland) are "intercontinental citizen passengers from U.K. ports." Using Mitchell's series B9, I have subtracted from the British row "all natives who left Irish ports, including to Great Britain" and put them in the row for Ireland.

[a]Calculated from adding the five columns to the left, then subtracting 1915–20 figures from Mitchell, 1976, series B8, 138–44.

[b]Denmark, Finland, Norway, and Sweden combined; Mitchell, 1976, series B8.

brought an even more abrupt and dramatic shift: compare only the decade 1871–1880 with that of 1881–1890 in the cases of Austria-Hungary, Italy, Russia, Spain, and Sweden. Even in the case of France, with the lowest rates of natural increase in Europe (and in that sense with the least population pressure) and with decidedly the lowest migration figures of any of the large European countries, the numbers nearly doubled. After 1890 the British, French, and (most steeply) the German emigration would subside, but the peak years for Austria-Hungary, Italy, and Russia (1901–1910) were still to come, and Spain's (1911–1920) and Portugal's (1921–1930) came even later.

Available railroad trackage and numbers of passengers carried on railroads tell a similar story (see table 2). Among New World countries the United States was decidedly the leader in railroad activity as well as in in-migrants. Argentina, Brazil, and Canada displayed sizable increases in those categories, with a big jump occurring about 1880 or shortly thereafter, continuing in the 1890s.

Much of this transatlantic activity took place in and among a few major European donors and even fewer American receivers. They included Austria-Hungary, Germany, Italy, Russia, Spain, Portugal, the Scandinavian countries, and the United Kingdom on the European side; and Argentina, Brazil, Canada, and the United States on the American side. The flow was not entirely west-bound by any means. An undetermined amount of return migration took place, very small for a few groups such as the Irish and the Russian Jews but very large for Italians and certain Slavic nationalities. One donor, Germany, also became a receiver; and one receiver, Canada, was a consistent donor as well.

There are a number of reasons for including these countries and not others. The bulk of the European migrants came from Britain, Germany, Italy, Russia, the Austro-Hungarian Empire, and the Iberian and Scandinavian countries. To account for what happened in those countries is to capture most of the emigrants. Also, the first five plus France and the Ottoman Empire constituted the European "Great Powers." Germany, Britain, and France were building territorial empires in Africa and Asia, and British investors were very active in Latin America. With

TABLE 2

Kilometers of Railroad Track in Service, Selected Years

	1860	1870	1880	1890	1900	1910	1920
Argentina	39	732	2,313	9,254	16,767	27,713	35,282
Brazil	223	745	3,398	9,973	15,316	21,326	28,535
Canada	3,323	4,211	11,036	21,164	28,475	39,799	62,450
U.S.A.	49,288	85,170	150,091	268,282	311,160	386,714	406,915

B. R. Mitchell, *International Historical Statistics: The Americas and Australasia* (Detroit: Gale Research Company, 1983), series G1, 656–58, 661–63.

TABLE 3

Overseas Migration to Major Receivers, by Decade (000 Omitted)

	1851–60	1861–70	1871–80	1881–90	1891–1900	1901–10	1911–14	1871–1914
Argentina	—	28	262	842	648	1,765	966	4,511
Brazil	122	98	218	530	1,144	695	581	3,388
Canada	—	176	343	887	341	1,644	1,258	4,649
U.S.A.	2,598	2,315	2,811	5,245	3,689	8,796	4,133	29,587

B. R. Mitchell, *International Historical Statistics: The Americas and Australasia* (Detroit: Gale Research Company, 1983), series B7, 138–42.

Britain leading the way, Germany rapidly catching up, and Austria-Hungary, Italy, and Russia following (mostly after 1900), industrialization and a rural-to-urban shift of population were touching all of these countries. Thus all, to greater or lesser degrees, were "first world," advancing industrial societies for their time. Several of them (Russia excepted) kept good demographic statistics. The Low Countries, Switzerland, and the Ottoman Empire were also donors, but not in numbers comparable to the others named. So to simplify the picture yet include the bulk of migrants, those countries and France do not figure in the discussion of donors.

The four New World countries were all increasing in population, opening up and exploiting raw frontiers within their territorial boundaries, and receiving the bulk of Europe's migrants (see table 3). The four were the largest New World countries in area and population except for Mexico. Mexico is not included here, however, because during the *Porfiriato* (1876–1911) it tried unsuccessfully to attract Europeans and instead exported people to the United States, especially after 1900, and it was not in the process of absorbing an internal frontier. Chile, Colombia, and Venezuela are not included because of their relatively small populations at that time; Uruguay, through a way-station for some numbers of migrants, was also small. Cuba received many migrants from Spain but few from anywhere else.

Size and Growth of National Populations

From about 1870 to about 1910, the four New World countries increased in population faster than any of the six largest European countries, with one exception (see tables 4 and 5).[2] Estimated Russian growth slightly outstripped Canadian (decisively up to 1900). In Europe the lowest increase by far was in France, as was true throughout the nineteenth century. Although the French emigrated far less often than their neighbors, their fertility rate was so low that total increase from the Franco-Prussian War to 1901 was less than 7 percent (0.2 annually). France and Russia (abnormally low and high) aside, growth in the larger European countries during thirty years ranged from Italy's 22 percent (0.7 annually) to Germany's 59 percent (2.0 annually). Italy was a major donor of emigrants and had a chronic surplus population in the nonindustrializing *Mezzogiorno*. Germany and Britain also contained certain areas undergoing rapid industrialization and urbanization, and they consequently attracted migrants. But they each included other areas as well where these processes were not happening; people were leaving those areas. Like Italy and Britain, Germany was also a major donor; however, at the same time, it underwent very rapid industrial and urban growth after 1886.

During the 1880s specifically, all of the European nations except France (lower) and Russia (higher) expanded in the range of 7 to 9 percent (0.7 to 0.9 annually). From 1900 to 1910, the post-1870 patterns continued except in Germany, which ceased exporting people, started importing them, and conse-

TABLE 4

Populations of Donor and Receiver Countries (in Millions)

	1860	1870	1880	1890	1900	1910	1920
Europe							
Austria-Hungary	33	35	39	43	47	51	—
Denmk-Norway-Sweden	7	8	9	9	10	11	12
France	37	36	37	38	38	39	39
Germany	36	41	45	49	56	65	—
Ireland	6	5	5	5	4	4	—
Italy	25	27	28	n.c.	32	35	36
Portugal & Spain	20	n.c.	21	23	24	26	27
Russia	74	85	98	118	133	161	—
U.K. (Eng.-Wales-Scot.)	23	26	30	33	37	41	43
Americas							
Argentina		2		4		8	
Brazil		10		14	17		31
Canada	3	4	4	5	5	7	9
U.S.A.	31	40	50	63	76	92	106

For Europe: B. R. Mitchell, *European Historical Statistics 1750–1970* (New York: Columbia University Press, 1976), 19–24, table B1. Austria-Hungary includes Cisleithania, Bosnia-Hercegovina, and Transleithania. Not all censuses were taken in years ending in zero; Britain, France, Italy, and some scattered other censuses were taken in years ending in "1." The figures given here are from the censuses closest to the date at the top of the column. Alsace-Lorraine is included in France before 1871 and after 1918, in Germany between those dates. Other boundary changes took place after 1918 and are not corrected for here. Russia conducted only one census (in 1897, showing 126 million); the figures here are estimates by P. A. Khromov, cited by Mitchell, 1976, 26. *For the Americas:* B. R. Mitchell, *International Historical Statistics: The Americas and Australasia* (Detroit: Gale Research Company, 1983), series B1, 47, 50, 51. U.S. censuses were taken in years ending in zero; Canadian in years ending in "1." Argentina's took place in 1869, 1895, and 1914; these are listed in the columns for 1870, 1890, and 1910, respectively. Brazil's took place in 1872 (listed here in the column for 1870), 1890, 1900, and 1920 and are so listed.

quently expanded by 15 percent in that single decade. That rate was probably not matched by any other European country in modern times. (The French population, in contrast, expanded only 14.6 percent in the *seven* decades between 1841 and 1911.)

The four American countries present a much different but very uneven picture. The Argentine growth rate from 1869 to 1895 was the highest, 135 percent, and the population nearly quintupled between 1869 and 1914. Total numbers, however, were small. Brazil grew more slowly but had a much larger population. Canada grew by far the most slowly. In fact it grew almost not at all before 1900, for a peculiar set of reasons. Although it was a country of high immigration, with frontier-like high fertility, Canada experienced very high emi-

TABLE 5

**Percentage Increase in National Population by Country,
1870–1910 and 1860–1920**

	1870–1910	*1860–1920*
Austria-Hungary	46	
Denmark-Norway-Sweden	38	71
France	8	5
Germany	59	
Ireland	−20	
Italy	22	44
Portugal & Spain	27	35
Russia	89	
U.K. (Eng.-Wales-Scot.)	58	87
Argentina	300	
Brazil	210 (1870–1920)	
Canada	75	200
U.S.A.	130	242

Calculated from table 4, above.

gration as well. After 1900, however, the emigration dropped sharply while immigration rose. Growth of the United States' population was close to the Brazilian rate, slower than the Argentinian, and faster than the Canadian. In total population, however, the United States was two to three times as large as the other three New World countries combined.

In population size and rate of growth, then, the United States does present unusual features. In both respects it was unlike the major European countries, growing faster than they were. In 1870 Germany's population was still slightly greater than the United States', while France and Britain were still not much smaller. But by 1890 the United States had surged well beyond any European country except Russia. Part of the reason was natural increase; another part was its net immigration, by far the largest of the New World receivers. Yet even that was not as "exceptional" as it seems. As J. D. Gould has pointed out, the United States' share of total European emigration "declined almost monotonically" from 1861 to 1910, and "in terms of *rates* (that is, immigration as a proportion of the population of the receiving country)," the United States was not in first place in any decade and rarely reached second place. It absorbed large numbers of people because it was already large. "The ability of [Argentina, Canada, Australia, and New Zealand] to attract larger numbers of immigrants [than the United States did] *relative to their own population* is one of the many reasons why it is desirable to consider inter-continental migration less exclusively in terms of migration to the U.S.A. than has been the case thus far."[3]

Among the other New World countries, Brazil came closest to the United States' growth rate in this period. Although its land area was 10 percent larger than that of the U.S., the Brazilian population in 1910 was only 26 percent as large.[4] If we look at the entire Atlantic region and in a very rough way consider rates of growth and sizes of population, as well as urban and industrial development not directly discussed here, then from the 1870s to 1914 the United States was the rising star of the New World, and Germany the rising star of the Old.

3

FERTILITY AND MORTALITY

Historical demography is concerned with population changes over time, and such changes can occur only from "natural" demography (the net balance of births and deaths) and from migration (the net number of people entering and leaving a population). Although this book is concerned primarily with migration, a quick look at natural demography is appropriate. Which among the Atlantic countries had high or low rates, and where did the United States fit among them? Did the changes result from a process of sequential "demographic transition" or from something else?

Every major European country except Russia kept annual tabulations of births and deaths. They were not kept in any of the four American countries although fragmentary figures exist for them as well as for Russia. In Europe, the French birth rate was the lowest, falling by not quite one-third between 1870 and 1914. It occasionally dipped below the death rate, creating negative natural increase for brief periods. Similarly high birth rates characterized Austria-Hungary and Germany, on the other hand, and birth rates in neither fell very much until after 1900. Empire-wide averages (as shown in table 6), however, concealed great local variations, and birth rates in areas such as rural Swabia and Bavaria were normally much higher than in Berlin and Munich. Italy's birth rate paralleled Germany's but did not drop as steeply after 1900. Birth rates in all three central European countries—Germany, Austria-Hungary, and Italy—outpaced the United States' after 1870.[1]

In England and Wales, fertility gradually rose during the late eighteenth and early nineteenth centuries, fell by about 20 percent between 1816 and 1846, rose again until 1870, and then began falling steadily. By 1900 it had dipped just below the American and Canadian levels.[2] In Brazil and Argentina, meanwhile, birth rates exceeded 40 throughout the period.[3] (By way of comparison, in

TABLE 6

(Crude) Birth Rates by Country, 1870–1914

Country	1870	1880	1890	1900	1910	1914
Austria-Hungary	39.8	37.5	36.2	35.0	32.5	29.7[a]
France	25.9	24.6	21.8	21.3	19.6	18.1
Germany	38.5	37.6	35.7	35.6	29.8	26.8
Italy	36.8	33.9	35.8	33.0	33.3	31.0
Russia-European[b]	49.2	49.7	50.3	49.3	45.1	43.1
U.K. (Eng. + Wales)	35.2	34.2	30.2	28.7	25.1	23.8
Argentina[c]	47.3	46.0	43.8	41.8	41.0	—
Brazil	46.5[d]		46.0[e]		45.0[f]	
Canada[g]	37.1	34.1	31.8	28.8	26.8	—
U.S.A.	37.1	33.6	31.2	28.5	27.3	26.6

B. R. Mitchell, *European Historical Statistics 1750–1970* (New York: Columbia University Press, 1976), series B6, 108–20; John E. Knodel, *The Decline of Fertility in Germany, 1871–1939* (Princeton: Princeton University Press, 1974), Appendix Table 2:1; Robert R. Kuczynski, *The Balance of Births and Deaths* (Washington: The Brookings Institution, 1931), II:41; W. R. Lee, ed., *European Demography and Economic Growth* (New York: St. Martin's Press, 1979), 35–77, on Austria-Hungary; U. S. Bureau of the Census, *Historical Statistics of the United States, Colonial Times to 1970* (Washington: Government Printing Office, 1975), series B5, I:49; Nathan Keyfitz, "The Growth of Canadian Population," *Population Studies*, 4 (June 1950), 55; Giorgio Mortara, "Pesquisas sobre Populaçoes Americanas," *Estudos Brasileiros de Demografia, Monografia No. 3* (Rio de Janeiro: Fundação Getulio Vargas, 1947), 86–90 (and also 294, for comparative growth rates of American and European countries, and 337–41, for comparative age and sex structures of national populations); O. Andrew Collver, *Birth Rates in Latin America: New Estimates of Historical Trends and Fluctuations* (Berkeley: Institute of International Studies, University of California, 1965), 60, 67; Ansley J. Coale and Melvin Zelnik, *New Estimates of Fertility and Population in the United States* (Princeton: Princeton University Press, 1963), *passim*. A useful table of several long-term estimates of U.S. birth rates is in Morton O. Schapiro, *Filling Up America: An Economic-Demographic Model of Population Growth and Distribution in the Nineteenth-Century United States* (Greenwich, CT: JAO Press Inc., 1986), 30.

[a]1913.
[b]European Russia only, not including Poland or Finland.
[c]Collver's birth rates for five-year periods (1870–74, 1880–84, etc.) rather than single years (1870, 1880, etc.).
[d]Mortara's calculation for the intercensal period 1872–1890.
[e]Same for 1890–1900.
[f]Same for 1900–1920.
[g]Canadian figures are for census years (1871, 1881, etc.) rather than 1870, 1880, etc.

1986–1987 the world's highest birth rates were in North Yemen (55) and Kenya (54), and the lowest in West Germany and Italy (10); Gambia's death rate was highest at 28, and Canada's the lowest among large countries at 7 (Qatar's was 2).[4]

The United States, despite the continuing proliferation of family farms through the 1880s and the persistence of high fertility in newly settled frontier-rural areas, was (with Canada) at the low end of the transatlantic fertility range.[5] At first glance, fertility appears lower in urban-industrial countries (France and Britain) and higher in rural-agrarian ones (Argentina, Brazil, Russia), but there are too many exceptions for the pattern to hold. Many parts of the United States, Canada, and France were very rural, although their national birth rates were low. No simple pattern of "modernization" emerges from birth rates, not at least by them alone. Instead, three patterns appear: first, the Central European type with birth rates in the 30s and falling slowly; second, the "third world" rates, to use today's term, in Argentina, Brazil, and Russia, all well above those of Central Europe and remaining high into the twentieth century; third, a low-rate group, including England-Wales, Canada, and the United States, all quite close, with France lowest. The United States and Germany, the two countries with fastest-growing populations as well as the most rapid industrialization, had quite different birth rates, and the American rate was lower, particularly between 1880 and 1910.[6]

Death rates are not so well documented as birth rates. Hard data are especially scarce for the New World countries, including the United States.[7] Intercountry data shown in table 7 have been gathered from several sources. Each number represents enormous labor by statisticians and demographers, especially for the New World countries where fertility and mortality were seldom measured directly and have had to be reconstructed with much difficulty.

In 1870 the range of mortality rates across Europe and the Americas was narrower than the range of birth rates. All of them were to decline from then until 1914. As the figures in table 7 show, France and England—among the large European countries—began the period with the lowest death rates. They were higher, however, than the prevailing rate in Massachusetts. How far back in time do these rates extend? Before the onset of large-scale urban and industrial development? Probably, although the spottiness of the data (especially the American) permits no firm answer. It seems clear that the French mortality rate remained fairly steady until 1900. English mortality in 1816, just after the Napoleonic wars, was about what it had been in 1701 or even 1601. Between 1816 and 1831 it fell about 10 percent, and then held steady until the 1870s, when it began a permanent fall—slowly at first, then very dramatically after 1900.[8] At the other end of the European mortality spectrum, Russia took until 1914 to reach the level that Germany had reached by 1870. Across the Atlantic, Argentina and Brazil closely paralleled Central Europe's mortality rates throughout the period. The United States and Canada, insofar as we know, almost certainly enjoyed the lowest mortality in the entire transatlantic region between 1870 and 1914.

Quite visible drops in mortality happened in Argentina, Canada, Germany, the United States, and a few other countries just around 1880. In Europe, as the historian-geographer Norman Pounds points out, "until [about 1850] the demographic picture was very broadly similar to that of the eighteenth century" with regard to births and deaths. Between 1850 and about 1880 both birth and death

TABLE 7

(Crude) Death Rates by Country, 1870–1914

Country	1870	1880	1890	1900	1910	1914
Austria-Hung.	29.4	29.7	29.1	25.2	21.2	20.3[a]
France	23.6[b]	22.9	22.8	21.9	17.8	17.7[a]
Germany	27.4	26.0	24.4	22.1	16.2	15.0[a]
Italy	29.9	30.8	26.3	23.8	19.9	17.9
Russia (Eur.)	35.0	36.1	36.7	31.1	31.5	27.4[a]
U.K.-Eng + Wales	22.9	20.5	19.5	18.2	13.5	13.8[a]
Argentina[c]	30.7	29.1	25.1	21.6	17.7	—
Brazil[d]	30.2	—	27.8	—	26.4	—
Canada[e]	—	—	—	—	—	—
U.S.A. (Mass.)	18.8	19.8	19.4	18.4	16.1	14.3[f]
(Registration Area)				17.2	14.7	13.3

For European countries: B. R. Mitchell, *European Historical Statistics 1750–1970* (New York: Columbia University Press, 1976), series B6, 108–20; also, for Italy, Antonio Tizzano, "Mortalità Generale," chapter 7 in "Sviluppo della Populazione Italiana, dal 1861 al 1961," *Annali di Statistica* (Rome: Istituto Centrale di Statistica, 1965), serie VIII, vol. 17. *For Argentina:* O. Andrew Collver, *Birth Rates in Latin America: New Estimates of Historical Trends and Fluctuations* (Berkeley: Institute of International Studies, University of California, 1965), 67. For Brazil: Giorgio Mortara, "Pesquisas sobre Populações Americanas," *Estudos Brasileiros de Demografia*, Monografia No. 3, vol. 1 (Rio de Janeiro: Fundação Getulio Vargas, 1947), 86–90. Mortara also worked out a life table for Brazil for 1870–1920: "Tabuas Brasileiras de Mortalidade e Sobrevivencia," *Estudos Brasileiros de Demografia*, Monografia No. 1 (Rio de Janeiro: Fundaçao Getulio Vargas, 1946); see also Pedro Calderan Beltrão, *Demografia: Ciencia da População, Analise e Teoria* (Porto Alegre: Libraria Sulina Editora, 1972), 173. Mortality rates for Canada are not certain before 1921; Nathan Keyfitz, "The Growth of Canadian Population, *Population Studies*, 4 (June 1950), and Warren E. Kalbach and Wayne W. McVey, *The Demographic Bases of Canadian Society*, 2d ed. (Toronto: McGraw-Hill Ryerson Ltd., 1971), find the data too fragmentary. *For the United States:* U.S. Bureau of the Census, *Historical Statistics of the United States, Colonial Times to 1970* (Washington: Government Printing Office, 1975), series B167, I:59 [since 1900 for the registration area] and series B193, I:63 [for Massachusetts]. (The "registration area" was the group of cities and states, then mostly in the northeastern United States, which registered births and deaths. Not all states required registration of these vital statistics until after 1930.) For a much more detailed analysis, but one that does not provide a single overall death-rate series, see Michael R. Haines, "The Use of Model Life Tables to Estimate Mortality for the United States in the Late Nineteenth Century," *Demography*, 16 (May 1979), 289–312.

[a]1913, since for most of these countries the 1914 death rate was skewed upward by war.

[b]1869, a more normal year for French mortality than wartime 1870.

[c]As in the birth rate table, these figures are five-year averages for 1870–74, 1880–84, etc.

[d]As in the birth rate table, these are Mortara's calculations for intercensal periods 1872–1890, 1890–1900, 1900–1920.

[e]No consistent series is available for the pre-1921 period.

[f]1915 not 1914.

rates showed a "slight downward trend." At that point a sharper change took place:

> The years from about 1880 until the outbreak of the First World War were a period of more rapid change. In all countries the death-rate tumbled *from about 1880 or shortly before*. Major epidemics had disappeared; living conditions, especially in the larger cities, had greatly improved, and there were no longer recurring food crises though it cannot be said that diet was everywhere adequate. *At the same time, in the 1880s and 1890s, the birth-rate dropped sharply.*[9]

In the United States as well, "it is unlikely that a sustained decline in mortality rates . . . occurred . . . before about 1880."[10]

That decline can be traced specifically to the conquest of infectious diseases, especially those affecting infants and children. A case study of Philadelphia for 1870–1930 revealed that some epidemic diseases, such as typhoid fever, smallpox, and scarlet fever, "virtually disappeared as causes of death." Infant and childhod deaths also fell off markedly, resulting in much improved life expectancy. The reasons, particularly for the decline in tuberculosis, are not entirely clear. Diphtheria antitoxin (1895) had some small effect. But clearly, such major killers as typhoid fever, smallpox, and intestinal dehydration diminished greatly because of public health officials who worked in a wide range of ways on behalf of the public's health.[11] In Hungary, for example, the Public Health Act of 1876 required registration of deaths, including a statement of the cause; sewerage and drainage; sanitary norms for homes, schools, and shops; regulation of medical and midwifery practice; compulsory smallpox vaccination, including animals; and state inspection of medicines and food.[12] Recent historiography generally agrees that filtered (later, chlorinated) water, sewer systems, and better living conditions were primarily responsible for lower death rates for the half-century following 1880.[13]

Not every advocate of improved sanitation, clean water, and pasteurized milk understood or advocated the germ theory being developed in Europe by Robert Koch, Louis Pasteur, and others. In fact American public health pioneers, and the medical profession generally, clung to "anti-contagionism," the conviction that disease was not carried by microorganisms but arose from filthy "miasmas."[14] Believing that filth bred disease and caused thousands of unnecessary deaths, they strove to clean up cities. Doing the right thing for the wrong reason, the public health pioneers in the United States (as well as their colleagues and counterparts in Europe) did much to reduce general mortality.[15] Aside from the long-known smallpox vaccination, medical advances, in contrast to preventive public health measures, were rare until sulfa drugs and antibiotics arrived in the 1930s and 1940s to usher in a whole new phase of mortality reduction.[16]

Did mortality start to fall before birth rates did—as the sequential version of demographic transition theory asserts? The idea, again, is that, at first, death rates fell while birth rates remained high (thus producing a surge in population size, independent of migration), and at some later time, for whatever reasons, birth rates finally fell, reducing the rate of natural increase and returning the two rates to some sort of equilibrium, at a much lower level than before the process began. As for death rates, we have just seen that they fell in several major Atlantic countries about 1880 or soon after. If the theory is correct, birth rates should have remained high for some time after that, until at some point they began declining and approaching equilibrium. Did they? Not in France; there they began falling in 1820, well before death rates declined, and well before any massive industrial growth which might have been causally connected to a downturn in either rate. Not in England; there the birth rate actually rose slightly in the middle of the nineteenth century, well after England's industrial and urban revolutions had become widespread; more Englishwomen were marrying and having children. After that, English fertility fell again, in the 1870s, almost simultaneously with the onset of mortality decline, and the downward curve of the two rates remained parallel from that time on.[17] Not in Germany; the variation among provinces was great, but across the whole empire, significant drops in both rates awaited the decade 1900–1910.[18] In West and Central Europe, the actual change did not match, or in fact reversed, the theory's postulated sequence.

As for the United States, the birth rate for whites fell steadily after 1800 (and for all we know, before), even though the population was 95 percent rural and industrialization had not yet begun—although transition is supposed to be linked to the onset of urbanization and industrialization. As Morton Schapiro wrote:

> The experience of the United States is particularly interesting in light of the fact that fertility rates began to fall by 1800 at the latest, while it appears that mortality rates were stable until the late nineteenth century. This violates one conception [the sequential one] of the demographic transition, which states that the decline in fertility is a lagged response to the reduction in mortality. Moreover, it is even in violation of a weaker version . . . which allows for the concurrent decline in fertility and mortality. Thus the experience of the United States is highly unusual. . . .[19]

But was it? France is another counterexample, and the United Kingdom, in a different way, is a third. The most support that can be teased from the statistics in support of transition theory is that, in some places, mortality started to fall about a decade or so before fertility did. Whether such a short timespan was sufficient for some kind of cultural adjustment to take place (or in fact if any verifiable adjustment took place at all) is conjectural. In Italy the fertility decline did not truly start until after 1910, a decade or two following the dip in mortality; and even in Italy differences between the developing North and the agrarian South weaken its support for the theory.[20] Russian birth rates declined after 1900, albeit from great heights to slightly lower ones. The Argentine rate gradually slowed after 1880, but the Brazilian rate, if it declined at all, did not do so until after 1900. Secular decline continued at about two or three points per decade throughout 1870–1914 in Canada and the United States. In sum, France, Canada, and the United States contradict the theory, since their birth rates began falling in the nineteenth century well before death rates did. England-Wales, Germany, and Austria-Hungary show births and deaths falling at about the same time. Of the large European countries, only Italy and Russia support the theory, and not solidly. In Argentina and Brazil mortality did decline before fertility did.[21]

An entirely different narrative of the relation between mortality and fertility declines may be offered, one that at least fits the facts, as well as recognizes the obvious, that both rates have indeed fallen in transatlantic and other countries in the past one-hundred-plus years. Rather than a sequential process of mortality decline, then population boom, and finally fertility decline—none of the steps in this "process" have ever been rigorously specified—there is another, nonrepeating explanation for the drop in mortality in each society. The lowering effects on the death rate of clean water, efficient sewage disposal, and better diet and living space—public health and public works, in a phrase—were becoming understood, along with the germ theory of disease, about 1880 in Central and Western Europe and North America. The technology of survival quickly spread to parts of eastern Europe and South America. This sanitation revolution was a one-time event rather than a repeating process, though of course sanitation practices had to be kept up and extended to remote areas. Fertility declines were chronologically and probably causally independent of it and could have occurred earlier, as happened in France, England-Wales, Canada, and the United States; or during it, as in Germany, Austria-Hungary, Italy, and Russia; or somewhat later, as in Brazil and Argentina; or much later, as in the present Third World.[22] Fertility declines remain to be fully explained. Neither demography, economics, nor history has done so as yet.

If lower birth and death rates mean modernity, then the United States was already, by the 1880s, at virtually the English level, despite the large and growing U.S. farm population. U.S. rates were also well below the South American and Central European rates. There is an apparent anomaly: the United States then had a relatively low birth rate but a growing farm population, which in so-called traditional societies means a high birth rate.[23] An answer (discussed in more detail in Part III) is that by 1880 agriculture in the United States was more commercialized and mechanized than agriculture elsewhere. In fact it had never been truly "traditional," as that term is used in modernization theory, in the first place. The most startling drops in American rural fertility had already happened, whereas in the 1870–1914 period much of Europe was just becoming affected by these changes. As for mortality, the American rate was low for those days. Thus the fertility and mortality history of the United States was different—ahead of—most or all of Europe. It was, in those respects, different. Was it unique or exceptional? Perhaps it was exceptional in the early onset of fertility decline, especially for such a rural population, although the French began almost as early. It was only slightly early in the timing of its mortality decline. It was about average in terms of general levels of fertility and mortality, and in the adoption and impact of public health measures. It contradicts the sequential version of transition theory; but so did some other countries.

4

MIGRATION

General Patterns and Motives

> You see, we nearly all came here to work hard for a few years, go back to Greece, buy a business or a taxi. Not to be rich; we know you can't be rich in a short period in another place, but to improve our life materially there. Not to stay permanent in Australia. Now it is proved by the reality that the contrary is happening. Only a few go back. Most of us are here.
>
> — From Wendy Lowenstein and Morag Loh, *The Immigrants*

Migration of people encompasses many kinds of geographical relocations. For centuries, and especially in the "swarming" of 1870–1914, Europeans and Americans traveled for various timespans (a harvest season or construction job, a year or two, or a lifetime), over various distances (the neighborhood, the home province, within their country, across national boundaries but within Europe, or across the oceans), and for various reasons (new land, new jobs, new freedoms, and so on). A full-scale history of European and American migration, describing each of these movements and relating them systematically, has never been done.[1] In the histories of all three continents—Europe, North and South America— migration has been a central and crucial constant. For the United States specifi- cally this has certainly been true. Frank Thistlethwaite once wrote that migration can be seen as the "central theme for a history of the American people . . . more lasting, because more profound, than [the frontier theme] of Frederick Jackson Turner; for settlers were emigrants before they settled and migration has more than the wilderness to do with American character and institutions."[2] Focusing on migration rather than on the frontier would also place the American experi-

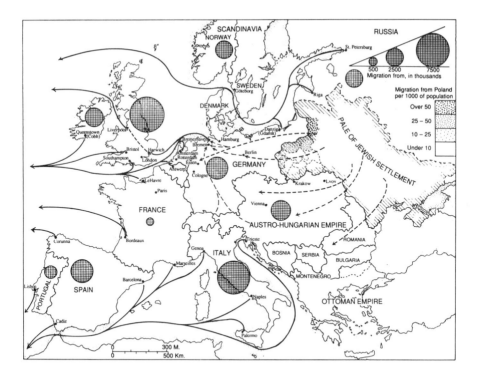

Map 2. Migration from Europe, 1871–1914 (*Map by Norman Pounds*)

Lines with arrows begin with the major ports of embarkation and the usual routes of passenger ships from them. Hatched circles indicate the numbers of migrants from each country (key at upper right). Railroad lines (generalized; a complex network was in place before 1890) are indicated by broken lines. Note the line from Harwich to Liverpool, across England; many migrants from north European ports traveled "indirect," that is, crossing the North Sea to Harwich and leaving from Liverpool for their transatlantic voyage. Sources of Polish migration and their densities appear at right.

ence within the broader transatlantic context rather than isolate it as something unique.

Intra-European migration itself is complex, extending from the distant past to the "guest worker" phenomenon of the late twentieth century. In the 1870–1914 period, migration within Europe—whether inside a country (Britons, French, Germans, Italians, and others did a great deal of this) or from one country to another—was in fact greater than transatlantic migration and included one or two million people every year.[3] "We know," stated two historians recently, "that the previously accepted wisdom regarding the lack of mobility of the rural European populations of the past was in serious error, that in fact a high degree of flux characterized many rural areas in the past."[4] Moves took place from one rural community to another, or to nearby cities. Kinship relations—a person's place within a family, and how it changed—influenced decisions on when and where to migrate, almost as much as did economics; indeed kinship and economics cannot really be separated. The young and unmarried, both men and women, were especially likely to migrate.[5] So much back-and-forth movement took place, both within Europe and across the Atlantic, that the terms "immigration" and "emigration" are cumbersome; historians find themselves better off with simple "migration." As one not too long ago wrote, "the immigration paradigm is being replaced by a model of international, often temporary, migrations in the framework of a segmented labor market comprising various areas of the Atlantic economies."[6]

Transatlantic migration began with the Norse voyages and expanded considerably after 1492. But, as the geographer Huw Jones has written, "for as much as three centuries after discovery," the Americas and other temperate regions "received a mere trickle of settlers."[7] Emigration to the Americas in the eighteenth century was more than a "trickle"; it was somewhere in the hundreds of thousands. But after 1815 the trickle became, to use the inevitable metaphor, a flood, well up in the tens of millions. The time was ripe.

> In the simplest terms, if migration is to take place there must be people who want and are able to leave where they are; countries which they wish and are permitted to enter; and an acceptable means for conveying them. The later nineteenth century not only provided the third of these more amply than any preceding period; it also met the first and second conditions more fully than any preceding period, and the second probably more than any subsequent period.[8]

Serfdom and other institutions hostile to migration had ended, while institutions helpful to migration and to economic development such as free labor, secure private property, and sources of credit had arisen. In that framework, mass migration began and grew.[9]

The total number of migrants will never be known precisely. Three recent, competent estimates put the total migrations of Europeans outside of Europe at 55 million, 1846–1924, of which perhaps 25 percent returned (hence net about

41 million);[10] or 55 to 60 million, 1820–1930;[11] or 65 million, 1800–1914, net about 50 million, of whom nearly 60 percent went to the United States.[12] Another estimate restricted to 1871–1915 is 35.4 million.[13] By 1930, perhaps 20 million European-born people were living elsewhere, and of those about 12 million were in the United States, roughly 2 million more in Canada, with 5 million in Argentina, Brazil, and elsewhere in Latin America. About one million lived in Australia, New Zealand, and South Africa, while well under a million lived in other European colonies and in Asia.[14]

The United States received more than the rest of the New World, and probably the entire world, combined (see table 8). Its absorptive capacity was thus exceptional in sheer numbers. But this was a function of size. In proportion to their populations, several other countries (Argentina, Canada, Australia, and New Zealand) took in more; and Canada, for a time in the late nineteenth century, gave more than it received.[15]

Sex ratios and age structures varied over time and in different places. Of the migrants to Argentina and the United States, generally more than 60 percent were male, or in the years immediately before 1914, more than 70 percent, but in Brazil and Canada almost half of the migrants were female. Males predominated in South Italian and some Slavic migrant groups, but after 1870 more

TABLE 8

Major Receivers and Donors of Migrants

Countries Receiving Over 500,000 Immigrants, 1820–1924

United States	1821–1924	33,188,000
Argentina	1857–1924	5,486,000
Canada	1821–1924	4,520,000
Brazil	1821–1924	3,855,000
British West Indies	1836–1924	1,470,000
Cuba	1901–1924	766,000

Countries Sending Over 1,000,000 Emigrants, 1846–1924

United Kingdom	16,974,000
Italy	9,474,000
Austria-Hungary	4,878,000
Germany	4,533,000
Spain	4,314,000
Russia	2,253,000
Portugal	1,633,000
Sweden	1,145,000

Imre Ferenczi, "Migrations, Modern," in Edwin R. A. Seligman, ed., *Encyclopedia of the Social Sciences* (New York: Macmillan, 1933), X:436.

than half of the Irish coming to North America were female. As for age, the young, if the term is defined broadly enough—15 to 45 years of age—predominated, as they do in most migrations, especially economically motivated ones.

No one doubts that the flow of migrants out of Europe accelerated in the nineteenth century, beginning in the 1840s and 1850s, then leaped forward after 1870 when steamships almost completely replaced sailing ships.[16] Early in the century, the voyage from the British Isles to North America took four to six weeks, plenty of time for contagious diseases to ravage passengers and crew. Up to and including the Irish Famine emigration of the 1840s, deaths from typhus, cholera, or other contagions frequently swept away 10 percent, and occasionally 25 percent, of the passengers during a crossing. In the 1850s mortality fell sharply, thanks to voluntary and government-imposed health and sanitary regulations and faster ships, which began to combine steam power with sails.[17]

The Irish Famine emigration was particularly brutal. A Canadian historian states that "between 1847 and 1851, forty British emigrant ships were wrecked with a loss of 1,043 lives," while aside from shipwreck, "the death rate on the crowded ships bound for America was nearly 17 out of every hundred, inclusive of those who died almost immediately after arrival." But by 1863, with half the traffic already under steam, the death rate was a fraction of 1 percent.[18] The shift from sail to steam is hard to pinpoint because it was gradual, and in the 1840s and 1850s the two power sources were combined on many ships. The *Royal William* made the first transatlantic crossing entirely under steam power in 1833, but not until 1884 did a ship (the Cunard line's *Umbria*) cross without any sails at all.[19]

The shift from sail to steam was not the only means by which marine technology sped up migration. The size of passenger ships, and their speed, increased almost continuously throughout the period to 1914. The two major German companies, the Hamburg-Amerika line ("HAPAG," out of Hamburg) and the Norddeutsche Lloyd (out of Bremen) began biweekly sailings to New York, often with stops at Southampton, in 1858; the schedule went to weekly sailings about ten years later. During the 1870s and 1880s the German passenger ships as well as those of the British White Star and Cunard lines and the French Fabre and Compagnie Générale Transatlantique were mostly in the 2,500 to 5,000 ton range, roughly 375 feet by 40 feet in size, and normally carried several hundred passengers although as many as 1,500 were occasionally packed into them.[20] Technical improvements in the stroke and bore of propellers and the efficiency of engines brought migrants westward ever faster.

Early in March 1871 White Star introduced the *Oceanic,* setting new standards of size and confort. At 3,708 tons, she was the largest ship on the waters, except for the problematic *Great Eastern,* and made 14 knots crossing the Atlantic in eight to ten days, while carrying a crew of 130 plus 200 cabin passengers and 1,000 more in steerage. The main saloon ran the full width of the ship, "which permitted the use of large outside windows and gave a feeling of lightness and airiness," while other novel refinements included individual chairs rather than benches in the dining saloon, coal-burning fireplaces with marble mantels in the bridal chambers, fresh and salt running water in staterooms, steam heat, and more (though little of this cosseted the steerage passengers). By 1873, seventeen companies were operating 173 steamships totaling over 500,000 tons between New York and Europe. The depression of the 1870s cut passenger lists in half, but prepaid tickets, at six pounds sterling or less, kept the stream flowing and ratified the transition from sail to steam.[21]

The Hamburg-America Line (HAPAG) developed a network of agents in various spots in Russia and East Europe from the early 1870s onward. Through them it served Russian Jews escaping from pogroms as early as 1871, and also German-Russian Mennonites and Bohemian farm families. The terrible cholera epidemic that killed thousands in Hamburg in August 1892 nearly shut down HAPAG for almost two years, but in the fall of 1894, together with the government of the city-state of Hamburg, it built another 25,000 square meters of port facilities, including baths, disinfection facilities, restaurants, sleeping quarters, churches and synagogues, and a music pavilion. Quarantines were enforced in accord with new rules, both German and American.[22]

In 1889 and 1890 HAPAG put in service the *Augusta Victoria* and the *Fuerst Bismarck,* each more than twice as large as its existing fleet (at 7,661 and 8,430 tons respectively). They promptly set records of about seven days from Southampton to New York, down significantly from the ten to twelve days of their older sister ships. In 1897 Norddeutsche Lloyd brought forth the "ship of the decade," the *Kaiser Friedrich der Grosze,* the fastest as well as largest ship (14,350 tons) on the transatlantic run at that moment. But larger ships quickly followed, and by 1911 and 1912 the *Kaiser Friedrich der Grosze* was dwarfed by White Star's *Olympic* and *Titanic,* at 46,000 tons, HAPAG's *Imperator,* at 52,000 tons, and in 1914 the *Bismarck,* at 56,551 tons.

HAPAG had grown from about a dozen passenger ships in 1871 to 21 in 1884, 95 by 1900, and 442 by 1914, with 1.4 million tons gross weight. Several other companies were not far behind. Almost exponentially, the leading British and German carriers, and others, expanded the passenger traffic from Mediterranean as well as North Sea and Channel ports to North and South America. The clear pattern is constant increase in size and speed, tough competition but occasionally pooling—any means to encourage passenger traffic.[23] Sailing vessels continued to be used up to about 1900 for long trips, such as from Hamburg or Southampton to Australia, carrying fifty to perhaps two hundred passengers. Until coaling stations were established, steamships could not carry enough fuel to travel those distances. But on the North and South Atlantic runs, much larger steamships had become the norm.[24]

Port cities on both sides of the Atlantic responded to the increase in traffic with sanitary regulations, quarantine facilities, and reception centers. New York's Castle Garden and Ellis Island had counterparts elsewhere. Hamburg's emigrant district of Veddel included boarding houses and hostels to lodge and feed migrants between their arrival by train and their departure by ship. The port also contained indigent aid societies, infirmaries, and a riot of ticket agents, porters, inspectors, innkeepers, expediters, and other service workers (and confidence men).[25]

Sanitation was inadequate. In 1892, for example, migrants arriving at Hamburg from Russia brought cholera with them. The city water supply became infected, and in six weeks in November and December nearly ten thousand people died. Bremen, Germany's other major port, escaped with only six deaths because its public health authorities had taken Robert Koch's advice and made sure the city's water was free of pathogens.[26] Such epidemics were fortunately rare. But the care and processing of several thousand migrants a day strained the resources of port authorities on both ends of the voyage.

Emigrants, who increasingly heard from relatives and former neighbors living in the New World of opportunities there, accordingly availed themselves ever more often of the expanding railway networks to reach the seaports. Those from the Austro-Hungarian Empire nearly always departed from Hamburg or Bremen; those from Russia went through Hamburg; and Germans themselves left from either of those ports or from a Dutch or French port. Swedes and Danes appear frequently on the Hamburg passenger lists. People leaving Italy embarked from Naples, Genoa, Trieste, or Marseilles; those from the Balkans, Trieste usually; and many from the Ukraine and the Russian Pale after 1900 used Odessa. By 1900 most emigrants had several options as to ports of embarkation, passenger lines, prices and accommodations, and of course destinations.[27]

During its 1870–1914 heyday, transatlantic migration involved tens of millions of people and, as Ferenczi and Willcox understood, resulted

> from the spontaneous decision of individuals on the ground of personal motives. Even when the current appears to be a collective whole, it is seen on closer investigation to be only a very loose association of interested individuals. . . . The typical representative of mass emigration in the nineteenth and twentieth centuries is the proletarian—an industrial or agricultural worker without means, though previously in many cases a small holder of land.[28]

Ferenczi and Willcox also state that emigration was not the result of "governmental policy," nor was it "a national undertaking,"[29] which is not quite true except in a relative sense when the 1870–1914 period is compared with the times before and after it. Governments and related agencies (for example, the Canadian Pacific Railroad) often promoted immigration, and governments (both donors and receivers) restricted it, though not as thoroughly as later. It is true that officially sponsored colonization efforts seldom resulted in mass population movements—Germans did not rush to East Africa, Italians to Libya, or Britons to India. Large British migration did go, of course, to colonies (future Dominions) in temperate zones.

Opportunity

Migrants sought better opportunities. As time went on those still in Europe very often learned of opportunities from family members or people from the same village who were already in the Americas. Chain or "serial" migration was common and natural.[30] Changes in legal status sometimes provoked migration; examples are the withdrawal in the early 1870s of German-Russian Mennonites' exemption from czarist military conscription, and the pogroms against Jews in the Russian Pale and Congress Poland after Czar Alexander II was assassinated in 1881. Few members of those groups ever repatriated.[31] Such cases aside, the pervasive motive for migration was economic improvement rather than religion, politics, or persecution.[32]

For some, opportunity lay in farmland, anywhere from northern Argentina to northwestern Canada. In North America, railroad companies whose governments had given them public domain land to help pay for (and provide users for) their lines actively recruited European migrants from the 1870s to the 1920s, bringing Volga Germans to Kansas in the 1870s and Ukrainians to Alberta in the 1920s. From the early 1870s to 1888, when drought and depression struck, homestead and railroad land on the Great Plains was an attractive option for many Germans, Scandinavians, Bohemians, and other Europeans. When agriculture recovered about 1900, North and East Europeans again started new farms on the High Plains, both in the United States (the Dakotas, Montana) and Canada. From about 1887 onward, most migrants to the United States sought nonfarming jobs. But Argentina and Brazil drew many Italians, Spaniards, and Portuguese to agriculture from the 1880s onward, and after 1900 Canadian prairie farmland attracted settlers from Britain and from eastern Europe.

For others, opportunity lay in factory, mining, or construction jobs; for a few, it meant employment in skilled trades or services. As a general rule, if farmland was the target, migrants were likely to stay in the New World. But if the target was labor for wages, migrants might well return to Europe or try another country, for their original aim was not settlement in the New World but improvement of life at home. Since the farm frontier in the United States was an unattractive option from about 1888 to 1900, Europeans instead looked toward cities or, in the West, mines (especially gold or copper mines) for opportunities. And their transiency increased. The Atlantic, with steamships making the crossing much less dangerously than sailing vessels, became a two-way street. After 1880 migration to the United States started changing not only according to national origins, as more South and East Europeans arrived, but more importantly it changed according to purpose: from settlement on farmland to wage labor in industry, construction, or mining. And as Caroline Golab wrote, "it is misleading to speak of 'immigrants' or 'emigrants' . . . there were only migrant-laborers. . . . It is the entity of the migrant-laborer and not time (before or after 1880), origin (northwestern versus southeastern Europe), or destination (farm versus city) that distinguishes the new immigration from the old."[33]

Continuity is a crucial point here: continuity in the practice of migration as a means of self-improvement and as a search for opportunity. The improvement might exist in a New World country, or it might exist at home—in fact it more likely existed at home for most Europeans. This was especially true after farm settlement made truly cheap land unavailable (though the saturation point was not reached until the 1920s in Canada). Much of the transatlantic migration was simply an extension of a long-established pattern of labor migration within Europe, even within countries or districts. Land-seeking migration, implying permanent resettlement, may well have been exceptional in the long history of transatlantic movements, even though it occurred in all four New World receiving societies.

The history of women as migrants has only just begun to be written. Women have been assumed generally to have migrated as wives or daughters, or as the second of a two-step male-female process, or simply as nonmigrants who waited while migrant husbands or fiances worked somewhere else trying to improve their finances. The reality was much more varied. Some women migrated alone, as adults, as labor seekers or land seekers. Others did become the first of a two-step process. Others, having once migrated, refused to return home with their husbands because of the personal gains they had made in the new country. Patterns varied from country to country, as was true of males, and will be noticed in subsequent sections.[34]

Repatriation

Repatriation—returning home after a season, a year, or a few years—was also a long-established pattern for many Europeans. The size of return flows is unclear because of poor or missing statistics, but it was large. Argentina's official statistics for 1857–1914 indicate that the number leaving was 43.3 percent of the number arriving. For Brazil between 1899 and 1912, the proportion may have been about 66 percent. For the United States (where departure figures were kept only after 1908) from 1908 through 1914, the proportion was 52.5 percent. For Canada, it was undoubtedly much higher. "An educated guess," Gould writes, "would be that for the period 1821–1915 . . . an overall return rate of 30 percent [is probably low], and a rate of 40 percent is quite conceivable. . . . Further, repatriation *rates* on the whole tended to increase through time."[35]

Within Europe, many groups were familiar with seasonal migration. North Italians through much of the nineteenth century migrated to nearby countries in the spring and returned home in the fall, with Piedmontese going to France, Lombards to Switzerland, Venetians to Austria. Indeed, more Italians migrated annually within Europe than to America until very late in the century. Saxons migrated to the lower Rhineland in early and middle century to supplement declining earnings in their cottage textile industry at home. Poles, especially women and children, migrated seasonally to the sugar beet fields of eastern

Germany well into the 1880s.[36] And Irish sought work in England, Spaniards in North America, Portuguese in France.

The roots of migration were sometimes ancient, as in the transhumance of shepherds and their flocks from low coastal areas to summer high ground in early modern Europe, which Braudel describes so vividly in *The Mediterranean*.[37] Yet intra-European migration continues today, as anyone can see in European railway stations at certain times of the year, or in Berlin's Little Turkey, or in the service sectors of Germany, France, and Switzerland with their many Yugoslavs, Portuguese, or Catalans. Migration for economic advantage has been a constant feature of European history for millennia, back to Roman or even Celtic times.

Migration specifically for wage labor began at least as early as the seventeenth century.[38] The new element in the late nineteenth century was steam power and cheap iron and steel applied to wheels and rails, hulls and propellers. But the social pattern of migration had existed long before. "Europeans have always moved in considerable numbers," and therefore "the modernization paradigm, which characterizes migration as a comparatively recent phenomenon, fundamentally distorts the historical experience of Europeans," two historians point out.[39] The new technology of travel simply extended the possibilities very greatly. The traditional, vast, labor-seeking migration quickly became transatlantic, much larger and much more transient than the transatlantic migrations of the sixteenth through the mid-nineteenth centuries.

Thus repatriation, a normal part of the old intra-European migration, became normal for transatlantic migration. The sea voyage was cheaper, more regular, and much safer. Loss of life was rare among steamship passengers. The HAPAG lost per year perhaps 150 out of 100,000 passengers, most of them infants, some born during the passage. Except for a rare tragedy, such as the collision and sinking of the Hamburg-America liner *Cimbria* in January 1883 off the Dutch coast, when about 350 died, the transatlantic voyage was safer than the old sailing ships by several orders of magnitude.[40] With increasingly strict and careful port and transit regulations concerning minimum square footage per passenger, more adequate food, water, and medical care, the passage in the steerage was becoming tolerable if not exactly comfortable.

Families could migrate and expect to arrive intact. The young male migrant worker, traveling by himself or with a group of men (probably from the same district), benefited from the improvements and from steadily more accurate information to help him decide whether to head for a New York construction gang or the docks of Buenos Aires. Some young Italians went to all of them. Young Poles also circulated widely in Europe, North Africa, and America.[41] Many young French Canadians moved to the mills of New England; young English-speaking Canadians, some born far down a sibling order on small farms in Ontario, tried and failed in the Cripple Creek gold rush of 1893 and then made their way to industrial cities in New York State. Others followed the frontier path, time-honored in Ontario as in the United States, and sought to create a farm and a family on the plains of Kansas, Nebraska, and the Dakotas, or in the prairie provinces.

For Europeans, repatriation was traditional and normal. It was, however, a new and disturbing thing for many old-stock Americans. For this reason it would affect the relations between receivers and migrants in the United States.

Part II

The European Donors

INTRODUCTION

Nearly every European country became a donor to the transatlantic migration of 1870–1914. The sequence here proceeds clockwise around Europe, looking first at Britain and Ireland, then Scandinavia, then dropping south to Germany, moving east to the Russian and Austro-Hungarian empires, and heading west to Italy and finally Spain and Portugal. This geographic journey also reflects very generally the migration's chronology, since in the period from the 1840s to 1914 British and Irish emigrated first, followed by Scandinavians and Germans, with East Europeans and Italians coming later, along with Spanish and Portuguese. The sequence also follows, therefore, the old-to-new migration to the United States, including the often-remarked-upon differences between old and new such as geographical source, timing, and the shifts from family to individual migration and from land seeking to labor seeking—shifts which were never sudden and complete but rather were contemporaneous and mixed. As will be seen, questions arise whether the family-to-individual and land-to-labor-seeking polarities really reflect the historical truth, especially when Latin America becomes part of the transatlantic picture.

France, it needs to be said right away, played little role in the migration. On balance, it imported people from elsewhere in Europe during much of the period. For a relatively large country its emigration was miniscule, never ranking among the top dozen European countries even in per capita terms. Of the few French people who did leave, many went to North Africa, not across the Atlantic or within Europe. France attracted migrants, especially from Italy, and otherwise met its labor needs from its own rural population. Belgium and the Netherlands were also nations whose emigration was small in absolute numbers and in proportion to population.[1]

Most of the data have problems of one kind or another, especially incompleteness and changing definitions of who was a migrant (temporary or permanent, first-timer or repeater, and so on). Figures for people leaving one country often do not match the figures for what should be those same people arriving in another country. Friedrich Burgdörfer, who compiled German statistics, noted that for German migrants the U.S. arrival figures are 30 percent higher for the 1870s and 17 percent higher for the 1880s than the German exit numbers.[2] The fact that the Germans used January-to-December years and the Americans used July-to-June years does not account for the differences, nor do other fairly obvious correctives. The Italian figures for emigrants are even farther apart from the figures for Italian immigrants of all the major receivers (Argentina, Brazil, and the United States). Although American researchers have often assumed that their national statistics are the most reliable,[3] New Zealander J. D. Gould found that "it comes perhaps as something of a shock to note that when the Italian statistics are used as a touchstone . . . it is the U.S. statistics which, of the three receiving countries, are most under suspicion of waywardness."[4]

Many emigrants left illegally and therefore went unrecorded. Some from Germany or Russia departed to avoid conscription or back taxes. Some East Europeans finessed the legalities when cholera or another disease caused Germany to close its borders, thus temporarily closing off access to the ports of Hamburg and Bremen. Some countries did not record emigrants. The United States did not do so until 1908, apparently thinking them either too few to bother with or that to do so suggested some lack of loyalty. Once people arrived in the haven for Europe's oppressed, would they ever leave it? Italy in 1901 changed its passport rules, hence the way it counted emigrants, thus affecting over- and undercounts. Nonetheless, the data do demonstrate trends. And, as with fertility and mortality data, they are of great help if one is sensible.

As the figures in tables 1 and 8 show, the British Isles accounted for much the largest single share of migration from Europe. The flow out of them was fairly steady over the forty-four years before World War I, with peaks in the 1880s and 1900s. Italy was second. Its migrants moved largely within Europe until about 1880, but increasingly they went to the United States, Argentina, and Brazil when passenger ships began sailing regularly out of Naples. Spain was third, contributing rising numbers as time went on, chiefly to Argentina and Brazil. The flow from Portugal, though smaller, paralleled that from Spain. Germany was fourth overall, but it ranked a clear second until the late 1880s when, singularly, Germans began staying home. The Scandinavian countries, Austria-Hungary, and the Russian Empire donated similar numbers, about 2.1 to 2.3 million each. Compared with the others, French emigration was negligible.

Migration as a proportion of home population still left Britain and Ireland in the forefront to 1900, when Italy and the Iberian countries passed them. Scandinavia followed in per capita emigration throughout most of the period. Germany, with large numbers of migrants (especially in the 1880s) but also the largest population on the Continent, was well behind in per capita terms. The same was true of Austria-Hungary, second in population. (See table 9.)

Throughout the period, virtually no government restrictions or quotas impeded the transatlantic flow (or intra-European flows either, except for Germany's requirement that harvest workers go home for the winter). If anything,

TABLE 9

**Intercontinental Emigration in Proportion to National Populations:
Average Annual Migration per 100,000 Inhabitants**

Country	1871–80		1881–90		1891–1900		1901–10		1913	
	No.	Rank	No.	Rank	No.	Rank	No.	Rank	No.	Rank
Ireland	661	1	1,417	1	885	1	698	3	679	5
Britain	504	2	702	3	438	5	653	4	1,035	4
Italy	105	8	336	8	502	3	1,077	1	1,630	1
Portugal	289	4	380	6	508	2	569	5	1,296	2
Spain	—	—	362	7	438	5	566	6	1,051	3
Norway	473	3	952	2	449	4	833	2	419	8
Sweden	235	5	701	4	412	7	420	9	312	10
Denmark	206	6	394	5	223	9	282	10	321	9
Finland	—	—	132	11	232	8	545	7	644	6
Germany	147	7	287	10	101	11	45	—	40	—
Aust.-Hung.	29	—	106	13	161	10	476	8	611	7
France	15	—	31	—	13	—	14	—	15	—
Neth'l'ds	46	—	123	12	50	—	51	—	40	—

Based on data in Imre Ferenczi and Walter F. Willcox, eds., *International Migrations*, 2 vols. (New York: National Bureau of Economic Research, 1929, 1931), I:200–201. In the 1881–90 decade Switzerland ranked ninth but was not among the leading dozen in other decades.

governments encouraged migration by regulating passenger health and safety (the United Kingdom, the Hanseatic ports), by enforcing military conscription, which encouraged evasion by migration (Germany, Russia), or by recruiting migrants (all of the New World countries at various times, usually through railroads or semiprivate "promotion societies").

5

BRITAIN
(ENGLAND-WALES AND SCOTLAND)

The United Kingdom consisted of England and Wales, Scotland, and Ireland. In the late nineteenth century "John Bull's other island" was politically unified with Britain; but its northeastern corner, Ulster, was culturally closer to Scotland than to England, and the Catholic majority in the rest of Ireland was distinct from either. All of them donated people in large numbers to North America and to the temperate regions of the Southern Hemisphere (Australia, New Zealand, South Africa), but not to Latin America. There the British impact was more economic than demographic. Over the entire period, British and Irish migrants usually went to the United States, choosing Canada second and Australia third.[1]

Migration out of England outpaced Ireland's for the first time in 1869. Although the Irish migration remained larger than the English in proportion to population, and in fact was the largest in Europe in that respect, the English exodus continued to outrun the Irish in absolute numbers.[2] The flow shifted toward Canada after 1900, as the figures in table 11 show. The figures in table 11 are derived from British exit data. American arrival data are considerably lower (the undercount was well over 50 percent in some years), possibly because the British counted not just emigrants but all passengers, while the Americans counted only steerage and third-class passengers who intended to stay, and omitted cabin-class passengers and "tourists."[3]

We will never know how many migrants repeated the voyage in steerage. Some no doubt traveled twice or several times. Even so, the rates of return were high, perhaps the highest of any European country, especially before 1900.[4] The 1890s brought fewer British and Irish to North America and sent more back home than did any other decade within the period, and out-migration remained only slightly greater in 1901–1910. In that decade startling changes occurred—great surges to Canada of English-Welsh (up fourfold) and Scottish (up tenfold). This strong increase continued until the outbreak of World War I.

Stating it broadly, emigration from England and Wales prior to 1930 clustered in two periods: 1879–1893 (almost one-fourth) and 1900–1914 (almost one-third).[5] From 1871 to 1900, 60 to 70 percent of the migrants from England-Wales and Scotland went to the United States, but only 37 percent did so in 1901–1914. From 1911 through 1914 more people from England-Wales went to Australia and New Zealand, and more than twice as many to Canada, than to the United States. Of emigrants from the United Kingdom, only the Irish continued after 1900 to proceed to the United States at much the same rate (90 percent or more) that they had since 1871.

Steamships made the Atlantic crossing cheaper as well as safer. A ticket from Liverpool to New York cost about $45 in 1860, but fell to about half that in the 1880s.[6] By 1886 more than sixty private societies had been formed to promote emigration, assisting English, Scottish, and Irish migrants to get to the Dominions as well as to the United States.[7] Both gross and net migration peaked in the 1880s, with 1887 and 1888 the leading years of the entire nineteenth century (see returns, table 10). Traditional histories of English migration have emphasized agricultural depression in remote counties as the main cause, something which indeed was true in Germany and Italy. But recent research, especially Charlotte Erickson's in the American passenger lists, has found that most of the migrants "gave a principal town as [their] last place of residence,"[8] thus making town dwellers overrepresented among the migrants, something which had not been true of the migrants of the 1850s.[9]

Moreover, English migrants had been working at urban-located jobs, not on farms. Those from a farm background, whether operators or laborers, declined in number; and by the 1880s they were "the least well represented" occupational group among the migrants to the United States.[10] In the large migration of the 1880s, 35 percent came from London, the West Midlands, or Lancashire, and another 25 percent from other urban counties. Most were common laborers, not farm workers. In that decade, only about one-sixth of adult male migrants were farm workers, whereas about one-third were non-farm laborers. People employed in "rapidly changing industries like textiles, iron and steel and engineering" were underrepresented among the migrants. Cornwall had the highest net emigration (as a percentage of its native population) of any English county, and certain counties in the West of England and on the Welsh border (Brecon, Herefordshire, Pembroke, Monmouth, and Montgomery) followed close behind it in rate of emigration.[11] Cornish miners were hard hit by sharp declines in tin and copper mining after 1866; and, very likely, the many Cornish non-miners who emigrated were in services or small artisanry dependent on the prosperity of the mines.

England, Wales, and Scotland not only donated migrants but also received them. The 1861 census reported about 727,000 Irish-born residents, many of

TABLE 10

Gross Migration from England-Wales, Scotland, and Ireland to the United States, British North America, and Australasia (000 Omitted)

	1871–80	*1881–90*	*1891–1900*	*1901–10*	*1911–14*
To U.S.A. from					
England-Wales	549	909	599	650	202
Scotland	87	178	117	186	67
Ireland	450	626	428	420	125
Total	1,089	1,715	1,145	1,255	395
To British North America from					
England-Wales	126	222	160	623	463
Scotland	26	35	17	169	133
Ireland	26	46	10	36	27
Total	178	302	187	832	622
To Australasia from					
England-Wales	201	272	103	186	236
Scotland	44	44	13	32	37
Ireland	61	56	12	12	12
Total	303	371	128	229	284
Gross Total, from					
All, to all	1,570	2,388	1,460	2,316	1,301
Returns					
From U.S.A.	N.A.	544	627	613	143
From B.N.A.	N.A.	79	96	227	128
From Australasia	N.A.	84	93	94	54
Total returns	N.A.	707	816	934	325
Net Total	N.A.	1,681	644	1,382	976

From N. H. Carrier and J. R. Jeffery, *External Migration: A Study of the Available Statistics, 1815–1950* (London: Her Majesty's Stationery Office, 1953), 95–96, table D/F/G (1). "Totals" are slightly different from sums of columns because of rounding. These figures differ somewhat from those for Britain and Ireland in table 1 above because Mitchell's figures in table 1 (his source is Ferenczi and Willcox, I:230–31) include migrants from Ireland to England, whereas the Carrier and Jeffery figures in this table include only persons going "direct to extra-European countries." Figures for returns are from Carrier and Jeffery, 97, table D/F/G (2).

them famine refugees. The number of native Irish in Britain dropped to about 632,000 by 1901, but they and their British-born children continued to be much the largest immigrant group in Britain. A much smaller contingent of Germans (33,000 in 1871, 53,000 in 1911), and Polish Jews (51,000 in 1875, 96,000 in 1911) formed the largest Continental groups, followed by clusters of Lithuanians, Gypsies, Italians, and even a few Americans. Employment levels varied; Germans often worked as commercial clerks, Jews in textiles, Irish at all levels although as a group they were residentially and occupationally discriminated against. Arrivals of East European Jews triggered the Tory-sponsored Royal Commission in 1903 that recommended restriction of "undesirable" aliens. The Aliens Act of 1905 ensued, leaving it to the Home Office's discretion whether persons would be let in, in contrast to the free immigration allowed since 1871.[12]

Migration from Scotland was more rural, and it was heavier. In the 1880s it took away 54 percent of the natural increase, and after 1900, over 75 percent, a proportion higher than anywhere else in Europe except Norway and Ireland.[13] The great majority went to the United States before 1900, but Canada increasingly became the Scots' preference and absorbed more than twice as many as the United States did after 1910. About 170,000 Scots entered Canada in the years 1910–1914 alone. In the 1870s twice as many males as females emigrated, but the sex ratio gradually became almost equal by 1914. Occupational statistics are unreliable before 1912, but in the 1912–1914 period about 47 percent of Scottish male emigrants qualified as skilled artisans, and another 21 percent claimed white-collar status; in both categories the proportion was greater among Scots than among English and Welsh migrants. Only 29 percent of the men were laborers, the majority of them agricultural. Of the women, 10 percent had middle-class occupations, 19 percent did garment work, and the remaining 71 percent were domestic workers "in private service or hotels."[14]

Women constituted about 37 percent of net migration from England and Wales between 1861 and 1900. Migration of family groups declined and migration of individuals rose steadily through those years and into the twentieth century.[15] As we shall see, the female cohort was larger among English migrants than among Italians and several Central European groups, but it was smaller than among the Irish.

From the late 1890s to 1914, Canada and the other Dominions received the lion's share of English, Welsh, and Scottish migrants. Reasons included discoveries of gold and other minerals in Canada, Australia, and South Africa; aggressive promotion by Dominion governments and railroads; the apparent scarcity of homestead land in the United States and its availability in Canada; job competition from South and East European migrants to the United States; and the eagerness of Canada and Australia to "purify the immigration stream"—that is, to attract British, not others. W. A. Carrothers wrote in 1929: "The Dominions [after 1900] were no longer considered as the dumping ground of the failures and misfits of the British Isles. . . . Emigration was no longer the last resort of the hopeless, but became the means of achievement to the hopeful."[16]

Never, however, did Britain's tropical outposts attract many migrants. As Colin Holmes writes, "between 1871 and 1914, when the British were busy painting the map red in the course of their imperial expansion, and when economic and social problems were becoming apparent in the heart of the Empire, immigrants and refugees continued to arrive."[17] All that time, of course, Britons continued to leave for North America and the southern temperate possessions.

Contrary to the stereotype of the pioneering English or Scottish family migrants who settled down on farms in the United States and Canada (though there were indeed many), a large share of the British migrants were migrant wage seekers. The rate of return migration, especially by the English and Welsh, was remarkably high, indeed "consistently higher than anywhere else in Europe."[18] As time went on, again refuting the stereotype, more and more of the migrants were single, or if not, they left their families behind to look, not for farmland, but for jobs that would earn them cash to take back to Britain. Comparing her findings about British emigrants in 1841 with data for those in the 1880s, Erickson found that in the 1880s migrants "travelled more often as individuals than in families. They were more likely to be labourers reporting no skills, and correspondingly younger. Only the Dutch . . . failed to conform to this pattern, remaining largely a family migration."[19] But when Erickson compared the 1841 group with another from 1831, she found that the 1841 migrants had already begun to reveal some characteristics of the "new immigration," which became the norm later in the century. Among them were "more lone travellers . . . more labourers, and a smaller proportion of farmers."[20]

Another historian sees labor migration from Britain beginning as early as the 1850s, "both as a harbinger of international labor mobility and as a refinement of the 'safety-valve' phenomenon in British life."[21] Labor migration was certainly evident by the 1880s. The ratio of migrants traveling as individuals to those traveling in family groups was about even in 1831 and about two to one in 1846–1854. But in the large 1885–1888 migration, "about eight times as many adult males crossed the Atlantic alone as travelled as part of a family group."[22] Some of these men were looking for farmland, but a larger segment sought jobs in construction, mining, factories, and certain trades, in order to return to England, if not richer, at least better off. The British, in this way, began the "new immigration"—labor-seeking, individual, often returning—almost twenty years before it developed as the common pattern among Italians and Central Europeans who migrated to North and South America.[23] The "bird of passage" whom official American opinion found so objectionable—and believed was Italian or Slavic—was, at the start, British. That ethnic coloration made the British invisible to American opinion makers and authorities. As the figures in table 10 indicate, "emigrant returns were about 35% in the 1880s; about 60% in the 1890s; about 40% in 1901–10 and about 20% in 1911–14."[24]

6

IRELAND

Return migration was much rarer among the Irish, and indeed was the lowest in Europe. In that and many other respects, their migration contrasted with the migration of the English, Welsh, and Scottish. After the Great Famine of 1846–1854, emigration—especially to the United States—meant at once exile, hope, necessity, and safety valve for the Irish.[1] It still does. The lead story in the Galway City newspaper of June 16, 1989, tells of Tony Kelly, who as a boy, along with his many brothers and sisters, cut grain for ten shillings a day (then US$2.40) on a local farm. He left home in 1951 for England. After eight months he took assisted passage for Australia, where he stayed five years. Next he went to Alaska, then to western Canada, and finally to San Francisco, where he prospered. In 1989 he returned to Galway and for $200,000 bought the farm on which he worked as a boy.

The local paper editorialized that "there are 'happy endings' to the stories of some of our emigrants; indeed many must have learned to live happily in their adopted lands, done well for themselves, and nurtured dreams of returning." No doubt "in many cases they go of choice," but others "are forced to go because there are not sufficient work opportunities here." The editorial closes by reminding readers of a recent scene in which "a father from Ballinrobe . . . broke down while telling the story of his departed children" and warning that Ireland "cannot afford to allow such things to continue to happen."[2] But they did happen for over a century and a half. Similar events and sentiments assuredly describe the Irish emigration from the pre-Famine years onward. Seasonal wage-seeking migration established itself well before the decisive event of the Great Famine. The *spailpín*, the young male migrant worker, moved about within Ireland and from Ireland to Britain during the summers in numbers upwards of 150,000.[3]

The fungal blight of July and August 1846, which destroyed the potato crop of that year, immediately changed migration from seasonal to permanent, from a day's crossing of the Irish Sea to a forty-days' crossing of the Atlantic, and from individuals to families. Because the fare to Montreal was about ten shillings below the New York fare, Canada received many of the Famine emigrants; about a third of those however, quickly proceeded to New England or New York State. The Canadian authorities described the autumn 1846 migrants as "clean and industrious, if poor." Later arrivals were not so highly regarded, impoverished and progressively ill-nourished as they were because of crop failures again in 1847 and once more in 1848. The 1847 migrants were severely afflicted with typhus and other diseases, and of the 110,000 who sailed in that year, at least one of six died on the voyage, in quarantine at Grosse Isle below Quebec, or soon after arriving.[4] Peasants who were reasonably secure at the beginning of 1846 were destitute by 1851 if they were still in Ireland. The 1851 Census counted 20 percent fewer Irish men and women than the 1841 Census, and 25 percent fewer in rural areas.[5]

When the famine and its economic consequences subsided in 1854, emigration fell abruptly and did not resume in heavy volume until the late 1870s.[6] At that time the potato crop failed again, causing a "mini-famine" and triggering large-scale emigration once more. The peculiar Irish pattern of marrying late, and in many cases not at all, was already developing. Celibacy and late marriage reduce fertility; so does migration, since emigrants give birth in other countries. Consequently the natural increase of the Irish people remained at a "virtual standstill" from 1880 to 1914, and was the lowest in Europe. Individual-level fertility did not decline from pre-Famine times to 1914, but the very low marriage rate—the large proportion of never-married persons—depressed the national level so deeply that, with emigration, Ireland continually fell in population. The heaviest migration came from the counties (mostly in the West of Ireland) with highest fertility.[7]

The broad characteristics of Ireland's emigration are these. The population of the country fell from 8 million on the eve of the Famine to under 4.4 million in 1911. More than 4 million persons emigrated. They were young and of working age; from 1850 to 1887, 66 percent, and after 1887, 80 percent, were in the fifteen-to-thirty-five age group. Most were sons and daughters of farm laborers and small farmers. Six counties, all in the west, provided about half of the migrants; on the receiving end, 85 percent went to the United States and three-fourths of those lived in seven states as of 1900 (see table 11). Most were literate, and in many cases spoke both English and Irish Gaelic.[8] When they left they were unmarried and traveled as individuals, whether men or women. In the post-Famine migration, family groups probably accounted for no more than a third of the migrants.[9] Nearly all were Catholic. Those who were not often preferred to go to Canada, where the Orange Order promoted immigration of Protestants.

Since few had any capital, vast numbers were financed by remittances or prepaid tickets from relatives or friends already in North America.[10] Steamships out of Liverpool and the Firth of Clyde began stopping at Londonderry, Cork, and Galway in the late 1860s, and by the 1870s Queenstown (now Cobh, which is Cork's harbor) and Moville (near Derry) surpassed Liverpool as the main Irish embarkation ports. Steerage fare to the United States reached $8.75 in 1894.[11] Private philanthropy, local governing boards, and American railroads all subsidized emigrants, but remittances were more important still—financing "over three-fourths of the total emigration," making it "a truly self-perpetuating phenomenon."[12]

The connections in the Irish case between migration and other demographic events such as births, deaths, and marriage are clear and in many ways exceptional. The Irish emigration from the 1870s onward shared certain characteristics with the Famine migration. In both cases the migrants were predominantly rural and were seeking opportunities (indeed, survival) either on North American land or in cities and towns. They included almost as many women as men. But the differences were marked. As noted above, the post-Famine migrants, women and men, left as individuals rather than as families. They were younger and in most cases without skills. The high proportion of single women, even more than the Irish proclivity to head for cities despite their rural roots, marked the Irish post-Famine migrants as different from other European groups.

For most of the 1871–1914 period, more Irish women migrated than men. Only in the 1890s did more males emigrate than females, and then not many

TABLE 11

Destinations of Irish Emigrants, 1876–1920 (000 Omitted)

To	1876–80	1881–90	1891–1900	1901–10	1911–20
United States	140	614	387	274	104
Canada	7	40	7	25	25
Australia	17	39	9	5	4
New Zealand	11	5	1	1	1
South Africa	0.1	0.4	2	3	1
Other Non-Europe	1	3	0.5	0.6	0.3
England-Wales	47	43	18	23	11
Scotland	37	27	10	15	4
Total	260	771	434	346	151
Annual Avg. per 1,000 pop.	9.6	15.0	9.5	7.9	3.4

N. W. Carrier and J. R. Jeffery, *External Migration: A Study of the Available Statistics, 1815–1950* (London: Her Majesty's Stationery Office, 1953), 101, table III. Another table may be found in W. E. Vaughan and A. J. Fitzpatrick, *Irish Historical Statistics: Population, 1821–1971* (Dublin: Royal Irish Academy, 1978), 264–65.

more. Females outnumbered males by a small margin in the two decades from 1871 to 1891, and by a large margin (55 percent to 45 percent) in 1901–1910.[13] In every other European country, males migrated in greater numbers than females: in Britain, as shown above in chapter 5, by about five to three; in southern Italy, by two or three to one; among some Slavic groups, as much as four or five to one. Why was Ireland different? Kerby Miller points out that the "status of women in rural Ireland had never been high," but worsened after the Famine, when arranged marriages (to preserve property) became the rule. Thus, "women lost even the freedom to choose their own mates, while the dowry system transformed them from independent personalities into a species of closely guarded property."[14]

Another author writes that a dowry "may be treated as a fine for the transfer of a redundant dependent female from one family to another." Before 1900, women routinely lugged two-hundred-pound sacks of potatoes, broke stones, and did " 'the work of cattle.' " The development of the national school system benefited females much more than males, because it gave them training that allowed them to escape this "oppressive demographic system. . . . National schools, evening classes and domestic economy courses were mercilessly exploited by country girls desperate to escape Ireland."[15] Joseph Wade, a returned migrant living in Mullingar, told an interviewer in 1955 that in the years around 1900,

the drudgery that girls had to go through in a farmer's place was terrible. She would have to milk all the cows, perhaps six or seven, [and] feed calves. All the milk vessels in those days were wooden. . . . She would have to mend and make clothing when night would come or evening fall. She would have to card and spin wool or flax until she would fall asleep over the wheel with fatigue. And worst of all with farmers' wives of those days, and their children, they would always be reminding her of the gulf that lay between their respectability and hers, and all that for £4 a year. What wonder then that that girl would save and scrape until she could get to America. Go she would. The sailing ticket was not too much in those days, £2 and 10 it was up to 1900. . . . It was wonderful what our emigrant [girls] accomplished. . . .[16]

Robert E. Kennedy states:

When women were gaining in social status in Britain and in urban America around the turn of the century, through what is generally called the emancipation of women, the status of young single women in Ireland was worsening. . . . The desire to escape from an unusually severe degree of male dominance (by northwest European standards) probably increased among young Irish females at this time. At the same time the proportion of single persons in the Irish population suddenly increased, and this alone would have led to more females among all emigrants.[17]

Although that rings true, male dominance was severe also in southern Italy, Iberia, and the Balkans; yet most migrants from those areas were men. The female majority among Irish migrants, therefore, probably resulted from the synergism of several factors. First, the undoubted male dominance (including pub life, which excluded women, and the puritanical clergy, which as Miller points out characterized the Anglicans and Protestants as well as the Catholics) together with the unremitting rural poverty placed most young Irish women in a situation no better than other young women throughout Europe. Second, the increasingly late age of marriage, a peculiarly Irish phenomenon, stretched out the time of life when migration was relatively easy and unencumbered; the numbers of years when migration was a practical option were greater than elsewhere. Third, many Irish already lived in the United States, and had since the Famine; young women who wished to migrate had relatives they could go to. Fourth, Irish women were literate and educated, at least to the American standard in many cases; they were employable upon arrival. And fifth, they spoke the language; except by choice they need not be ghettoized for an indefinite period after arrival.

Opportunities abounded for young Irish women as domestic servants in the Gilded Age, when upper-middle-class American families required a "Bridget" or two. When white-collar jobs proliferated after 1900, Irish women increasingly became American office workers, shop clerks, or teachers. The ease of leaving Ireland and entering gainful employment in the United States simply did not exist for young Italian or Croatian or Polish women, regardless of the degree of male dominance in their societies.[18] And, as Miller has observed, men were scarce in rural Ireland, and those who were around "were less-than-attractive marriage prospects, in either an economic or a romantic sense."[19] The departure of so many young women, in turn, further reduced the Irish fertility rate. Uniquely in Europe, migration from Ireland—because it was so heavily female—not only removed the migrants themselves from the population, but also prevented the population from achieving more than a flat rate of natural increase.

The female migrants, however, did contribute to alleviating economic distress in Ireland. They dutifully sent home money or steamship tickets. As Arnold Schrier states, return migration to Ireland consisted more of dollars than of people. "It was Irish girls who contributed the lioness' share," and thus they helped pay the rent, repair thatch roofs, replenish livestock, and build country churches.[20] Nonetheless, the Irish economic situation, especially in rural areas, made emigration desirable or necessary for many young people. As a United States consul summarized it in the 1880s:

> The farming class emigrates in consequence of the severity and irregularity of the laws appertaining to land, non-security of tenure to the tenant at will, and the facility afforded speculators in purchasing over the heads of others; and again because of the non-subdivision of the land into small holdings. Seventy per cent . . . go to the United States—that country being the easiest and cheapest to reach. Then some member of the emigrant's family, relatives, neighbors or friends have, it generally happens, gone there before them. They are impressed . . . with . . . a hope that

at some future time they may possess a home for themselves and families, which . . . here seems impossible.[21]

Inheritance of land began to become impartible before the Famine and was generally so after 1852. One child inherited the parents' farm, and the others were encouraged to emigrate.[22] Farming shifted in the late nineteenth century from crop tillage to livestock raising, requiring the average landholding to become larger and reducing the demand for young farm workers. Miller points out that insecure land tenure, uncontrollable rents, unavailable freeholds, and most fundamentally, Ireland's smothered existence within the British free-trade economic orbit—an agricultural appendage to industrialized Britain—ensured that Ireland would remain "a fundamentally 'sick' society."[23]

Not surprisingly, then, return migration to Ireland was chronically the lowest in Europe. Every village had its "Yank," its Tony Kelly of the nineteenth or early twentieth century, but the salient fact was how few they were.[24] Returnees were sometimes young women, who at twenty-five were considered old to be marrying in America but young by Irish standards, and who were now economically more independent. Some were men who had accumulated the funds to buy a pub, a farm of their own, or a country store. But Irish migrants never became "birds of passage," unlike the English and most other Europeans. Even when they returned, their presence spurred further emigration by confirming "the illusion that New York was but the next parish over from Galway."[25]

The bulk of Irish migration did not occur during the Great Famine of 1846–1854, but between the 1870s and World War I. It took place despite the urgings of Irish nationalists such as Thomas D'Arcy McGee that young people stay and strengthen the country and despite the fulminations of the clergy who emphatically warned that migrants would lose their immortal souls in the fleshpots of America.[26] This migration was the largest in Europe for the size of the population, and it was the only one which lowered the population by any amount; in fact it halved it. It uniquely included a female majority. And eighty-five percent of the migrants went to the United States.

The reasons for all of those peculiarities are still unclear. Economics, as usual, played a crucial role, but Miller is persuasive in claiming that the majority "were not involuntary exiles." He insists that most were "voluntary emigrants who went abroad in search of better economic and social opportunities. . . . They emigrated voluntarily, in order to better themselves; and they could, at least in theory, have remained in Ireland."[27] Yet they left in droves and seldom came back. For the women, certainly, migration brought a measure of independence and freedom of personal choice in every aspect of their lives, not simply an income. Migration was an open route, indeed virtually the only route, to self-fulfillment. Equally needy women elsewhere in Europe, for reasons of culture and language, did not have that opportunity.

7

SCANDINAVIA

The four Scandinavian countries together sent almost as many people to the New World as did either the much more populous Austria-Hungary or Russia. As the figures in table 9 indicate, the Scandinavian countries led most others in numbers of emigrants in proportion to population. In that respect Norway was second only to Ireland. The departures from each of the four were as shown in table 12. Besides its high rate, Scandinavian migration was unusual in other respects. It began early and nearly all of it went to the United States. Emigrants started sailing west from some parts of Sweden and Norway in the 1840s and 1850s. By 1871, so many Swedes and Norwegians were already living in the United States that serial migration kept the rate of flow unusually high for the next several decades.

The documents for Swedish and Norwegian migration history are exceptionally good. Accurate local record keeping, which began in the eighteenth century,

TABLE 12

Gross Migration from the Scandinavian Countries (000 Omitted)

Country	1871–80	1881–90	1891–1900	1901–10	1911–20
Denmark	39	82	51	73	52
Finland	—	26	59	159	67
Norway	85	187	95	191	62
Sweden	103	327	205	324	86

B. R. Mitchell, *European Historical Statistics 1750–1970* (New York: Columbia University Press, 1976), series B8, 135.

created the longest continuous series in Europe and has permitted more precise statements about Scandinavian migrants and their behavior than for any other group. Although Denmark's migration statistics are not as complete, other sources enabled Kristian Hvidt to compile an accurate register for the 300,000 migrants who left between 1868 and 1914. The Swedish sources even suggest an answer to the vexing question of whether emigrants left because they were unusually enterprising and intelligent or because they were unable to survive and succeed at home. Local Lutheran pastors were obliged to describe the mental abilities and skills of their parishioners and record their judgments. Comparing migrants with stay-at-homes, these records reveal that all over Sweden, "emigrants generally made higher marks than the rest of the population. They were brighter in school, had a wider picture of the world, and were the kind of persons to whom it would occur to leave their habitual surroundings."[1]

Like migrants elsewhere, Scandinavians sought better life chances. Jon Gjerde's study of Balestrand, a district on the shores of Norway's Sognefjord, demonstrates that people there were not starving or even underemployed. Farm output in fact rose in the nineteenth century. But all the arable land was owned and occupied, inheritance was impartible, and thus even the noninheriting children of landowners (not to mention tenants and laborers) faced stagnant futures.[2] In Rättvik, Sweden, which Robert Ostergren studied, real rural poverty was also uncommon; but the land had been so minutely subdivided since the eighteenth century that a new class of crofters and landless peasants had emerged, and since prevailing custom required even those lucky enough to acquire land to care for close relatives who had none, "prospects" were not good for a great many young people.[3] Partible or impartible, there was simply not enough land to provide more than a moderate or meager future. In Denmark as well, the desire for economic and class improvement, more than other motivators, triggered migration. The direction taken by migrants, however, depended less on sheer market forces than on family ties and local traditions; migration agents tried to persuade Swedes to go to Canada, but they continued to flow to the United States, where friends or family were already established.[4]

Other motivations did operate in some cases. After the Danish-Prussian War of 1864, North Schleswig became German, which prompted Danes to leave there in unusual numbers. Religion also motivated many Danes who had converted to the Baptist or the Mormon faith in the nineteenth century; tens of thousands left for America, where there was no established church. Religiously motivated emigration from Denmark, per capita, may have been the greatest among European countries.[5]

About one and a quarter million Swedes migrated between 1851 and 1930. Three-fourths of them left in 1868–1873, 1879–1893, and 1900–1913—periods marked both by agrarian crises or other economic problems in Sweden and, at the same time, by vigorous economic activity in the United States.[6] Of the four nationalities, Finns were the latest to join the mass migration. Although a few departed as early as 1864, not until the 1880s, a stagnant decade in

Scandinavia, did heavy Finnish emigration begin. Much of it came from the Swedish-speaking east coast of the Gulf of Bothnia and continued even more strongly from there after 1900.[7]

Swedish migration was heaviest from several provinces west and south of Stockholm, particularly Hallard, Jönköping, Värmland, Kronoberg, Kalmar, and Alvsborg, in that order. Close by to the west were the southeast and south central regions of Norway, from which its migrants came in greatest numbers. Northern Sweden, along with the areas around Uppsala and Stockholm, contributed least to overseas migration. Those cities and Göteborg attracted internal migrants and contributed only lightly to the overseas flow.[8]

In Norway, the area around the Sognefjord and the south central districts of Valdres and Hallingdall lost population at the greatest rates, well above the rate of Cornwall, which had the highest rate in England.[9] From Denmark, the greatest numbers emigrated from the Baltic island of Bornholm and the southern Zealand district of Lolland-Falster. Copenhagen contributed above-average numbers, as did the northern tip of Jutland and areas near the German border, and market towns generally.[10]

Scandinavians migrated internally, within Europe, and overseas, as did other peoples, but with some peculiarities. Swedes and Danes (Norwegians and Finns less often) migrated within their borders, usually from countryside to towns and cities. Seldom did any of them go to other European countries, which is not surprising since those countries were part of the mass migration themselves. Scandinavians chose the United States overwhelmingly, more often than the Irish did (see table 13).

Norwegians often came from isolated communities. To get to Bergen from

TABLE 13

Overseas Destinations of Scandinavian Emigrants, 1869–1914
(Percentages)

From	To U.S.A.	Canada	Latin America	Other[a]
Denmark	89.1	4.7	3.3	2.9
Finland[b]	93.0	6.2	0.3	0.5
Norway	95.6	3.8	0.0	0.6
Sweden	97.6	1.2	0.6	0.6

Kristian Hvidt, *Flight to America: The Social Background of 300,000 Danish Emigrants* (New York: Academic Press, 1975), 162, table 13.1 (his source is Ferenczi and Willcox, II:299). The exception is the small Icelander migration, of which (1871–1925) 15 percent went to the United States, 84.8 percent to Canada, and 0.2 percent to Latin America (Hans Norman and Harald Runblom, *Transatlantic Connections: Nordic Migration to the New World after 1800* [Oslo: Norwegian University Press (Universitetsforlaget AS), (1988)], 70).

[a]Australia, New Zealand, South Africa, and elsewhere.

[b]1901–1923. From Norman and Runblom, 70, table 5.

Balestrand one had to cross two fjords and travel eighty miles; to Oslo it was over two hundred miles. The migrants re-created those communities as well as they could in a few places in the upper Midwest of the United States. Thus they usually remained as overwhelmingly rural as they had been in Norway.[11] This tendency preserved ethnic patterns (or retarded assimilation). Even in the 1980s a psychological gulf separated the two Iowa towns of Decorah, a Norwegian and Lutheran settlement, and Spillville, which is Czech and Catholic, although they are less than a fifteen-minute drive apart. Swedes and Danes, however, spread themselves much more widely around the midwestern and western United States.[12]

Latin America never attracted more than a few thousand people from the entire Scandinavian emigration. A Swedish publicist named Johann Dam persuaded 108 people, mostly from Stockholm, to emigrate to Santa Catarina in southern Brazil in 1868. Soon "destitute," they hardly formed a basis for chain migration. In 1890 the Brazilian government recruited and subsidized a group of about 2,000 Swedes, mostly families, for Rio Grande do Sul. Again, since living conditions were harsh, no more followed. It is easy to understand why there was "no continuous stream of migrants from Sweden to Latin America," as Harald Runblom puts it.[13] About 14,000 Danes went to South America between 1869 and 1924, three-fourths of them to Argentina, where they created "concentrated Danish settlements" in the provinces of Buenos Aires and Mendoza. But these were rare. For whatever mixture of cultural and economic reasons, Scandinavians did not graft well to Latin America. The Northerners "found themselves in miserable circumstances," suffering "material want and cultural dissolution," even to the point where the Swedish government evacuated several hundred Swedes from Brazil in 1912.[14]

Canada attracted a few thousand Icelanders, who created agricultural communities west of Winnipeg. Larger numbers of Danes, Norwegians, and Swedes went to Saskatchewan, Alberta, and British Columbia. Some farmed, while others worked on railroads or in construction, or, as Finns often did, in lumbering. By the 1880s Scandinavians were coming to the United States, not only out of "land hunger," but also to find wage-paying jobs.[15]

In all four mainland countries, internal labor-seeking migration was hardly anything new (although Ostergren's migrants from Upper Dalarna had not been travelers previously). The basis for transatlantic migration already existed in the culture, ready to burst forth when the means (steamships) of travel and the opportunities in the United States became available.[16] For people in remote towns in the Norwegian fjords or on the Bothnian coast of Finland, with a prepaid ticket booked all the way to Chicago or Minnesota, the United States probably seemed a more promising target than Stockholm, Bergen, or Copenhagen. For Scandinavians, as in the case of British migrants, the distinction between the "old" land-seeking immigration and the "new" labor-seeking immigration breaks down. They coexisted at least as early as the 1880s. Scandinavians and Britons shared with South and East Europeans the characteristics of "new" immigrants.

The overwhelming tendency of Scandinavians to go to the United States resulted from active recruitment by shipping companies and their agents, from friends and relatives already there who by letter or sometimes in person urged those at home to come over, and from the prepaid tickets or cash remittances they sent. Once chains began, they repeated and nourished themselves, as they did among the Irish. In the 1880s and 1890s, prepaid tickets financed one-fourth of the Danish migrants and half of the Swedes. For those hundreds of thousands of people, Hvidt concludes, "we can almost say that . . . the decision to emigrate was made in America."[17]

During the years 1905 to 1914, probably about one-third of Norwegian male migrants and two-fifths of the females crossed to America on prepaid tickets.[18] As in other European countries, letters from America helped develop a tradition of migration from some remote places such as Balestrand. "The most traditional regions often became the hotbeds of America fever."[19] Steamship companies employed hundreds of emigrant agents and recruiters throughout Sweden. Their agents encouraged people to migrate, and booked space on trains and ships for those who decided to.[20]

The customary route began with a coastal ferry or a train to one of several ports: in Norway, Trondheim, Bergen, or Kristiania (Oslo); in Sweden, Göteborg; in Denmark, Copenhagen; and in Finland, Vaasa and Hangö. Scandinavian ships took the migrants across the North Sea to Hull, where they boarded trains for Liverpool. They then made the transatlantic crossing on British liners. British companies wrote 90 percent of the tickets from Sweden in the 1880s and captured much of the Norwegian (even Icelander) traffic as well.[21] Exceptions included the few who took trains to Hamburg or Bremen and then a German ship to New York, as well as passengers on the Danish Thingvalla Line from Copenhagen direct to New York. From there railroads led to Chicago or points in the upper Mississippi Valley.

How old were the migrants and what proportions were male and female? What fractions were rural or urban? Did they travel in family groups or individually? What classes and occupations did they represent? Finally, how many returned? All of these questions, and what changes took place over the years from 1871 to 1914, may be answered better for the Scandinavians than for most groups.

Just over half of the migrants were fifteen to thirty years old, and the fifteen-to-twenty-four cohort was especially overrepresented among Danes and Norwegians. Urban migrants were older, on average, than rural ones by a few years.[22] The clear majority of the Danish migrants were men, 61.4 percent for the 1868–1900 period, ranging between a high of 65 percent for 1866–1870 and a low of 57 percent in the 1890s. Adult females constituted 36.7 percent. While young men went directly overseas, women from rural areas often migrated to towns or to Copenhagen to work as domestics or as unskilled operatives. Thus they bore out one of E. L. Ravenstein's "laws," which he based on the behavior of English migrants, that more women migrated within their country, and over shorter distances, than men.

Among Finns, the sex ratio was more heavily skewed toward males. Of the Finns who started leaving *en masse* about 1880, 80 percent were male, and, though the proportion dipped to 60 percent in the late 1890s, it remained at about 65 percent after 1900. The Swedish and Norwegian migrants were much more evenly distributed—usually 50 to 55 percent male. The Mormon migration of some twenty thousand from Denmark before 1904 divided almost exactly between males and females (as was true of the Mormon migration from Illinois to Utah in the late 1840s); it was distributed almost normally in age because it included so many already established families.[23]

Migration in family groups gave way over time to individuals traveling by themselves or with nonrelatives. In Norway, "what had begun [in mid-century] as a family exodus ended as a migration of unmarried youth," especially young men from the countryside. Fifteen to twenty-five years of age, they made up one-fourth of the Norwegian migrants of the 1860s; by the early 1900s they accounted for two-thirds.[24] Families traveling together provided 60 percent of the Swedish migration in the 1840s, but only 42 percent in the 1870s and 25 to 26 percent after 1900.[25] Earlier Swedish migrants included better-off farm families, traveling in groups of perhaps several dozen, benefiting from chains of kinship and information. After 1890, landless young men and women predominated, and differences lessened between internal and international migrants. Very few of the early, family migrants returned—they had reconstituted their society in Minnesota and South Dakota. But the post-1900 migrants, much more footloose, returned more often.[26]

Among Danes, the figures were almost identical. Only among Finns did family migration persist as late as the 1890s, when it too was overtaken by individual migrants.[27] Females more likely traveled in family groups (in Denmark, 21 percent of adult males and 37 percent of adult females). But, as Hvidt perceived, adult women migrants included two different subgroups: married women going with, or following, their husbands and children; and younger, unmarried women who were job seekers and, "from a social point of view, little different from the [young unmarried] male emigrants."[28]

Young women migrated to market towns and capital cities, or across the Atlantic, for the same reasons young men did. In traditional rural areas, the sexual division of labor only intensified those choices. The work there was heavy, the hours long, and the future decidedly unpromising. In the Balestrand district, men cut hay while women raked it and lifted it to racks. Young women were responsible for the livestock, which meant "rigorous work" began at six in the morning, when the milkmaid cleaned up the night's manure and fed and milked the cattle. All day she carried hay, twigs, and dozens of buckets of water, often over considerable distances. In the evening she had to feed and milk the cattle once more. The day's work done, she could look forward to a night's sleep in the barn, where the plowboys also dwelt.[29]

A young woman in such a situation might hear that in America women did not work in the fields except perhaps at harvest time, or that windmills (instead of women) pumped the water, or that housemaids and cooks earned in America as much cash in a week as Scandinavians earned in a month even in Stockholm. She might learn that instead of hoeing sugar beets in southern Sweden in a team with twenty other women, led by a male overseer, she could do her own housework in Minnesota, where teams of horses pulled reapers and combines to bring in the family's harvest. She might be tempted to emigrate.[30]

The countryside and the towns both contributed to migration from Scandinavia. Although urban population increased more rapidly than rural (as was happening elsewhere in Europe and in the United States), the majority of people remained rural through 1914. More often than not, emigrants came from rural backgrounds. Landless farm laborers, especially after they married, lacked the means to emigrate. Yet cotters (tenants who paid their landlords in services and retained some of what they produced), the noninheriting sons and daughters of landowning farmers, and most of all, unmarried maidservants and farmhands, all had high rates of emigration.[31]

Though a minority in absolute numbers, migrants from towns and cities were overrepresented in comparison with their presence in the general population. The Danish story resembles what was happening in England: "idyllic little towns without any new factories or workshops usually produced a great[er] number of emigrants" than did rapidly industrializing ones, and provincial towns provided an undue share of emigrants.[32] In Denmark, migrants from towns actually outnumbered country people after 1900.[33] Many, perhaps about half, of the "urban" migrants from larger cities such as Stockholm, Bergen, and Kristiania had begun their lives in rural areas and had moved to those cities some time earlier. This stepwise migration was especially true of women, who first left the farm to become domestics in the city and then made a second move overseas.[34]

The emigrants, by occupation and background, thus included disproportionate numbers of young men and women who were being marginalized by the unavailability of land. They also were attracted to urban-located wage opportunities, either in the home country or in America. Farm owners did not need to migrate; landless farm workers often could not; cotters and others in the middle often did. In Sweden, fragmentation of farms into dwarf holdings because of partible inheritance encouraged emigration. Whether land went to one heir or to many, the shortage of it provoked departure. Inheritance of a subdivided dwarf plot was a slow way to fail in life, whereas impartible inheritance clarified a hopeless situation from the start. Non-farm people also left; from villages and cities alike, journeyman craftsmen and apprentices were also well represented among the migrants. So were domestics and industrial laborers—occupational categories which in truth meant men and women who were young and not yet skilled.[35]

Örebro *lan,* a district about eighty miles west-southwest of Stockholm, had one of the highest emigration rates in Sweden. Hans Norman, who performed a multivariate analysis on its sources, found that little migration came from fertile flatlands and much from less arable forested or mixed-vegetation land distant from the district town. But while nearness to a town encouraged internal migration, an "emigration tradition, i.e. an early start of emigration," was crucial above all else in producing overseas migration from a particular area.[36] This fact helps to explain for Stockholm and Copenhagen what Baines and Erickson noticed regarding London: transatlantic emigration from the central city was heavy, but from nearby districts such as the English Home Counties it was light.[37]

In another important respect, Scandinavian migration was quite unlike British and very much like Irish migration. Scandinavians seldom returned. The rate of repatriation rose from the 1880s into the early twentieth century as more individuals and fewer families migrated, but it rose from a tiny base. Sweden (which kept the best records in Europe for return migration) counted returnees at 5.8 percent of emigrants in 1881–1890, 23.5 percent in 1891–1900, 20.1 percent in 1901–1910, 45.6 percent in 1911–1920, and 29.9 percent in 1921–1930, for a fifty-year average of 19.0 percent.[38] The Norwegian rate may have been smaller, approaching the Irish rate.[39] Danish sources are spotty; based on the United States return figures for 1908–1914 (the earliest that exist), the Danish rate was 8.6 percent, but this figure is probably too low; more likely Danes returned at a rate not much different from that of the Swedes.[40]

Those who did return were frequently males, some still quite young but others in the thirty-five-to-forty age group. Very often they went back to the rural areas from which they originated—80 percent of the Swedes returning to Västernorrland did so—and to their former occupations. As Hans Norman points out, they differed greatly in this respect from the Italians, Greeks, and Slovaks, among others, many of whom used the Atlantic as a highway, crossing back and forth several times.[41] Of the minority who returned to Sweden (in one studied area, at least), half re-migrated to the United States.[42] It may be that not only return migration (over once and back) but also multiple migration (two or more round trips) was rarer among Scandinavians than among British and many other European migrants. Impressionistic evidence suggests it. In any case, Scandinavians, once gone, usually stayed gone.

8

THE GERMAN EMPIRE

The German Empire which Otto von Bismarck unified under the crown of Wilhelm I of Prussia in 1871, and which became truncated in the peace settlement of 1919, dominated the middle of Europe between those dates. Second only to Russia in population and area, it stretched unbroken for about 1,000 miles from present-day eastern France (about 150 miles east of Paris, the border of Lorraine) beyond Königsberg, the capital of East Prussia, later Kaliningrad in the Russian Federation. Until the late 1880s this Wilhelmine Reich provided North America with more migrants than any other political entity except the United Kingdom. After the late 1880s it retained its own natural increase, took in migrants from Eastern Europe, and by 1910 reached a population level higher than that of West Germany in the 1980s. The rate of natural increase in the late nineteenth century hovered around 1 percent per year (0.7 percent during high migration in the mid-1880s) but jumped to about 1.5 percent after 1900, quite unusual for Europe. Germany, with 43 million people in 1875, nearly matched the 45 million then in the United States. If through some impossible turnabout the migration had flowed in reverse, from the United States to Germany, for the next forty years, the two countries would have remained fairly close in population size.[1]

Because of its large population, the German Empire never ranked higher than seventh among the countries of Europe in per capita emigration, the rank it held in the 1870s. But the migration of over 1.3 million people in the 1880s—though it gave the Reich only tenth place in per capita migration—made it in that decade the second-largest donor behind Britain.[2] Germany also figured importantly in migration history because it contained the North Sea ports of Bremen and Hamburg, the most accessible embarkation points for migrants from east of the Elbe, whether German or non-German. Many Germans from the Rhineland, Baden-Württemberg or Bavaria, on the other hand, found Antwerp or Le Havre more convenient.[3]

In the context of the other European donor countries, Germany shared an early start with Britain, Ireland, and Scandinavia. German colonists migrated to Brazil in the 1820s and to the United States in various waves beginning in the 1830s.[4] Almost half a million Germans came to the United States in the three years from 1852 through 1854, causing a slightly greater per capita loss to the German areas than in the numerically peak period of the early 1880s.[5] Like the Irish and Scandinavians, Germans had roots in the United States firm enough by the 1870s to keep return migration at a minimum. Of the well-established groups, only the British came and went frequently, perhaps because only they were regarded as culturally equal or superior to the receiving society.

In this context, German migration—at least from certain parts of the Reich— was heavy and relatively permanent. The bulk of it, but not all, went to the United States—between 1820 and 1928, about 5.3 million (89.2 percent) of the 6 million Germans who emigrated. In the 1860s the United States' share was 94.5 percent; in the 1880s, when German emigration peaked, 92.2 percent. The United States attracted its smallest proportion, 70.8 percent, in the 1920s. A small but measurable number of Germans migrated to South America. Brazil became the second country of German emigration, with about 3.3 percent (112,000 by the German statistics) between 1871 and 1928, and Argentina the third, with an indeterminably smaller number. By German figures, 64,000 went to Argentina, but by Argentine figures, 118,000 did so.[6]

The statistical sources on German migration involve uncertainties and gaps which, except for the Scandinavian figures, are endemic to all migration statistics; some have already been mentioned. Consequently we may face the problem here and be done with it. (See table 14 for discrepant statistics.) The German data were first analyzed in this context in 1930 by Friedrich Burgdörfer, writing in Ferenczi and Willcox, and the problem has still not been fully explained.[7] (As we will see, similar problems cloud analysis of Italian and other migrations.)[8]

The problem is a double one: first, the difficulties inherent in comparing any sets of statistics compiled at different times for different purposes; and second, the discrepancies between donor and receiver countries in counting what should have been the same people (already mentioned in connection with British and Irish migration to the United States and Canada). Comparability problems include those of definition and outside influences. Which migrants were leaving permanently, which ones were leaving for a season or two, and which ones were tourists or on business trips? Between the first two categories especially, the migrant-passengers themselves had no idea where they fit because their futures were anything but clear. Return migration, and whether it was planned from the start or resulted from failed expectations, will always remain a statistical conundrum because of these unclear definitions. Laws regarding tax collection, conscription, and public health quarantines were variously enforced; unauthorized migration to avoid them consequently varied. Discrepancies between European

TABLE 14

German Migrants to Five Countries: Discrepancies between Emigrant and Immigrant Statistics (000 Omitted)

Emigrants = German figures; Immigrants = Receiving Country's figures

	1871–80	*1881–90*	*1891–1900*	*1901–10*	*1911–20*
To U.S.A.					
Emigrants	555.9	1,237.1	478.9	255.2	63.8
Immigrants	718.2	1,453.0	505.2	341.5	143.9
To Argentina					
Emigrants	1.5	8.4	6.4	4.6	4.2
Immigrants	3.8	14.2	8.7	19.3	22.2
To Brazil					
Emigrants	20.7	18.8	12.5	4.1	1.7
Immigrants	16.9	21.5	12.5	17.5	26.2
To Canada					
Emigrants	—	—	—	3.2	3.3
Immigrants	—	—	—	18.6	20.2
To Australia					
Emigrants	—	—	—	1.5	1.2
Immigrants	—	—	—	13.7	14.2

Friedrich Burgdörfer, "Die Wanderungen über die deutschen Reichsgrenzen im letzten Jahrhundert," 1930, in Imre Ferenczi and Walter F. Willcox, eds., *International Migrations*, 2 vols. (New York: National Bureau of Economic Research, 1929, 1931), II: 336, 355–56, giving per-decade totals. For annual figures, and series for Canada and Australia, see Burgdörfer's essay (1930) reprinted in Wolfgang Köllmann and Peter Marschalck, eds., *Bevölkerungsgeschichte* (Cologne: Kiepenheuer & Witsch, 1972), 294, 296.

and New World migration figures sometimes lay in record keeping. For example, American immigration figures for long periods did not include first- or second-class cabin passengers, who were taken off before the steerage passengers, or overland arrivals from Canada, whatever their origins. Arrivals at Castle Garden and, after 1892, Ellis Island were classified as "German" if that was their language, but many were Austrians rather than Reich Germans. After the North German Bund abolished passports in 1867, emigrants were more difficult to track, especially if they left from non-German ports such as Trieste, Genoa, and Copenhagen. Burgdörfer concluded that "the actual number is probably nearer the German totals than the [United States']. The German figures are too small because they make certain omissions and start from too narrow a definition. The American immigration statistics are too large because they define an emigrant too broadly, and because they include German-speaking emigrants who lived outside of Germany."[9] Fortunately the two sets of figures are reasonably close until 1900, by which time the great bulk of German migration to the United States had already happened.

Burgdörfer offered several explanations for the discrepancies. Germans going to Canada and Australia often went "indirect," that is, through British ports. Germans in Canada often went first to the United States and were recorded as going there, while Germans heading for South America gave that as their destination rather than specifically Brazil or Argentina.[10] All of the explanations are helpful but not fully satisfying, nor have better ones been offered in the sixty years since Burgdörfer wrote. One should simply keep in mind that in the peak year of German migration to the United States, 1882, the American figures exceeded the German by more than 61,000, or 24.4 percent. The Hanseatic city-states of Hamburg and Bremen, however, did keep detailed and presumably accurate figures on embarkations from their ports. Beginning in 1871 the new Imperial German Government used that information for extensive statistical reports that shed much light on the German side of the migration.[11]

As noted above, migration from Germany started early. It also finished early. The overseas migration of Reich Germans fell off sharply in the late 1880s as urban industrial jobs proliferated. Migration within the German-language area, much of it seasonal, had a long history before 1871, notably in areas that were beginning to industrialize and where landless peasants had to gain some income from cottage industry; migration to the Netherlands—"Hollandgängerei"—had taken place since the late eighteenth century, for example.[12] Internal migration, or *Binnenwanderung,* continued in greater numbers after the consolidation of the Reich, as did international migration (*Auswanderung*). The migration swelled as an agricultural transformation pushed peasants off the land and contracted as Germany industrialized swiftly after 1885. The German Empire was the only country within Europe that was for decades a major donor of people but then became a net receiver.

Population pressure in itself did not induce people to leave Germany. In the late nineteenth century, the heaviest migration came from some of the less densely populated provinces, which were undergoing agricultural changes that lowered the demand for farm labor (see table 15). As was happening in England and Sweden, areas around large industrializing cities were underrepresented in the overseas migration because they absorbed the potential labor force nearby. Earlier in the century, the upper Rhineland and the west (Hesse, Westfalia, Thuringia) produced the most migrants, many of them (like Scandinavians) young people otherwise facing bleak futures on small plots—dwarf holdings of a couple of hectares or less—that had been subdivided through inheritance to a point below survivability. In the 1870s and 1880s, eastern and northeastern

TABLE 15

German Provinces with Highest and Lowest Rates (per 100,000 Population) of Transatlantic Migration, 1871–1914

	1871–74	*1880–84*	*1890–94*	*1900–04*	*1910–14*
Pomerania	695	1,234	474	65	24
West Prussia	329[a]	1,154	672	113	40
Posen	531	866	623	173	58
Schleswig-Holstein	460	866	287	79	50
Bremen	428	852	521	162	89
Saxony	67	130	73	22	17
Silesia	58	117	56	14	10
Anhalt	64	102	42	14	3
East Prussia	329[a]	91	98	30	18
Alsace-Lorraine	35	42	50	37	22

Rearranged from Friedrich Burgdörfer, "Die Wanderungen über die deutschen Reichsgrenzen im letzten Jahrhundert," 1930, reprinted in Wolfgang Köllmann and Peter Marschalck, eds., *Bevölkerungsgeschichte* (Cologne: Kiepenheuer & Witsch, 1972), 307. Rank is that of 1880–84; the order was not greatly different at other times between 1871 and 1914. Rate is average annual number of migrants per 100,000 population.
[a]East and West Prussia combined.

provinces produced many of the migrants, also because of the unavailability of land, but in this case because of the predominance of large estates.

Young Germans seldom had a chance to acquire land. While their fathers and grandfathers might have worked on the estates as contract workers (*Instleute*) protected to some extent by feudal rights, the abolition of serfdom and the mechanization of farming so depressed wages that migration proved very attractive.[13] Small farmers and tenants feared that they and their children would become proletarianized. As in Sweden and Norway, no system of inheritance worked advantageously for young rural people in the late nineteenth century; partible inheritance, the practice in southwestern Germany, was still driving people out in the 1880s and 1890s; nonpartible inheritance, as in Schleswig-Holstein, Hannover, and Oldenburg in the north, provided noninheriting siblings with a cash payment but no land, thus making American farmland very attractive and accessible.[14] Migration became particularly heavy from the eastern border provinces of West Prussia, Pomerania, and Posen. There the largest estates, having lost their German labor force, replaced it with Polish migrants from Russian and Austrian Poland.[15] Provinces where mining and industry were developing, such as Silesia and Alsace, absorbed their own young people and more.[16]

Migration within Germany included many peasants and workers who lacked the wherewithal to get to Hamburg or Bremen and strike out across the Atlantic. Remittances or prepaid tickets from those already in the New World helped a large proportion—a good one-third, according to an American consul in Bremen in 1890—of the transatlantic migrants.[17] Those not so lucky migrated instead to the booming industrial towns and cities such as Essen and Köln, in the Ruhr, and Berlin and Breslau. Thus less densely populated provinces lost people faster than the more densely settled Brandenburg, Saxony, and Silesia.[18] As a result of these migrations, the Reich's labor force rose from 17 million in 1882 to over 25 million in 1907, despite Germany's loss of a net 5 million from emigration in the seventy years before World War I. (The answer to this seeming contradiction was that most of the out-migration had taken place before the late 1880s). A few years later, in-migration from nearby parts of the Russian and Austrian empires rose sharply. As Klaus Bade states succinctly, "from the mid-1890s on . . . Germany exported fewer and fewer people, but ever more goods. Soon she was forced to import people from abroad."[19]

The German economy, stagnant during 1875–1880, began inching forward in the early 1880s and accelerated into rapid growth on broad fronts after 1886. The depression that began in 1873 lasted for several years in Britain, France, Germany, and the United States. Recovery began in the United States in 1879 and soon devolved into a remarkable period of expansion that lasted until 1893, led by railroad building, urban construction, manufacturing, and agriculture. The French and British economies remained anemic through the 1880s, but the German economy was "sharply distinguished" from them by "growth and prosperity, particularly after 1886."[20] Chemicals, metals, electrical equipment, urban construction, railroads, canals, and transatlantic shipping were only the most visible of the developing sectors. The rise in agricultural productivity reduced the demand for farm workers. The flourishing labor market became more urban-located than ever, and swarming internal migration was the result. The late 1880s were as vigorous in the Reich as the early 1880s were in the United States; the prosperity cycle which began in 1879 in the United States followed in 1886–1887 in Germany. And it kept happening. Germany avoided the hard times that wracked the United States from the Panic of 1893 through the rest of the 1890s. In the twenty years leading up to 1914, the German economy grew steadily, except for two brief crises in 1901 and 1906, at a robust annual rate of 3.3 percent.[21]

The seven- or eight-year lag between the German and the American prosperity cycles of the 1880s and the consistency of German growth once begun, together with flat German and exuberant American agriculture, help to explain why German internal migration was large throughout the period and why overseas migration was so great from 1879 through 1886 and then receded permanently. Except (as was true in Sweden) for a few thousand Germans recruited to Brazil in 1890–1891 to meet sharp labor demand following the abolition of slavery,

German migrants overwhelmingly opted for the United States, going to cities as well as farms. Emigration through Hamburg swelled by a factor of eight between 1877 and 1881, but the proportions changed—that of workers doubled while that of farmers (proprietors and tenants alike) fell by more than a third.[22]

Conditions of working-class life made migration attractive in the early 1880s but increasingly less so a few years later. One worker recalled how, as a child, he traveled with his family in 1881 across northern Germany. The whole family migrated, working from early spring to late fall, from agricultural districts to sugar factories in Magdeburg or Braunschweig, or to other industries in Hannover, Oldenburg, or Schleswig-Holstein. They migrated from Pomerania and West Prussia to Berlin, meeting a mixture of Kashubs, Masurians, Latvians, Galicians, Hungarians, and Slovaks.[23] For a family such as his, passage to America could probably have come only from remittances or a prepaid ticket. Yet by 1891, a skilled worker in Berlin could live with his wife and two children in a "clean and decent" apartment on an annual income of 1,700 marks, which approximated the average annual income of a skilled worker in America ($400).[24] For the skilled, at least, the cash incentive to emigrate had disappeared.

Prior to the late 1880s, however, several incentives operated. Bismarck's anti-socialist law, in effect from 1878 to 1890, encouraged social democrats and class-conscious laborites to leave. The Bismarckian *Kulturkampf* did the same for Catholics.[25] And the economic inducements remained. The U.S. State Department asked its consuls in Europe in 1885 to describe economic conditions in their districts that might affect migration. Their reports from Germany leave little mystery about why migration remained high at that time. Consul-General Brewer in Berlin found the "necessaries of life" costing more in Berlin than in New York, with wages lower; every family member had to help, including women: "The laboring women here are accustomed to perform the hardest of manual labor, on the farm, in the shop, about the mines . . . such as would only be performed by the strongest of men in the United States."[26] The rock-bottom expenses for a laborer in Berlin were $186 a year, but his wages were $123. A stonemason, living with his wife and three children in a village outside Berlin, made 95 cents for a twelve-hour day, or $238 a year (he was idle for four months). Although his expenses were $301, he could use a small plot to grow potatoes and keep a goat and a hog.

Berliners in fact were relatively well off. The consul in Breslau reported that Silesian male farm laborers made, in cash and food, between $53 and $78 a year, females between $45 and $60. Artisans and female field workers migrated every spring from Silesia to Prussia, Poland, Hungary, and Saxony; "the women work in the fields of Saxony during six or seven months in each year, receiving about 36 cents per day, and return to their homes at the commencement of winter with their saved earnings."[27] But Silesia represented an extreme of poverty. Provinces in the west and northwest such as Rhenish Prussia, Alsace, and Thuringia produced few migrants unless several successive crop failures occurred. The consul in Leipzig even reported—for the first time—that emigration was ebbing because local industry was picking up and exports were high. Change was in the air.[28]

Until it happened, however, conditions for the laboring classes in both cities and rural areas was unenviable. For farm women it must have been almost unendurable. Every consul's report commented on female workers. In general they earned half of what men earned. That imbalance contributed to another; men more easily scraped together the money to emigrate, and did so, leaving a female-skewed sex ratio in some areas, thus making marriage and some escape from wage labor more difficult for the women who remained. Groups of women performed stoop labor in the fields, overseen by a male, as in Sweden. Women worked in quarries, in the needle trades, as glassblowers, and as bookbinders. Farm work for them could be brutal. The American consul in Sonneberg, Thuringia, painted this picture:

> American readers will hardly understand how it can be that the severest part of existence in this whole region falls to the lot of woman. But such is the fact. She is the servant and the burden-bearer. . . . The position of wife and mother appears to shield her from no hardship. . . . Her sex is liberally represented in most of the manual-labor occupations of the district, even to mining and foundry work, but far less liberally in any branch of clerical or professional life. . . .
>
> Thus it is seen that the chief pursuits of women in this district are not of a gentle or refining character. They perform by far the greater part of all the out-door manual service. The planting and the sowing, including the preparation of the soil therefor, is done by them. I have seen many a woman in the past few weeks holding the plow drawn by a pair of cows, and still more of them 'toting' manure into the fields in baskets strapped to their backs. They also do the haying, including the mowing and the pitching; likewise the harvesting; after which they thresh much of the grain with the old-fashioned hand flail. They accompany the coal carts through the city and put the coal in the cellars, while the male driver sits upon his seat. They carry on nearly all the dairy business, and draw the milk into town in a hand cart—a woman and a dog usually constituting the team. 'I have just written to my wife,' said [an American traveler recently], 'that it is a very serious thing to be a dog in Germany, or a cow, or a woman.' "[29]

As was the case in Britain and Scandinavia, the mass of migrants comprised young people, 55 to 58 percent male. The age and sex structure of the German overseas migration remained fairly stable from the 1870s to 1914.[30] Changes did take place, however, in occupations and family status. Through the 1870s and well into the 1880s, rural people predominated, whether independent, smallholding peasants who could sell their holdings and buy better ones in the American Midwest, or noninheriting children of peasant families whose emigration rested on parental support or remittances from the United States, or farm laborers who managed to get passage and then to step onto the low rungs of the economic ladder there. Independent artisans and craft workers accounted for a substantial minority. Until then, the migration was "appropriate to early industri-alization and characterized by the emigration of lower-peasant and lower-middle-class elements, either as families or as individuals."[31]

After 1890 the idea circulated in Germany that the farm frontier in the United States had filled up. The basis for this was the Census Bureau's announcement that the frontier had closed, although settlement continued for some years. In any case industrial opportunities within Germany were multiplying. Thus the farm-family migration, in Mönckmeier's words of 1912, "belongs to history. . . . The great majority of German immigrants go now to cities and industrial areas and only increase the proletariat. . . . They are workseekers, not homeseekers."[32] Before 1893, however, most German emigrants continued to travel as members of family groups, to a greater extent than other North Europeans. Even in the peak years of 1881–1885, family migration was strong, and for the decade 1881–1890 58 percent of Germans migrated as family members. In the follow-ing decade the proportion fell to 48 percent and continued to slide to 39 percent during 1911–1920; but the total numbers were much smaller by then.[33]

Throughout the period, however, females made up about 55 percent of family migrants while males constituted 64 to 71 percent of migrants traveling alone.[34] Male heads of families sometimes went first to find "a new existence in the new land," and the family followed after he had done so.[35] After 1890, as family migration became much less common, so did the emigration of women. German emigration, shrunken as it then became, consisted of labor-seeking young men, a "proletarian mass emigration."[36]

The shift from family to individual migration should not be overstressed. It was one of degree. Individuals seeking labor (skilled or not) rather than land formed a substantial minority in the 1870s and earlier. Unfortunately no one has researched the numbers as Erickson did for British migrants, or as others have done for parts of Scandinavia. But it seems likely that in the German case as well, the "new immigration," in the sense of labor seeking rather than land seeking, began well before 1880. In the first five years of the 1880s, almost a million Germans emigrated, 90 percent of them overseas. In the second half of the 1880s, nearly half a million Germans emigrated overseas; but 142,000 others migrated *into* Germany, most of them from the Russian and Austro-Hungarian empires. The tide turned in the late 1880s. By 1895 "the German mass emigra-tion of the nineteenth century was closed," and the German Empire had become a net importer of people.[37]

Return and repeat migration among Germans is not well documented. It apparently happened at a much lower rate than among the English and at a level closer to that of the Scandinavians. Mönckmeier noted that "many" Germans returned, and that "today [1912] in Germany there are many such 'Amerikaner' living in part on their American earnings." But useful statistics do not exist.[38] One would expect that a migration of which the majority (before 1890) were land-seeking families would produce relatively few returnees. And German-American and Teuto-Brazilian communities and communal institutions were sufficiently well developed to placate homesickness. Although Burgdörfer noted an unusually strong return movement in 1893–1894, when the United States abruptly collapsed into depression, by then the emigration had almost stopped. The mass migration of the early 1880s did not reverse itself.

The Hamburg authorities, when they concerned themselves with returning migrants, addressed their efforts chiefly to keeping out public charges. They passed regulations on the funding of returnees and on penalizing ship captains who might dump pauper returnees at the docks. The harbor police were to check before the arrival of a ship to see whether penniless passengers were on board, and if so the captain was enjoined to forbid them from landing.[39] By that time, the ports of Hamburg and Bremen were as crowded as ever, but with the many peoples of Austria-Hungary and Russia; no longer with Germans.

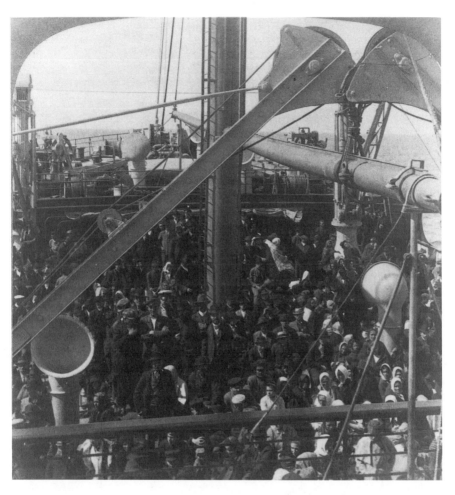

Emigrants leaving Bremen, about 1890, on the *Königin Luise*. Courtesy of the Library of Congress.

Steerage children playing on deck of the *Friedrich der Grosze,* about 1911. Courtesy of the Library of Congress.

The interior of Castle Garden, New York's disembarkation point before 1890. From *Harper's Magazine,* March 1871. Courtesy of the Library of Congress.

Migrants arriving in the "Land of Promise," 1901. Courtesy of the Library of Congress.

Buenos Aires' Immigrant Hotel, a Southern Hemisphere Ellis Island. Courtesy of the Library of Congress.

Dining room of the Immigrant Hotel, Buenos Aires, about 1920. Courtesy of the Library of Congress.

Argentine immigrants' farm home, near Buenos Aires, probably about 1915.
Courtesy of the Library of Congress.

Brazil, São Paulo state. View of the village of the *colonia* Nova Odessa. Courtesy
of the Library of Congress.

Coffee berry pickers, about 1920, in Brazil, probably São Paulo state—a more typical setting than the *colonia*. Courtesy of the Library of Congress.

The expansion of steamships, 1871–1914. Four pathbreaking vessels: (*a*) the *Oceanic,* 1871; (*b*) the new *Oceanic,* 1899; (*c*) the *Olympic* (the better-fated sister ship of the *Titanic*), 1911; and (*d*) the *Imperator,* 1913. The change in transatlantic passenger capability did not end with the shift from sail to steam about 1870 but continued as vessels were built ever larger, from those of 1,500 to 2,000 tons in the early 1870s to behemoths of more than 50,000 tons by 1914. After N. R. P. Bonsor, *North Atlantic Seaway* (Prescott, Lancashire: T. Stephenson & Sons Ltd., 1955).

The *Lusitania*'s first arrival in New York Harbor, September 13, 1907. Courtesy of the Library of Congress.

The rudder of the *Imperator*, in service from 1913. Courtesy of the Library of Congress.

Homesteaders Mr. and Mrs. Tom Ogden en route from England via Massachusetts to Bingley, Alberta, spring 1910. Courtesy of the Glenbow Museum, Calgary, Alberta.

9

AUSTRIA-HUNGARY AND RUSSIA, JEWS AND POLES

East and south of the German Reich lay the great multiethnic empires of Russia and Austria-Hungary. Hundreds of miles distant from the Atlantic, they were nonetheless very much involved in the Atlantic demographic pool. Not to return until 1919, the Polish nation had disappeared from the political map in the partition of 1795, dividing the Polish people among all three empires. Yiddish-speaking Ashkenazi Jews were concentrated most heavily in Austrian Galicia and Russian Lithuania and Poland but lived also throughout what is now Belorussia and the Ukraine. The migration from these areas touched every group; it was a generalized phenomenon, in Ewa Morawska's phrase, of "colossal dimensions," participated in by what was supposed to be a traditional peasant society. Yet 30 to 35 percent of the "adult agrarian population of . . . Hungary proper, Slovakia, all of Poland, the western . . . Ukraine, Subcarpathian Rus', Transylvania, Croatia-Slavonia, northern Serbia and Slovenia, lived or worked in places different from that of their birth."[1]

The East European peasantry, not strangers to migration and never a static group in any case, grasped quickly the potential economic profit and psychological exhilaration of transatlantic migration. Austrians, Hungarians, and Czechs migrated in the 1870s to take up farmland in Kansas and Nebraska. Poles migrated extensively across Germany but also went to Brazil and the United States. Slovaks started leaving their northern Hungarian counties of Spis, Saros, and Zemplen after a crop failure in 1879 underscored their bleak chances there.[2] Croatians, Slovenes, Rusins, and other national groups also contributed to labor-seeking migration across the Atlantic, principally to the United States, beginning about 1880 and continuing most strongly from 1901 to 1914.

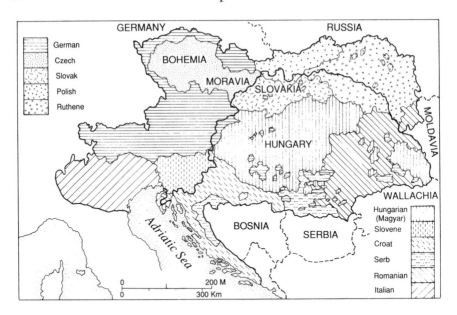

Map 3. The Austro-Hungarian Empire before 1914 (*Map by Norman Pounds*)
Shown are eleven major ethnic groups.

While the long-established, often seasonal migrations within Central and East Europe were proto-industrial and could be done by wagon or even on foot, transatlantic migration *en masse* had to await the arrival of railroads to take passengers from remote villages to expanding cities and thence to the ports of Bremen and Hamburg. Railroads linked western Austria with central Hungary in the 1860s and became networks first in Germany, then in Austria-Hungary and Congress (Russian) Poland by the 1870s. The Balkans lagged—Serbia's first line opened in 1878—as did their emigration.[3] The railroad networks effectively created worldwide competition in agricultural products and punished the inefficient, whereupon the railroad provided a way out for the young workers made redundant by it. The American economist Emily Greene Balch recounted what a Ruthenian priest in Galicia told her about how migration began from that area. Following the end of serfdom, land continued to be subdivided below the survival point, while home crafts could no longer compete against factory goods. In about 1875 a new railroad opened, leading from the edge of the Carpathians to the already existing line from Lvov to Kraków. Not long after that an out-of-work Polish weaver made his way to New York. He wrote a friend at home about how promising things were, and from that point on, despite opposition from employers and the authorities, the Galician emigration was under way.[4]

The railroads required to bring those millions to Hamburg, Bremen, Trieste, and, later, Odessa were in place north of the Balkans by the 1870s. With land still available in the Great Plains and wages much higher than at home, migration to the New World became an attractive option.

Bremen and Hamburg serviced the mass of East European transatlantic migrants. Of the 1.84 million who left Austria between 1870 and 1910, 1.3 million used the two northern German ports.[5] Of the 64,000 western Pomeranians who exited during 1871–1880, 60,500 went through Bremen and Hamburg, the remaining few from Antwerp and Szczecin. That pattern continued in the 1880s.[6] Emigration through the Hanseatic ports had always included people traveling by themselves as well as families, but as sail gave way to steam, and as Germans gave way to East Europeans, the proportion of wage seekers as opposed to land seekers slowly rose. Families continued through the 1880s to account for 60 percent of the emigration, but by then some were young Jewish couples rather than German peasants. By 1895, Wolfgang Köllmann and Peter Marschalck point out, the migration had shifted from "preindustrial" to "a class-conditioned form of migration typical of a highly industrialized society."[7]

In 1879, 24,864 persons migrated through Hamburg, 7,059 "indirect," via British ports, the rest "direct" to New York and other New World destinations. Of the direct passengers, 15,595 sailed in 53 steamships (average: 294) for the United States, 992 in 13 ships (average: 76) for Brazil, and 979 in 68 ships (average: 15) for Argentina, Chile, the West Indies, and elsewhere. One sailing vessel departed with 126 passengers for Australia, 27 others with the remaining 113 passengers to other destinations.[8]

In 1880 the destinations remained about the same but numbers rose 177 percent. The *Lucania*, sailing on February 25 for New York, included roughly one passenger in ten who gave an address in the United States, suggesting some repeat migration. Among the mass of German names were a few families of Hungarian Jews. Sailing on the *Frisia* on March 10 was the Holsteiner farm family of Hans Harms, his wife, Elise, and their eight children, aged nine and under; but of the 511 passengers individuals outnumbered family members. On the *Westfalia*'s sailing of March 17 was a group of six families (29 persons) from the same town in Hungary; five other families (28 persons) had left another Hungarian village.[9]

Then in 1881 came the peak of emigration from the German ports. Over 247,000—184,000 German, 63,000 non-German—departed from Bremen, Hamburg, and Szczecin. Of the non-Germans, 56 percent came from Austria-Hungary, 15 percent from Russia, 15 percent from Sweden, Norway, and Denmark, and 11 percent from the United States. Of those listed as German, almost 70,000 (38 percent) came from the three northeast provinces of West Prussia, Pomerania, and Posen and may have included Poles, Kaszubs, and Jews.[10] Of all these people, only 155 died at sea, of whom 127 were infants or children aged ten or under.[11]

The ships kept sailing, and as they did the passenger lists gradually changed. By early 1882 groups of as many as fifty young men from Saros and the other Slovak counties were a common feature along with Germans traveling singly and with families. In early March 1882 a number of Jewish families from Ujkely, Hungary, sailed on the *Suevia,* the *Wieland,* and the *Bohemia* along with men named Bodnar, Waczewski, Kalacz, and Smolka and others from Saros. The *Lessing*'s sailing of February 1 for New York included a large group of Slovak men from Szepes, another group from Gorlice, and eighty-five people from Saros, of whom only seven were female. Jews—sometimes mothers and daughters—came from Marienpol, Kovno, Yaroslav, and Odessa in Russia. Some Jews traveled as work groups. One ship in February 1882 carried nineteen men, aged twenty-one to twenty-five, all from Kiev, all listed as "Handl"—tradesmen—but Jewish migrants traveled as families more frequently than did Poles or Slovaks. Already in January the Meyer Hamburg family of two, the Lifschitz family of six, the Bernstein family of six, the Schwartzburg family of eight, and many others passed through Hamburg from Kiev and Kishinev in flight from pogroms. Germans, Poles, and Slovaks were often listed as "Arbeiter"—laborer—or "Landsmann"— farmer or farm worker; Jews often as "Schneider" (tailor) or some other kind of craftsman. In the column for occupation, adult women were nearly always listed simply as "frau" or "ledig"—married or single.[12]

In 1886, for the first time, non-Germans outnumbered Germans sailing from Hamburg and Bremen, and by a large margin—100,000 to 67,000. The number of migrants from Russia and Poland nearly doubled, but that of Germans declined. West Prussia, Pomerania, and Posen contributed a little more than one-third of their 1881 contingent (still 35 percent of the reduced German total), while of the non-Germans Austria-Hungary contributed 41 percent (half from Hungary), Russia 32 percent, and the United States 14 percent (a mixture of Europeans making second trips and Americans returning home); Scandinavians (11 percent) were the only other sizable group.[13] For the next several years threats (and realities) of cholera, typhus, and smallpox infection from Russia and Austria-Hungary caused the German authorities to close the borders to migrants from time to time, most notably in late 1892 and 1893 when Hamburg was devastated by cholera. Hamburg had passed new sanitary regulations in 1887 and believed they were working, but the micro-organisms proved otherwise, killing ten thousand.[14] In 1897 the Imperial German Government passed a comprehensive emigration statute for the first time. By then dockside Hamburg and Bremen were lucrative operations servicing East European—but not German—migration.[15]

Most of the East European migrant groups shared certain characteristics. In regard to some of these, the Jewish group was the major exception. Yet even it was not exempt from the relative poverty and slow rate of development of the two eastern empires, especially compared with Germany. Serfdom was a thing of the past, but the not too distant past, in most of the region. It was abolished in East Elbian Germany in the Napoleonic era, in Austria and Hungary after the upheaval of 1848, in the Russian Empire in 1861, and in the Ottoman Empire (which included much of the Balkans) not until World War I. Despite serfdom's disappearance, vast tracts remained in the hands of large landowners everywhere in the region—Junkers, nobility, or aristocracy—who, through the organs of the state, governed "in their own interests."[16] (The same remark could have been made of Brazil and Argentina, as will be seen.) Add to this the institutions of entail and impartible inheritance, and the result is an extremely rigid, impenetrable system of landholding.[17] Tenants, sharecroppers, and agricultural day laborers abounded. The better-off ones could support themselves on a few hectares, but many others formed a landless proletariat, who found seasonal work for 150 to 200 days a year:

> Their standard way of life was one of slow starvation. They lived in unhygienic, overcrowded slums, on an average yearly income of hardly more than a hundred dollars. . . . Children were underfed. . . . There was usury, and compulsory labour for women; 96 percent of the farm servants lived in buildings which also housed stables. Disease was rampant; tuberculosis ravaged the countryside, and infant mortality was very high. . . .[18]

These unfortunates contributed to the mass of seasonal workers who migrated within Germany and the other two empires. They simply lacked the means to sail from Hamburg or Bremen. People who were slightly better off did just that, so that Austria witnessed a net loss of 1.3 million persons between 1871 and 1910, equal to over 28 percent of its natural increase. Hungary in the same period lost almost 1.4 million; Russia, about 1.5 million. From the Balkans the emigration before 1900 did not exceed 500,000 for various reasons (communal landholding and lack of access to railroads, among others), but it too expanded after 1900, thanks to new railroads, remittances, and prepaid tickets.[19]

The mechanization of agriculture and other aspects of the "agricultural crisis" that made East and South Europe uncompetitive with New World producers also promoted emigration throughout the region. Landowning peasants increasingly lived under the threat of becoming marginalized, they or their children foreseeably being pushed downward to cotter or even day-laborer status. Taxes, military conscription, changes in family relations, and unpredictable events—"a flood, a conflagration, a new American tariff, an outbreak of phylloxera in the vineyards, or a treaty admitting Italian wine at a lower rate"—could all serve as expelling forces, while recruitment by emigrant agents, the opening of new rail and steamship routes, and encouraging news from friends or relatives already overseas could all make departure attractive.[20]

Migration should not be thought of as a purely negative act, a desperation measure to escape a hopeless situation. If it had been, return and repeat migration would not have been so common. The leading authority on Hungarian emigration states that Hungarians "regarded their stay abroad as temporary, and only wanted to improve their economic position at home with the money earned abroad."[21] Morawska has stressed that emigration displayed "a 'positive' thrust" toward an envisioned accomplishment:

> The economic calculation was obvious: in Austrian *kronen* it meant an unheard-of purchasing power enabling one to afford a full hectare of land for a single year's savings or four cows in six months or a large new brick farm building in nine. . . . Indeed, the enormous amounts of money that had accrued to East Central European peasant households as the result of American migrations, made plainly visible as they were turned into land, cattle, brick houses, barns, etc., only augmented the hopes of those who had not yet gone themselves and fortified their belief that America was the peasant Eldorado.[22]

The impact and availability of the United States began later for Central and East Europeans than for the groups discussed above. Although there were clear signs that America was attracting Slovaks, Bohemians, and some others from 1880 onward, their migration did not happen broadly and in strength until the late 1890s. Like earlier groups, the East and Central European migrants were peasants, whether landless or not; but unlike earlier groups, and with a few exceptions, they returned (and often emigrated and returned again several times), probably because the transatlantic voyage became ever easier. Their migration also continued longer. Thirty years after Germans had ceased coming to the Americas, several East European groups continued to arrive in Canada. Ferenczi and Willcox concluded that between 1899 and 1924, 6,502,109 people from East Central Europe migrated overseas, most of them to the United States, and noted the ethnic distribution shown here in table 16.[23]

These generalizations cover much of the reality of the migration from Central and East Europe, but a few details specific to each major group are worth noting. In the Austrian part of the Dual Monarchy, ethnic Austrians were much less numerous among the migrants than were Jews, Ruthenians, and Poles from Galicia, and Croats and Slovenes from Dalmatia and Carniola. Czech migration,

TABLE 16

Ethnic Distribution of East European Migrants (in Percentages)

"Hebrews"	27.1	Ruthenians	4.0
Poles	22.1	Russians + Ukrainians	4.0
Germans	8.5	Lithuanians	3.9
Slovaks	8.5	Finns	3.3
Magyars	8.3	Czechs	2.3
South Slavs	7.1	Romanians	2.3

Julianna Puśkaś, "Hungarian Migration Patterns, 1880–1930: From Macroanalysis to Microanalysis," in Ira Glazier and Luigi De Rosa, eds., *Migration across Time and Nations: Population Mobility in Historical Contexts* (New York: Holmes & Meier, 1986), 238.

which had been fairly heavy in the 1870s and 1880s, was slight after 1900, exhibiting a timing closer to that of German, rather than other Slavic, emigration. The Czechs stood apart from other Austro-Hungarian groups in that their migration started and ended earlier, was often "a permanent withdrawal of entire families,"[24] and targeted the frontier of farm settlement from Texas through Kansas, Nebraska, and the upper Missouri Valley. In fact the Czech farm-family migration of the 1870s and 1880s to Kansas and Nebraska was very little different in any respect except language (and to some extent religion) from the German migration to the same places at that time; but it was very different from the labor migration of their fellow Slavs—Poles, Slovaks, and others—from the 1880s to 1914. Of all migrants from Austria proper between 1876 and 1910, 83 percent went to the United States, 8 percent to Canada, 5 percent to Argentina, and 3 percent to Brazil.[25]

Hungarians also migrated to all four New World receiving countries, as well as to Germany and other parts of the Austro-Hungarian Empire. After 1899, however, 98.5 percent of Hungary's overseas migrants went to the United States. Well over half were young men, "landless peasants and underpaid industrials who hope[d] to win fortune across the seas and return as they have seen others do, with capital accumulated."[26] In the peak years of 1905–1907, Hungary's emigrants, overseas and intra-European, were 73 percent male and 27 percent female; 60 percent aged between 20 and 39; and 69 percent "agriculturists" or "agricultural and day laborers."[27] Ethnic Magyars migrated most heavily from the northern counties bordering on Slovakia, rather than from central Hungary. Budapest, like major cities in Sweden and Germany, seemed to soak up the migrant youth around it, who sought work there rather than overseas. As Julianna Puskaś sums it up, "everywhere [in Hungary], mass emigration began in regions far from the industrial centers, in those lacking in natural resources and in regions in some way . . . already familiar with emigration."[28]

To American mines, foundries, and steel mills these people went—Magyars mostly to New York and New Jersey, Slovaks and other non-Magyars to Pennsylvania, Ohio, and Illinois; and in the 1920s, as the American door closed, to Canada, South America, France, and Belgium. And many did return to Hungary with money to buy fifty to seventy acres and thereby transform themselves into wealthy peasants. Puskaś calculates that over 50 percent who emigrated to the United States returned in three to five years. But who started the chain and why these people went where they did remain unknown, as with most other emigrating groups.[29]

Slovaks, as the Hamburg passenger lists show, began migrating as early as the 1870s. A disastrous crop failure in 1879 in the Slovak counties of northern Hungary spurred hundreds of young farm boys to leave.[30] By 1899, 43 percent of emigrants from Hungary were Slovaks, a proportion four times greater than their share of the general population. They were often repeaters; by 1906, one-fifth of Slovaks migrating had already been in the United States. Whether they worked in a wine-growing colony in Georgia in 1894 or in a Pittsburgh steel mill, their "dearest wish" was to save money and take it home.[31] By 1908–1910, fifty-nine went home for every hundred who arrived in the United States, and nearly all of the new arrivals joined family or friends already there. "At times," June Alexander writes, "when firms desperately needed labor, foremen promised jobs to employees' friends or relatives if they would send for them." And when Slovaks became foremen themselves, they hired those whom they knew.[32] How it all began is poorly recorded; Slovaks from Zemplin, and a few from Saris, were actively being recruited to Allegheny, Pennsylvania, in 1882 by a Zemplin native, John Leniansky. Personal contacts must have operated in many more cases.[33]

Slovak young women, like their Irish counterparts, often migrated by themselves or in groups, finding positions as domestic servants in the United States. "America," Balch observed, "is to them even more of an Eldorado than to the men. Instead of three or four dollars a month a girl has American wages and almost no expenses. If she secures a good place she is treated with more respect, if not also more kindness, than she is used to. . . . and—glory of glories—she wears a hat."[34]

Croatians and others from what is now Yugoslavia also migrated because of agricultural depression, the intrusion of capitalism into agriculture, and the specifically South Slav problem of the breakup of the traditional extended-family landholdings (the *zadruga*). Home industries among this rural people were devastated by factory competition, and in the mid-1880s and again in 1900–1901, the phylloxera plague destroyed Croatia's vineyards. The emigrants were, before 1914, over 86 percent rural; and in 1901, when South Slav migration began in force, 90 percent male. Theirs was an almost purely labor-seeking migration. But although most intended to return, relatively few apparently did. Instead they sent substantial remittances: "Tile replaces thatch, taxes and debts are paid, field is added to field, better tools and more cattle are bought, phylloxera-smitten vineyards are replaced with immune vine stocks, churches are built and adorned"; villages for the first time received street lights and clean water, land values rose, life improved.[35]

Russia was not a major country of transatlantic emigration except for the Jews and Poles living there. Of the 2,361,000 people who left the Russian Empire between 1899 and 1913, 41 percent were Jews, 29 percent Poles, 9 percent Lithuanians, 7 percent Finns, 7 percent Russians, and 6 percent Germans.[36] Migration statistics did not always distinguish carefully among ethnic Russians, White Russians, Ukrainians, Ruthenians, Jews, Poles, and others who migrated from some place in the Czarist Empire. A net 78,000 true Russians may have settled in the United States during the 1901–1910 decade, but that figure may be too high.[37] Russia actually gained some tens of thousands of people from Germany and Austria-Hungary each year during the 1880s, as the net residue from a seasonal flow of more than a half-million.[38]

The Volga Germans, a small group of several thousand emigrants, deserve mention because of their later visibility in the United States and Canada. In the

1760s, Catherine the Great enticed with land grants and exemption from conscription the first 25,000 to come from Germany to the steppe frontier of the lower Volga valley. About twice that number arrived between 1803 and 1823, settling near the Black Sea several hundred miles west of the earlier group; and a final contingent of some 25,000 arrived in the western Ukraine and Volhynia between 1830 and 1870. In 1874 the czar's war minister Dmitri Miliutin revoked the draft exemption, a severe blow to the pacifist Mennonites in the Volga colonies. Almost simultaneously, C. B. Schmidt, an agent of the Atchison, Topeka and Santa Fe Railroad, arrived among them and persuaded them to buy much of the railroad's grant lands in Kansas. The Mennonite Volga Germans emigrated *en masse*. They were a rare case of emigrants who left for essentially religious reasons. Catholic and Lutheran Volga Germans, however, also left Russia for the Great Plains then and through the 1880s; their motivation was not religious but land-seeking, of the same sort that spurred Scandinavians, Reich Germans, Czechs, and British of the stereotypical "old immigration." A few went to South America. As was usually the case with land-seeking migrants, few returned. Most of the Volga Germans did not migrate at all, or did so within Russia, and through rapid natural increase numbered 1.7 million by 1917. Their choice was unfortunate. Later, "Stalin erased the Volga Germans from history," except for the descendants of those who emigrated to the Americas.[39]

The largest two groups who left Russian lands were Polish Jews and Polish Christians. Of all Polish migrants, the United States received only about one-fifth, because so many never left Europe but formed part of the large flows into Germany.[40] By one estimate, about two million Poles migrated within Europe, and another million overseas, between 1870 and World War I. A second estimate suggests nearly five million, with the United States receiving three million, Brazil 115,000, Canada 45,000, and Argentina 30,000. A third estimate states that of 1,250,000 "who left Russian Poland for good in the period 1871–1914 some 800,000 went to the U.S.A., 200,000 settled in . . . Brazil [and] Canada; 200,000 migrated to [Asiatic] Russia . . . and some 50,000 went to Germany and other European countries," while Austrian and Prussian Poland contributed still more. The total is confused by return migrants, repeaters, those who went first to Germany and then overseas, and those classified as Germans, Russians, or Austrians although they were ethnic Poles. If the total is uncertain, the general direction of the flows is clear enough; the United States received the great majority of the transatlantic Polish migrants.[41]

Emigration from Polish lands moved in general from west to east. Poles in Prussia left first, followed by those from Austrian Galicia, and finally those from the Russian-ruled "Kingdom of Poland" created at the 1815 Congress of Vienna. The timing of the abolition of serfdom—Prussia first, Russia last—may have helped produce this shift.[42] Within the German Empire, tens of thousands of ethnic Poles from West Prussia to Upper Silesia migrated to Saxony, Brandenburg, Mecklenburg, and other provinces in the 1870s, and had been doing so since 1815 or before (and were known as *Sachsengänger,* or *Chodzenie na Sasky*). Beginning as a seasonal migration, some of it became permanent. Polish and Ukrainian young women also migrated, often to make money during their fiance's three years of military service.[43]

In 1885, the skittish German government required all non-Reich Poles to return after each season.[44] It is not clear how much that inspired Russian and Austrian Poles to shift from German to overseas migration, but it probably helped. More general reasons for emigrating included "surplus population," that is, a large cohort of young people for whom no local labor market existed, coupled with available transportation, active recruitment, and the other usual reasons for labor-seeking migration. At the close of the 1880s, nearly thirty years after serfdom ended, one-eighth of the adults in Congress (Russian) Poland had no land of their own; the average holding of peasants who did have land was nineteen acres, compared with the average noble estate of 1,436 acres. "With such a social structure," Walter Willcox wrote, "with an almost complete absence of peasant lease-holders, with low wages in agriculture, with industry unable to absorb the surplus population, supplementary work or emigration was a necessity for the agricultural laborer or small peasant."[45] As was true elsewhere, the heaviest migration, in rates or numbers, usually came from less urban and less industrial provinces. Young people living in or near Warsaw or Lodz found plenty of jobs in those booming cities.

Polish migration, like that from other places, is best explained by economics. It may also, however, have been tinged by status aspirations. Morawska has seen in letters from emigrants in the United States and Brazil, writing back home, a fear of "proletarianization" had they stayed home; Krzysztof Groniowski notes that Poles coming to the United States "entered the working class but with the course of time a group of petit bourgeois and of bourgeois started to develop."[46] In the United States, Poles at first targeted farm states, founding Panna Maria ("Virgin Mary") in Texas in 1855, and later settled in Wisconsin, Minnesota, and the Dakotas. But from the 1880s onward, Poles coming to the United States usually went to industrial cities. By 1900, 95 percent were working in coal mining, steelmaking, meatpacking, and other industries. Half of them lived in Chicago, Detroit, Pittsburgh, Cleveland, Milwaukee, New York, and Buffalo, another 20 percent worked in the coalfields of Pennsylvania—and a few braved high mortality rates in the copper and gold mines of California, Colorado, New Mexico, and Utah.[47]

In Canada the order was reversed: Poles went first to urban Ontario and later to farms in Alberta and Saskatchewan. In Brazil, most went south to Parana, Santa Catarina, and Rio Grande do Sul, unlike the Italians, who so often in the late nineteenth century went to São Paulo. Because of bad harvests in Russian Poland and high labor demand in Brazil, the "Gorączka Brazylijska"—Brazil fever—ran hottest in 1890 and 1891 and continued for some years. Poles also went to Argentina, usually working in Buenos Aires and other cities, though some tried farming in Misiones and Chaco provinces.[48]

Jews were pouring out of the Russian Pale of Settlement and Congress Poland well before 1881. From Germany a probable 140,000 Jews had emigrated in the twenty-five years before 1871, and another 50,000 to 60,000 between then and 1914, most of them to the United States.[49] The East European Jewish migration, however, was much larger. Beginning in the 1870s, much for the usual reasons of comparative economic opportunity and easier transportation, it was spurred in the early 1880s and again after 1900 by successive waves of pogroms in Russia and in Congress Poland. The Jews in the czarist empire were forbidden to own real estate, to farm, to migrate freely, to be civil servants, to teach, or to practice law, or to live in areas other than designated towns and cities. They were far less than second-class citizens; such a status would have been enviable. Hence the pogrom: since Jews were outside the law in so many ways, organized public violence against them was punished lightly if at all.[50]

The assassination of Czar Alexander II in early 1881 set off pogroms of unprecedented harshness, coupled with further restrictive legislation, driving many Jews into crowded towns and miserable poverty. In the first year and a half after passage of the "May Laws" of 1882, "the Jewish population of the town of Tschernigov rose from 5,000 to 20,000 souls, so that four people had to find a living where previously it was difficult enough for one to earn bread." Housing became nearly impossible to obtain and jobs doubly difficult to find because Jews were ineligible for municipal employment ("civil service," therefore proscribed occupations) such as tram drivers, construction workers, porters, waiters, and the like.[51]

Jewish migration out of Russia thus became virtually necessary for survival. The period from May 1881 to May 1882, according to historian Jonathan Frankel,

should probably be regarded as of unique importance in modern Jewish history. It was not a time of culminations as was 1943–44 (the climax of the Holocaust) or 1948–49 (the establishment of the Jewish state). On the contrary, it was a time of beginnings, when many seeds were scattered, most to wither away, a few to take root and grow.[52]

Flagrant anti-Semitism spread through the Russian upper classes as well as through the peasantry, and spread geographically from Poland and Lithuania to the Ukraine, where by 1903, at Kishinev, the worst pogrom took place. Frankel notes that beginning in late April 1881, "twelve extra carriages were being coupled on to every train leaving Kiev for Berdichev and Belaia Tserkov," then proceeding across the border of Austrian Galicia to Brody, and on to Lvov, Kraków, Berlin, and finally Hamburg and its ships.[53] In early 1881, 1,200 Jews every week—enough to fill a Hamburg-Amerika liner—took that route to the United States.

Between then and 1903, possibly as many as 15 or 20 percent returned to Russia, many of them young unattached males or older persons, some temporarily. The pogroms abated for more than fifteen years. Then came the Kishinev massacre, after which "most people agree[d] that the best solution for Jewish problems was [e]migration. Before then opinions divided, many thinking that pogroms would pass."[54] They did not. For another four years they continued, the worst occurring over twelve days in October 1905, when in hundreds of outbreaks more than eight hundred people died, many more were injured, and property damage exceeded thirty million dollars. No outbreaks happened in Poland and few in White Russia, but the Ukraine was especially hazardous.[55]

Violent anti-Semitism explains much of the rush out of the Russian Pale. Its quieter forms, together with oppressive economic conditions and lack of opportunity, help explain Jewish migration from Galicia and elsewhere in Austria-Hungary. Simon Kuznets argues persuasively that even without the pogroms, economic transitions would have spurred emigration. With such persecution, the age and sex structure of Jewish emigration included many more women and children, thus a smaller proportion of young men, than most other groups. Family migration (sometimes just young couples and sometimes parents with children) characterized Jewish migration to a degree not seen since the North European land seekers of the 1850s to 1870s. Return and repeat migration happened less often, especially after the Kishinev episode. Since Jews had been kept off the land in both empires, the proportion of skilled craftsmen was unusually large. The stereotypical Jewish peddler or tailor or retailer, and after a time in America the doctor or lawyer or accountant, originated in the legal disabilities of Austria-Hungary and Russia.[56]

All told, the pre-1914 East European Jewish migration to the United States alone approached 2 million: 381,000 from Austria-Hungary, 81,000 from Romania, and 1,557,000 (77 percent) from the Russian Empire, including Congress Poland. The northwest part of the Pale, including the districts of Kovno, Vilnius, Minsk, and Grodno, contributed 29 percent of its Jews; the southwest (Volhynia, Kiev) also 29 percent; and Poland (Warsaw, Płock, Suwalki, and elsewhere) 27 percent.[57] These people settled mainly in American cities, but sizable numbers chose Latin America or Canada. In the late twentieth century it was not rare for a Jew in the United States to have cousins in Buenos Aires, Toronto, and Tel Aviv. Unfortunately, Hitler and the Nazis left few cousins in Lithuania, Poland, Galicia, and the Ukraine. In the 1871–1914 period, however, brothers followed brothers, and families followed in turn, whether observant or nonreligious, most young, most skilled and used to town life, most not to return. The Jewish migration was decidedly labor-seeking rather than land-seeking, but at once more highly skilled, more organized in families, and more permanent than any other labor-seeking group. The peculiar legal disabilities together with persecutions suffered by the Jewry of the two empires largely explain those differences.

10

ITALY

Italy's population rose from 28 million in 1871 to 35 million in 1914. Its natural increase was obviously high, because also during those years 14 million people left Italy. About 44 percent went to other European countries, 30 percent to North America, and 24 percent to South America. The remaining few went to Italy's not very successful colonies in Africa. Of the New World receivers, the United States took 4.2 million, or 29 percent of the total; Canada 149,000, or 1 percent; Argentina 1.8 million, or 13 percent; and Brazil 1.2 million, or 9 percent. This transatlantic migration of 7.3 million made Italy the second-largest donor country in Europe, behind Britain (not including Ireland) with 7.9 million. Most Italian migrants roamed within Europe until the late 1880s, but from then on the great majority crossed to South or North America, raising Italy to the leader in sheer numbers of migrants from the 1890s on, and the leader in proportion to population between 1901 and 1914.[1]

Regional differences of every kind abounded in the recently unified Italian Kingdom. As is still true, however, differences were most stark between North and South. In a very rough way, Italy resembled the leading donor of emigrants, the United Kingdom. Italy had its peasant South, like Ireland though poorer, and its industrializing North, like England though less developed; and both regions contributed to migration. Northwestern Italy produced a large share of emigrants at the beginning of the period, but as that area industrialized, central and southern Italy supplied increasing proportions. Venezia and other parts of the northeast, suffering a chronic agrarian crisis as did the *Mezzogiorno,* contributed a steady one-third. Italian migrants were preponderantly male—83 percent in the intra-European migration of 1876–1880, 75 percent in the much greater transatlantic migration of 1896–1900. In certain years, such as 1888, 1891, and 1895, however, when opportunities were especially attractive (or recruitment most effective) in Brazil, women accounted for 33 to 38 percent of the migrants.[2] Speaking generally, one can say that northern Italians had a long tradition of migration within Europe and continued it through the 1871–1890 period. While such migration was often seasonal and made up of young men, almost half of the northern Italian migrants to Brazil were female. In the pre-1914 period, southern Italians went overseas, and most were male; but in the years just before World War I, and again for a time after the war, women and children joining husbands or fiances made up a large minority.

Italian migrants, certainly the peasants, showed foresight and energy in using migration to improve their situations, as indicated by much evidence. Lombard peasants started going to Brazil and Argentina in 1877, and Ligurians, Piedmontese, and Venetians soon followed, all preferring unknown possibilities to known impossibilities under large landowners.[3] Waldensians, a small religious sect who had lived in the mountains southwest of Turin and migrated seasonally to France since the Middle Ages, began leaving for Uruguay in the 1870s and to Entre Rios province in Argentina in the late 1890s. They were undoubtedly in tight straits economically, although not destitute. Described as "independent thinkers and decision makers," they obviously had the imagination and courage to begin new lives in South America.[4]

Much the same has been said for the larger migration from southern Italy, including Sicily. Life in America, even in New York's tenements, could improve the migrants' social lives as well as their economic condition. Migration would also improve their children's chances, providing dowries for daughters and education for sons. Time after time, Italian migrants attempted to re-create the village life they left behind. Sicilians, Calabrese, and others, through chain migration, depleted their home communities and rebuilt them in the eastern United States or Argentina.[5]

Transatlantic migration for some Italians became an option after other measures for improvement did not bring enough results. Sicilian artisans in the 1870s and 1880s attempted to better themselves by migrating from the mountains to Palermo; others formed mutual benefit societies to protect themselves against oppression by the upper class. A coalition of Sicilian artisans and peasants revolted against the landowners in 1892–1894, a drastic step though without permanent effect. The situation for many was intolerable. Migration for such people became the best response to political failure and continuing economic problems. Again the evidence reveals that the migrants were not the destitute and desperate but enterprising people able to make cooperative decisions.[6]

Expelling factors operated powerfully. Absentee landlords—gentry, nobility, the church—refused to modernize agricultural methods or invest in improvements. Peasants worked under labor contracts that forced them to overexploit the soil. As few as one in six of the peasants of Calabria and Sicily owned land. If they did, it was often a holding too small to provide a family income and too far from home to permit normal family life. The system forced men into migrant labor. Conditions for peasants in the industrializing northwest were better; yet in northern provinces such as Venezia, where industrialization lagged, even a slight decline in crop prices could be ruinous for the peasants.[7]

A crisis everywhere in agriculture struck Italy from 1879 to 1883. Production disincentives led to great reductions in output and in land under cultivation. Crop returns hardly paid for subsistence, much less for mortgages and taxes. Since production meant only hard work for nothing or less then nothing, large tracts lay fallow. Introduction of more up-to-date farm methods was out of the question. Deterioration of roads increased the costs of shipping crops. In such an impasse emigration, not only of husbands and fathers but also of wives, mothers, and children, became an almost heaven-sent alternative. In the late 1880s the demand by Brazilian coffee planters for family migrants seemed an optimal solution for both. Sicily, traditionally a major producer of wheat, suffered in the 1880s from American competition, as did some areas of Germany and East Europe. In wheat-producing communes of Sicily's interior, violent political-economic protest erupted in 1892–1893.[8] The Sicilian migration to Tampa, for example, arrived in force after the suppression of rural protest leagues in 1894, and the bulk of it came from one interior town. Santo Stefano Quisquina provides a fine display of both serial and return migration; the statistics for 1891–1913 indicate that 119.6 percent (!) of the village's 1881 population emigrated.[9]

Late industrialization prompted migration even more than did demographic pressures,[10] and government protectionism squeezed the peasants further. In 1887, Italy placed a protective tariff on imported wheat, paralleling German tariffs begun in 1879, but neither resulted in any relief for peasants. While Prussian Junkers and southern Italian *latifundistas* both benefited for a time, the rural workforce inclined further toward emigration.[11] In fact the 1887 tariff linked the interests of industry and agrarian protectionists against the interests of the *contadini*. In the end, it provoked a tariff battle with France that harmed the southern small producers of wine, oil, and other products while leaving untouched the *latifundista* grain producers.[12]

A massive inquiry by government-appointed experts into economic conditions in agriculture revealed crisis conditions among peasants almost everywhere in Italy.[13] Protectionists, who as in other countries tended to be nationalists on more than just economic issues, urged that Italy build colonies in Africa as the solution. However, Liberal Prime Minister Sidney Sonnino pushed through laws in 1888 and 1891 making migration easier, on the grounds that emigration was an individual right as well as a safety valve for Italy.[14] Problems continued, however, without Rome's taking effective direct action. Absentee ownership and dwarf farm plots plagued southern peasants, as did drought, malaria, and earthquakes.[15] Agriculture mechanized and rationalized along with industry in the North, but in the South, industry remained craftsmanship, agriculture remained premodern, and surplus labor, much of which was being absorbed in the North, emigrated.[16]

In such a predicament, Italian peasants sought new destinations. The recently built rail and steamship networks allowed an Italian to get to North or South America for less than the rail fare from Genoa to Königsberg in East Prussia.[17] Not surprisingly, migration became heavy. Northern Italians usually headed for Brazil and Argentina, while southerners more often went to the United States (and, years later, to Canada). The reasons for this distribution were partly accidental. The end of slavery in Brazil coincided with severe agrarian crisis in Venezia, setting up a strong supply-demand relationship which, once begun, continued through recruitment networks and immigrant letters. Genovese, and Ligurians generally, however, usually sailed for Argentina.[18] Southerners found the Naples–New York crossing quick and cheap. Their relative poverty and their initial plans to return made short-term, low-status industrial or service jobs in the United States acceptable.

In the 1880s the ocean began to teem with Italians seeking distant, and temporary, opportunity, increasingly in North America rather than in northern Europe. In 1880, only 5 percent of Italian emigrants went to the United States; in 1914, 43 percent did. The shift was gradual. In 1882, 58 percent of migrant Italians left for other European countries. In 1886, however, only 48 percent did so: 21 percent to France, 11 percent to Austria, 8 percent to Hungary, 3 percent to Switzerland, 2 percent to Germany, and 3 percent to other destinations. For the first time, the Americas received more Italians than Europe did—Argentina 23 percent, the United States 17 percent, and Brazil 7 percent.[19] Eager recruitment brought over a quarter-million Venetians to Brazil between 1891 and 1897. Thereafter the bulk of Italian migration went to the United States from the provinces south of Rome, with Sicily the chief source in the years just before World War I.[20]

The most accurate description of specific aspects of the Italian migration emerges from Ira Glazier's random sample of 10,330 Italians who crossed between 1880 and 1900.[21] Naples led the embarkation ports, accommodating perhaps 75 percent of migrants to the United States, with Palermo a distant second and Genoa third. Some Italians, many of whom had already migrated to France, left from Le Havre and Marseilles.[22] Glazier's sample includes twenty-two ships, of which ten were British (of the Anchor Line and Henderson Brothers, running directly between Naples and New York), five French (the Cyprien Fabre Line), five Italian (Navigazione Generale Italiana, from Sicily), and two North German Lloyd. The crossing to New York took, on average, twenty-one days. Six deaths, five of them infants or children, took place en route among the entire sample. Campania produced 24 percent of the migrants, the Abruzzi and Molise 12.5 percent, Sicily 9.5 percent, Basilicata 8 percent, Calabria 7.6 percent, Puglia 1.5 percent. Another 8.4 percent came from central and northern Italy; the origin of 28 percent is unknown. Clusters came from certain localities within those regions: 60 percent of migrants from the Abruzzi-Molise came from Campobasso and Isernia, and another 20 percent from Aquila; Salerno provided 31 percent and Avellino 28 percent from Campania; Potenza provided 84 percent from Basilicata; Catanzaro and Cosenza provided 44 percent from Calabria; Palermo provided 62 percent from Sicily.[23]

The entire group came from 1,529 towns, but 216 towns contributed 56 percent of the migrants, suggesting the strong migration chains that have been noticed by historians of Italian settlement in the United States.[24] Glazier found that migration from southern Italy began in remote mountain areas with the least progressive farming.[25] Italy thus matched the pattern seen also in Prussia, Hungary, and Scandinavia. Isolated areas, where land ownership was immutable and income from agriculture increasingly poor, generated overseas migration to a greater extent than did urban or other more densely populated areas.

In Glazier's sample, half of the Italian migrants were between twenty-five and forty years of age, and in that predominant cohort, males outnumbered females 4.35 to 1 (3 to 1 in the whole sample). About 65 percent were agriculturists—a few owners, many landless. Half migrated by themselves, half with families—individuals more likely from the hills, families from Naples, Palermo, or other large cities.[26]

As in other European countries, the poorest Italians migrated, if at all, within Europe. The sons and daughters of small landholders, and upwardly mobile tenant farmers and their children, populated the ocean liners. From Sicily came not only the rural proletarians but also artisans, small businessmen, and small landowners—all told, a petty bourgeoisie. Individualistic and acquisitive, suspicious of landlords, clerics, notaries, and other authorities, they adapted easily to Argentina and the United States.[27]

Many young men crossed to the United States in the spring, worked until the late fall, saving and sending money home, and returned for the winter. Others left Italy after harvest in October or November and arrived in Argentina's springtime. These migrations resembled the age-old seasonal transhumance of the Mediterranean.[28] However, in exchanging wage work on *estancias* or in great cities for sheep and pastures, the new transhumance was different, perhaps even "twisted and inverted."[29] Three-fourths of the emigrants were male, nearly all in their working years,[30] as were the returnees, who came back not as failures in America but as great successes, their plans carried out.[31] Southern Italians were as mobile as any other group in Europe. They decided carefully whether to go to South America, with its easier cultural adjustment, or to the United States, with its shorter voyage, quicker cash wages, and seasonal employment on railroads or in construction.[32]

Firm figures on return and repeat migration among Italians have never existed. Census data indicate, however, that it always took place, probably at about the 50 percent level from either Argentina or the United States before 1900, and more frequently between 1900 and 1914. Women and children returned as well as men.[33] Women, though a minority, made up a fairly constant segment of the migration. Gabaccia estimates that upwards of two million women returned to Italy from the United States, a considerable number but lower than that of male returnees. Consequently, although females made up only 25 percent of recent Italian migrants, they constituted 46 percent of Italians living in the United States at the census of 1920.[34]

The vast Italian migration extended and continued very old Mediterranean practices. The post-1880 migrants traveled farther and to different places than before, and there were more women among them, especially in the flow to Brazil in the 1890s. The migration was a reasonable and traditional response of a clever people to adverse conditions and attractive opportunities.[35]

11

SPAIN AND PORTUGAL

The two countries of the Iberian Peninsula present the historical synthesizer with a problem that only time will remedy: the lack of sources, primary or secondary. Available census and migration data are not so complete as those kept in northern Europe and South America. Monographs on the demographic, social, economic, and cultural dimensions of the migrants are extremely few. Probably the stifling impact on social research of the two long-lived and reactionary regimes of Franco and Salazar prevented Spanish and Portuguese scholars from emulating either the French *Annalistes* or the recent American social-history school. In any event, social history in general, not to mention such branches of it as women's history, has yet to take its place beside kings, courts, generals, and prime ministers on the Iberian library shelves. As a result, what follows is a rather skeletal description of Iberian migration. Patches of flesh and blood will be added once the Iberians arrive in the Americas (see Part III below).

Spain contributed the third largest number of transatlantic migrants of any country. Spain and Portugal together sent 4.7 million people across the Atlantic between 1871 and 1914. In both, births exceeded deaths in most years by considerable margins; both had traditions of labor-seeking migration within Europe; and neither had begun industrializing significantly. As the colonizers of most of Central and South America, they retained strong ties of language and culture with Argentina and Brazil. Spanish ship-passenger statistics begin in 1882 and show 40,721 Spaniards traveling to the Americas that year. Of that number, 30,730 went to Cuba, still a colony of Spain until 1898; 3,245 went to Argentina; 2,247 to Brazil; and 57 to the United States (none to Canada).

As in Italy, migration accelerated as passenger ships became larger and chains of information grew stronger. Of the entire Spanish migration to the Americas recorded between 1857 and 1914, three-fourths took place after 1900. Until

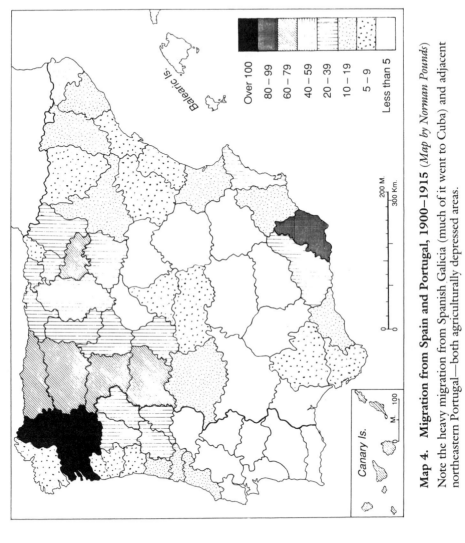

Map 4. Migration from Spain and Portugal, 1900–1915 (*Map by Norman Pounds*)

Note the heavy migration from Spanish Galicia (much of it went to Cuba) and adjacent northeastern Portugal—both agriculturally depressed areas.

1902, Cuba remained the leading destination. In the following year Argentina took the lead and kept it, nearly always by large margins. In the five years from 1911 through 1915, Argentina received 403,000 Spaniards (or about two-thirds of the total), Cuba 136,000, Brazil 32,000, Uruguay 12,000, Mexico 7,000, and the United States 6,000, with several thousand more scattered from Chile to the Caribbean.[1] Cuba's independence did not deter Spaniards from going there, and a Spanish government ban in August 1910 on assisted emigration to Brazil (similar to the Italian ban of 1902) reduced the flow to Brazil but certainly did not stop it. When Italy restricted the flow of Italians to Argentina in 1911, Spaniards responded to Argentine recruitment and filled the gap. When the Moroccan crisis flared up in 1912, draft-liable men aged eighteen to twenty-one hastened to Argentina, making that year's emigration the largest Spain experienced.[2] In 1914, 89,193 Spaniards shipped out for American ports, and of them 48,343 went to Argentina, 24,572 to Cuba, 5,764 to Brazil, and 3,017 to the United States. In almost every year from 1882 to 1914, Brazil was the clear third choice. Legal restrictions on emigration from Spain, very tight up to the 1850s, gradually relaxed, "passing from one extreme to the other" between 1853 and 1903, when passports and governmental permission were no longer required.[3]

Spanish population grew slowly in the nineteenth century. The cause was not, as in France, low fertility; rather, it was high mortality, especially among infants. As one Spanish writer lamented in 1897, "the population [in France] barely grows because too few are born. In our country, it barely grows because too many die."[4]

However, in northern and northwestern Spain—Galicia, Asturias, Leon, Old Castile, and Navarre—population rose fast enough to encourage substantial emigration.[5] In the 1880s, the Canary Islands, among the provinces of Spain, had the highest rate of emigration, most of it to the Caribbean, and also the highest birth rate.[6] Synthetic dyes began driving down the demand for cochineal, the Canaries' main product, after 1870; while in Galicia problems regarding farm credit, landlordism, and tenant contracts became increasingly frustrating to peasants.[7] The Galician provinces of Pontevedra and La Coruña followed the Canaries closely in emigrant numbers, but donated most of their emigrants to Argentina and Brazil.[8]

By the 1911–1915 quinquennium, however, Galicia and neighboring provinces were leading the emigration. The *Gallego* provinces of Lugo, Orense, and Pontevedra all had per capita rates over 10 percent. Coruña's was 9.7 percent and it produced the largest actual number of emigrants, 61,560. Oviedo and Leon, immediately to the east, contributed over 77,000 between them. Of the eight leading emigrant-providing provinces, six were in the extreme northwest of Spain. Only the Canaries and Almería, on the southeast coast, were located elsewhere. On the other end of the scale, Badajoz and Huelva, in the far southwest, and Cuenca, in the center, had emigration rates below 0.2 percent; the least emigration, in general, came from central and southern Spain. Madrid and

Barcelona, the two largest cities, also ranked near the bottom, confirming the pattern observed elsewhere in Europe that capital or other large cities absorbed the potential emigrants from nearby rural areas.[9]

As in other parts of Europe, nineteenth-century changes in the feudal land-holdings of the church and large transhumant sheep owners led to a rise in agricultural productivity. That perhaps encouraged higher fertility, perhaps not. Nevertheless, population did rise with productivity, while acquisition of small-holdings remained difficult. Only Catalonia began to industrialize significantly and absorb its own excess rural population. The other northern provinces, where peasant tenancy was the rule, contributed emigrants well beyond the national rate. Primogeniture and high fertility strongly encouraged younger sons to marry late or to move on.[10] As in Sicily, Poland, and other wheat-growing areas of Europe, an agrarian crisis struck Castile in the late nineteenth century, and Castilians migrated, as did others similarly disadvantaged by international grain competition.

Galicia, the northwesternmost region of Spain, exemplified the Spanish situation. Between 1850 and 1930, fully half of the Galician male population emigrated either temporarily or permanently in the face of rising population, no industrialization, and the difficulty of acquiring land or earning a living wage by working for landowners. When productivity rose, it made farm workers increasingly redundant, as in Scandinavia. Migration became a safety valve, allowing a "massive exodus" from rural Galicia, most of it overseas to Spanish America.[11] Young *Gallegos* completed the harvest and then, in September, October, and November, boarded ships for Argentina, Brazil, and Cuba.[12]

The Spanish emigration to Argentina mixed the *golondrina* type—the seasonal wageworker—with longer-staying artisans and families. The Spanish authorities found to their surprise that nuclear families and others staying at least two to five years outnumbered the *golondrinas* among the Argentine-bound; *golondrinas* simply made more exportable cash and paid lower ship fares if they chose the shorter voyage to Cuba. As for the Brazil-bound, the 1912 migration from Spain, totaling 25,577, included 21,534 persons traveling in family units and only 4,043 who went as individuals, thus helping to explain why the females, numbering 11,223, almost balanced the males (14,354). The great majority of the Brazil-bound, about 23,000, listed themselves as farmers or farmhands.[13]

Like other Europeans, Spaniards did not limit themselves to transatlantic routes but continued to move from rural areas to provincial capitals and other cities.[14] They also returned home to Spain in large numbers. Between 1882 and 1914 nearly four returned for every five who left. The Cuban Revolution gave Spain a net inflow of about 110,000 transatlantic migrants in 1897–1899, contrasting with a net outflow of 153,000 in 1895–1896. After the great invasion of Spaniards in 1912, the Argentine government in 1913–1914 tried to retain them by settling them in land colonies; yet large numbers returned to Spain anyway.[15] A strong characteristic of Spanish migration was its volatility, most marked in the late 1890s but evident at other times too. As was true of southern Italians and most East European groups, men outnumbered women by two or three to one, and most gave their occupations as general or farm laborers.[16]

Portuguese emigrants were fewer than Spanish and chose somewhat different destinations. Otherwise they shared important features. Portuguese migrants increased gradually from the 1870s, when they averaged about 13,000 a year, to an annual average of about 21,000 from 1886 to 1890. Their numbers soared briefly to about 42,000 in 1895, nearly all of them going to Brazil, and then stayed in the 15,000 to 20,000 range until 1904. Gradually rising thereafter, the annual figure peaked at 89,000 in 1912 and averaged over 75,000 during 1911–1913.[17] Usually, between 1900 and 1911, the proportion of females was only 19.3 percent of the total. A startling rise in the number of married women emigrating occurred after 1906, especially in the heavy years of 1911–1912; they came particularly from mountain villages in and north of Vila Real, bordering on the Spanish Galician province of Orense.[18] Also, as in Spain, the heaviest emigration consistently happened from September through November, after harvest, and the lightest in early summer, reflecting the ties of these peasant migrants with the soil and its economy.[19]

Ninety-five percent of Portuguese migrants went to the Americas, about 70 percent to Brazil. More surprisingly, the United States was the second choice (though a distant one), the largest annual number 14,171, coming in 1913 chiefly from the Azores, whose fishermen had worked the New England coast for hundreds of years. Third choice was Argentina, whose Portuguese arrivals peaked at 4,959 in 1912. Of mainland Portuguese emigrants, 92.5 percent chose Brazil, the largest Portuguese-speaking country in the world. Portugal's African colonies, led by Mozambique and Angola, attracted no more than a tenth of the total, sometimes only a few dozen, even in their best years.[20] Colonies proved no better a sponge of excess population for Portugal than they did for Germany and Italy.

Repatriation figures, which were not kept until 1919, paralleled the high Spanish rate at that point, and probably would have earlier.[21] As was true of Spaniards, the Portuguese had a long history of intra-European migration and repatriation; going to the New World meant a change of target, not of strategy. Portuguese men had migrated to Spain and France, seeking work and returning home at the end of a season, since the early eighteenth century if not before.[22]

The northern regions of Tras-os-Montes and Beira Alta, which border on Spanish Galicia, contributed far more emigrants than did other parts of Portugal. During 1909–1913, the district of Bragança, the northeasternmost in the country, had an annual rate of over 3 percent, followed closely by Vizeu, Vila Real, and Guarda just south of Bragança. The Azores and Madeira also contributed more than their share. Emigration least affected the central and southern districts and Lisbon; as elsewhere, the capital apparently captured many migrants who might have gone overseas had they lived in more remote areas. Central Portugal, especially the districts of Portalegre and Evora (the Alentejo region), displayed the very lowest rates; there some farmland actually remained unused and young people were less pressed by land scarcity, as was true also in neighboring Extremadura across the Spanish border.[23] The clear pattern in Portugal was that the northernmost districts provided the highest numbers and rates of emigrants, excepting only Porto and Viana do Castelo on the northern coast, which were near the middle of the rank order. This pattern was evident by the 1880s and continued through 1914.

The great majority of Portuguese emigrants were, not surprisingly, farm workers and agriculturists of various degrees of attachment to land. A visible minority were artisans, especially carpenters, stonemasons, and others in the building trades; some few were domestic servants. About 60 percent of the migrants of 1893–1913 were illiterate, 67 percent in the big year of 1912, as was true of other Continental emigrants, when the peak years included the highest proportions of unskilled and illiterate persons. Also, at least 75 percent were described as "of humble condition."[24] From 1911 to 1914, family emigration including married women rose sharply, and in the case of Bragança, the number of females almost exactly matched that of males in 1912 and 1913. Fernando Emygdio da Silva speculated that subdivision of landholdings may have contributed to the high rates of family migration in the northeast, where both subdivision and emigration were strongest. In the latifundist south, emigration was infrequent. Evora, with the largest average landholdings, had the absolute lowest emigration rate, while Bragança, the top emigrant district, had the smallest average landholdings.[25]

Reasons for emigration resembled those found in Spain and southern Italy: the lack of capital, public funds, and local industry meant that excess rural population could not be absorbed. The result was "demographic saturation of the fields in the north of the country," thence expatriation.[26] Portuguese, both men and women, continued to emigrate to other European countries, and also to Brazil, for these structural reasons. In Portugal, as in much of Spain and southern Italy, industrialization and urbanization had hardly begun prior to 1914. As in other parts of Europe in similar socioeconomic situations, emigration of rural people continued at high rates. Where economies were rapidly industrializing and cities were mushrooming, as happened in Germany from the late 1880s onward, people stopped leaving and others started arriving.

From Ireland across to Russia and southwestward to Portugal, Europeans of almost every ethnic coloration participated in migration inside their own countries, to other European countries, and to the New World. Not all migrants came from rural areas, but most did. Those who lived fairly close to political capitals or industrializing cities often preferred to go there rather than cross the Atlantic. As a very general rule, transatlantic migrants came from the more remote districts of their respective countries.

Women migrated as well as men. In the Irish case, unique in Europe, virtually half of the migrants were women, a great many of them single. In East and

South Europe, on the other hand, males predominated, but they also returned in greater numbers, the result being a more balanced sex ratio in New World immigrant communities than in the migration process itself. The very poorest did not cross the Atlantic unless recruited or assisted; otherwise the transatlantic migrants were not the most destitute or desperate, although many were without capital of their own. Some, more typically in the 1870s and 1880s, had been landowners or the children of landowners and came in search of fresh land, whereas the majority, beginnning in the 1880s, sought remunerative nonagricultural work. But these generalizations have many exceptions. Wage seekers were leaving Britain and Germany, for example, before 1880; and Poles and Ukrainians continued coming to Canada as homesteading farmers well into the 1920s. Where these Europeans went in the New World, and what happened to them, now needs to be told.

Part III

The American Receivers

INTRODUCTION

On the western side of the Atlantic lay the major receiving nations: Argentina, Brazil, Canada, and the United States. As in Europe, migration flowed in more than one direction. Europeans went west to the New World, but some returned eastward; small numbers of people born in the Americas went to Europe; and north-south flows (both ways) existed between Brazil and Argentina and their neighbors in small numbers, and between Canada and the United States in quite large numbers. Some migrants stayed, some repatriated; some went to rural areas, others to cities; some succeeded in finding what they migrated for, others failed. Some migrants intended to make a fresh start in the New World, others to go back with enough to improve life at home or simply to survive another season. In any case, land or jobs were of the essence in all four countries. The United States was no exception.

Each of the four played a different role in the transatlantic migration story.[1] Because of their similarities in geographical and population size, Argentina has sometimes been compared to Canada (and to Australia), while Brazil and the United States have always been the *colossi* of their continents. Differences among the four are obviously great, but they shared a receptivity to European migrants, and implicit comparisons of the two pairs—Argentina-Canada, Brazil-United States—are worth remembering. The donor nations last looked at in Europe—Spain, Portugal, Italy—appear first here; the donors first considered above—Britain and Ireland—surface only later. To a larger extent, North Europeans traveled to North America, while Mediterraneans went to South America. But there are important exceptions: Italians, East European Jews, and some other peoples went to both.

12

ARGENTINA

Argentina underwent a remarkable expansion from the 1860s to 1914. Population rose from 1.7 million in the first national census in 1869 to 7.9 million in the third, in 1914. The gates were wide open; as the statesman Juan Bautista Alberdí announced, "gobernar es poblar"—to govern is to populate.[1] Migrants from Europe formed a greater part of the population in Argentina than in any other country (three and a half times the proportion in Brazil), and by 1914 the foreign-born and their children accounted for 58 percent of the 7.9 million.[2] No country, including the United States, had nearly so large a proportion of immigrants; no other country's capital was 70 percent foreign-born, as Buenos Aires was for more than sixty years. The 1914 census revealed that 30.3 percent of the national population was foreign-born, more than twice the proportion ever reached in the United States.[3]

Before 1900, the majority of immigrants came from peasant backgrounds and sought places on the land or in agriculturally related work in the extremely fertile, recently opened provinces within reach of the coast. From the 1890s onward, migrants increasingly stayed in larger cities, particularly Buenos Aires. In 1895, the city of Buenos Aires was 74 percent foreign-born; the provinces of Córdoba, Buenos Aires, Entre Rios, Mendoza, and La Pampa, 44 percent; and the rest of the country, 11 percent. In the 1914 census the proportions were, respectively, 72 percent, 51 percent, and 20 percent. When the Argentine-born children of immigrant parents are added to their parents, one sees clearly an overwhelmingly European, particularly Italian, people and culture in the capital and in several of the richest provinces.[4]

A liberal immigration law, passed in 1876 and revised in 1887 and 1889, removed almost all restrictions and also provided for lodging and maintenance, hostels, and other support. The law favored building a labor force in both

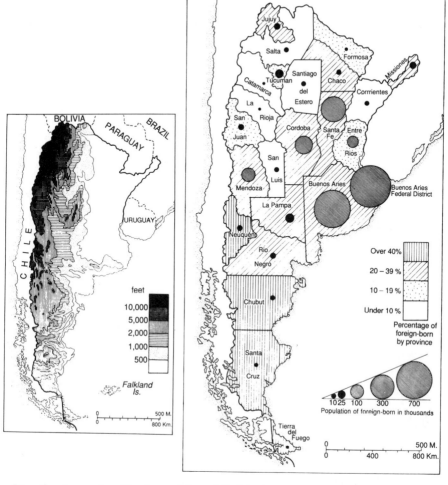

Map 5. Argentina. Physiographic and Political (*Map by Norman Pounds*)
The vast pampas included Buenos Aires and La Pampa provinces and most of several others northward to the borders of Paraguay and Brazil, nearly 1,000 miles with practically no land higher than 500 feet (152 meters) above sea level.

agriculture and industry.[5] Not until 1931 did a restrictive law pass.[6] President Domingo Faustino Sarmiento favored immigration during his term (1868–1874), and his successor, Julio Roca (1880–1886, 1898–1904), did so even more; the conventional wisdom was that mass European immigration was essential to develop the nation. Briefly stated, the pattern was acceleration during the 1870s, boom in the 1880s, followed by a halt and net loss during 1889–1895 because of political and financial upheavals. During Roca's second presidency, immigration soared through 1914. Although much of it was seasonal by then, many people visited once or twice and then stayed.

Between 1871 and 1914, 5.9 million Europeans came to Argentina, of whom 2.7 million returned and 3.2 million remained—the bulk of them in Buenos Aires, in the larger provincial cities, and on the land in Santa Fe, Córdoba, and Entre Rios provinces.[7] The cities of Buenos Aires and Rosario increased ten times over in forty years, while Sante Fe province expanded at a "vertiginous" rate, from 41,000 in 1858 to 397,000 in 1895.[8] Italians and Spaniards accounted for about 80 percent of the migration to Argentina, with Italians more likely to stay. Of gross migration, 1857–1926, 47 percent were Italians, 32 percent Spaniards; of those who stayed, 1860–1910, 55 percent were Italians, 26 percent Spaniards. The French were a distant third at 4 to 5 percent, and no other European nation contributed so much as 2 percent.[9] Many immigrants recorded as Spanish or French were in fact Basque.[10] Following well behind the Italians and Spanish, before 1890, were French (often Basques), British, Swiss, people from Austria-Hungary, and Germans; between 1890 and 1920, Russians, Austro-Hungarians, Germans, and British; and after 1920, Poles. Many later immigrants were Jewish.[11]

Before 1900, northern Italians outnumbered southern, but from 1900 to 1913 the numbers were nearly equal. As seasonal workers, recruited in Italy to work the harvest for four or five months during the European winter, they took up a larger share of the migration than before.[12] An undefined number of Italians also traveled between São Paulo and Buenos Aires, forming "a link, albeit weak, between the Argentine and the Brazilian labour markets."[13] Lord Bryce, the peripatetic Englishman best known for his book of observations on American culture, also visited South America about 1910. He noted that north Italians "take to the land," while southern Italians "stay in the towns and work as railway and wharf porters, or as boatmen." The reason may have been that southern Italians arrived in Argentina later, when land was less available than it had been in the 1870s and the booming 1880s when northern Italy became linked by steamship to Buenos Aires.[14] With Buenos Aires only a few weeks by steamship from Italian ports, and with the third-class fare about fifty dollars, Argentina was an attractive option.[15]

These Italian and Spanish migrants had demographic profiles already noted as they left Europe: 70 to 73 percent male; two out of three single; more than half in their twenties and thirties.[16] Although male migrants outnumbered females 2.3 to 1 in the 1880s and 2.7 to 1 during 1901–1910, the sex ratio in the foreign-born population was not that distorted. In the 1895 and 1914 censuses the ratio was 1.7 to 1 nationally, and more balanced than that in immigrant-filled farm provinces. Females returned and repeated migration less often; once in Argentina, married and with children, they more likely stayed.[17]

In several ways Argentina in the 1870s to 1890s resembled the North American West at the same time. Flat, semi-arid, and nearly devoid of white settlement, the pampas had much in common with the American and Canadian Great

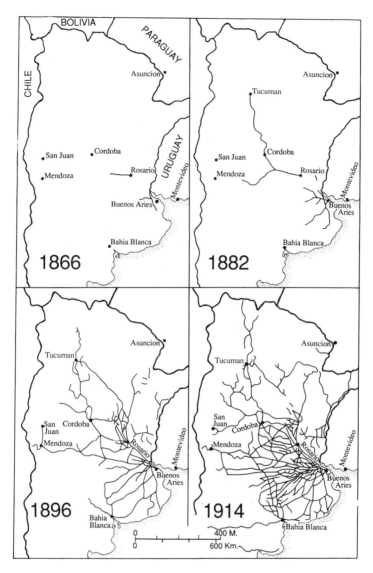

Map 6. Argentina's Railroad Network, 1866, 1882, 1896, 1914 (*Map by Norman Pounds*)

The network's expansion began in earnest after the "Conquest of the Desert" (that is, destruction of the Araucanians) in 1879. The isolation of Mendoza, San Juan, and Tucuman had ended by the 1890s. By 1914, as shown, the bulk of the network (and the target of migrants) lay across the southern pampas, from Bahia Blanca through Buenos Aires province to Rosario and Cordoba.

Plains. In both areas, railroad companies (using foreign capital and government bounty) began stretching lines into the interior. In both areas, military suppression of the natives occurred between 1876 and 1879: as Sitting Bull surrendered the last independent remnant of the Sioux nation, General Julio Roca destroyed the Araucanians and thus completed the "conquest of the desert."[18] Native tribes were suppressed north of Santa Fe and Patagonia.[19] Central authority replaced *caudillismo* in the provinces, and agriculture began to become oriented to international markets. The railroad reached Tucuman in the far northwest in 1876 and Mendoza, at the foot of the Andes, in 1885, linking them with the Atlantic. Until then and since their founding in the sixteenth century, the only safe way to reach those interior cities had been over the Andes, through Chile or Bolivia. Roca strongly backed railroad building across the pampas, and trackage rose from 732 kilometers in 1870 to 2,313 in 1880, 9,254 in 1890, 16,767 in 1900, and 27,713 in 1910. These lines brought settlers to the provinces and, soon after, their grain and livestock to seaports.[20]

Up to 1879, the relatively small immigration to the then-unsafe pampas included North Europeans (Germans, Swiss, French, British). However, in the mass immigration after that, North Italians predominated and "were accommodated harmoniously as small holders, share croppers or tenants."[21] The Italians had been coming since the mid-1850s and settling in agricultural colonies. By 1895, when Argentina held 735 colonies covering six million hectares, probably three-fourths of the people in them were Italian immigrants or their children. Indeed, three-fourths of the Italians who arrived in Argentina before 1897 went into agriculture, comprising seven-tenths of all of the foreign-born who lived on the land.[22] The economic expansion that began tentatively in the late 1860s exploded into a major boom from 1879 to 1891. It ended as a result of the failure of the London financial house of Baring Brothers, which set off a drastic credit contraction in Argentina and other parts of the world whose financial progress depended on British investment. Immigration stopped as well. Financial health and immigration both resumed, however, in the late 1890s and continued to 1914 and beyond.[23]

Thus in broad ways the timing of aboriginal "pacification," railroad building, and prairie-pampa cultivation was coincidental in Argentina and North America. Yet important differences existed between Argentine and North American frontiers. In his 1912 book, Lord Bryce was struck by how much "Argentina is like western North America. . . . It is the United States of the Southern Hemisphere." Yet he also saw that Argentina "is a country of great estates. . . . Though a tendency to subdivision has set in and will doubtless continue, *estancias* of sixty thousand acres are not uncommon; and the average holding is said to be even now about six square miles." Consequently, the land held "two classes, the rich *estancieros* or landholders, and the labourers."[24] Carl Solberg, writing in the 1980s, is equally blunt: in the Argentine pampas, "land remained concentrated primarily in the hands of a small group of wealthy and powerful owners. Most pampa farmers were renters. In Canada (and the United States), by contrast, small individually owned farms characterized prairie land tenure."[25]

The contrast between North American smallholdings (except for parts of Texas) and Argentine *latifundia* was indeed striking. A tradition of large land-holdings had started with royal grants in Spanish colonial times and continued beyond 1879, when the government made extensive pampa tracts available to private holders, thus reinforcing and extending the previous pattern. "The Conquest of the Desert did not presage the rise of a small farmer class," Solberg notes; the newly opened land went to a few of Roca's soldiers, and the rest was auctioned off to speculators and the already landed.[26] Land laws of 1853, 1862, 1876, and 1884 attempted to promote colonization in various ways but did nothing to interrupt the concentration of ownership.[27] Provincial governments, dominated by the large landowners, were hardly eager to execute a broadly distributive homestead policy. In the meantime, the central government promoted unrestricted immigration and railroad development. The predictable result was that "Argentine agriculture was built on the systematic exploitation of the nation's tenant farmers. . . . property ownership remained highly concentrated . . . the educational system was primitive . . . the roads were abominable, and . . . the agricultural marketing system was left in the hands of grasping grain merchants."[28]

A new land law of 1903 managed to transfer some fairly remote public land in the territories to smallholders, but by then the accessible and profitable pampas had long since been alienated.[29] In Argentina, then, land laws existed but did not have the function, as in the United States, of transferring title from the public domain to smallholders. An effective homestead act did not exist. No rectilinear survey had been carried out, and clear title to a defined tract was hard to come by.[30] The upshot was that while an agricultural ladder existed in Argentina, whereby an Italian or Spanish immigrant could climb in economic and social position, it was harder to climb than in North America. After the mid-1890s, the top rung, outright ownership, was almost always out of reach. If an immigrant arrived in the 1870s or 1880s with skills, intelligence, and some luck, he could do well. Mark Jefferson, an American sent by the American Geographical Society to survey the Argentine frontier, described the success story of Carlos Brebbia, a stonemason born in Como, who arrived in Santa Fe in 1872, made his first money on a public construction project, and started buying land. Some of it he rented to tenants, themselves immigrants who arrived later. He became a wealthy railway contractor, and his six sons included a grain broker, a commander in the navy, and an accountant. But Brebbia was an exception.

More typically, in Casilda colony in southern Santa Fe province, Jefferson found an Italian family with nine children who farmed twenty-five hectares (sixty-two acres) of their own land, but it had cost them twenty years' work. All of the Italians at Casilda "had prospered and had good houses of burnt bricks with solid roofs."[31] The colony system (*colonización privada*) worked well for many immigrants to Santa Fe and Entre Rios in the 1880s (as it did, also untypically for the country, in Brazil's Santa Catarina state about eight hundred miles to the northeast).[32] As James R. Scobie describes the process, colonies involved assisted migration. Developers paid the steamship fare of a potential colonist, brought him to a *lote* of thirty-six unplowed hectares on the pampa, and let him get to work. If the colonist did work, he "stood a fair chance" to pay off his loans and become owner of the land.[33] On the way to ownership, the migrant might begin as a farm worker (*peon*) for wages and keep, or more likely as a sharecropper (*mediero*), turning over half the harvest to the *estanciero* who provided implements, seeds, and enough food to get started, as well as the land. On the next rung of the ladder he became a tenant (*arrendatario*), leasing the land for a fixed period, providing draft animals, tools, and labor by himself and his family, but keeping all or most of the harvest. This form of tenancy, which worked especially well in 1887–1895 in Santa Fe, permitted the migrant finally to grasp the top rung of the agricultural ladder, independent ownership.[34] But not many achieved that height, and virtually no one did so after the 1890s.

In the late 1890s, the price of land in the pampas rose sharply, beyond the reach of all but the luckiest migrants. After 1900, Argentina's flourishing economy depended on improved cattle requiring alfalfa rather than wild grass, as well as on successful wheat crops for international sale. In part of Córdoba province, Italians owned a third of the land by 1906, and this probably inspired the many migrants freshly arriving from Italy. Mark Jefferson remarked:

> They may well have hoped to have the same good fortune. But in this they were to be disappointed. They could have work there only as renters. There was no more land for sale. The *latifundia* were to be kept intact. . . . Long, long ago the Creole landowner found his leagues of worthless land had become a fortune and made up his mind to part with no more of them. They had, it appeared, an astonishing value—if gringos [that is, Italians] could be got to work them. Long before the colonies had crept from Santa Fe into Cordoba the colonies were *renters'* colonies, with little chance that the renter would acquire ownership.[35]

Tenants often found themselves in an "alfalfa contract," a four- or five-year lease requiring them to break the pampa soil and raise three or four wheat crops and, in the final year, a crop of alfalfa to be used as pasturage for thoroughbred cattle. The tenants made little progress toward owning their farms. The five-year contract ended, and they left "to make room for fine cattle."[36] As of 1900, fewer than two of five farmers in Santa Fe and Buenos Aires provinces had achieved ownership, fewer still after that.[37] By 1914, Argentina's economy had become enormously productive in per capita terms, but the country had reached its peak in area of land under cultivation, as the United States was shortly to do.[38]

The land no longer attracted migrants. Latifundism went unchecked, with 70 percent of migrants on the land working as sharecroppers or tenants. *Arrendatario* status was about all one could aspire to, unless one moved to a city or returned to Europe.[39] The immigrants of the 1880s, and their children, had often become landowners (and tenacious ones) by the 1900s, putting out land to tenants and sharecroppers and hiring mechanized combine teams, using migrant workers, for the harvest. Cheap migrant labor, mechanization, and closed access to land ownership—not simply, by then, the *estanciero* elite—throttled the colonization movement.[40] Not all tenant farmers were poor, and many were employers themselves.[41] But the repatriation rate rose after 1900, *golondrinas* accounted for a larger share of migrants, and Italians headed for the cities, especially Buenos Aires.

Argentina then moved into a second stage of its immigration history. In the first, during the 1880s boom, emphasis lay on "populating the desert," building the railroads, and creating the wheat and cattle export economies. In the second, post-1900 phase, new immigrants could become *arrendatarios* at best (70 percent of whom were foreign-born as late as 1914),[42] more likely sharecroppers or migrant workers, on the land; or they could become wage earners (or better) in the cities. The result for the country was "expansion without development," as some economists put it; "not development but a process of proletarization coinciding with rapid urbanization without the industrial development to justify it."[43] By this time, as Scobie observes, Argentina had a city rather than a frontier.[44] And the city had its class contrasts and ethnic variety—shantytowns of "the newest and poorest" from southern Italy and southern Spain, "a large and not very desirable element among whom anarchism is rife," as Lord Bryce sniffishly noted.[45]

In Buenos Aires and other cities, nonetheless, migrants from Italy, Spain, and elsewhere actually found a good measure of upward mobility after 1900. They could start at the bottom and move much farther up than they could in the countryside. Working-class immigrants saw their sons become businessmen, white-collar workers, civil servants—that is, successful, middle-class urbanites. By 1914, "an amazing 30.4 percent" of immigrants had risen from manual to middle-class positions.[46] In the 1895 and 1914 censuses, immigrants predominated overwhelmingly in the proprietorships of industry and commerce, constituted the majority of commercial and industrial employees and the liberal professions, and were underrepresented among domestics and artisans.[47]

In manufacturing, the foreign-born outnumbered native Argentinians more than four to one after 1895. Among owners of all sorts and sizes of industries, over 90 percent were foreign-born in 1895.[48] An Italian consul in Argentina reported in 1893 that "the vendor of ices becomes, say, a liquor dealer, the fruit seller a restaurant or hotel keeper, the tailor a cloth merchant, the bricklayer a building contractor."[49] While the old-stock Argentinians remained predominant in livestock raising, either at the top as *estancieros* or at the bottom as *peones,* immigrants, especially Italians, took over manufacturing and retailing, both as owner-employers and as employees.[50]

In a peculiarity of the Argentine situation, almost none of these immigrants, despite their economic and social success, ever became naturalized citizens. The result was to encourage migrants to return home and to migrate again, to prevent them from becoming a force promoting development strategies such as tariff protection, and to cut them off from the political-economic elite.[51] As late as 1914, after several million immigrants has arrived in Argentina, only 2.3 percent of the foreign-born in Buenos Aires and 0.9 percent in the rest of the country had been naturalized.[52] To be sure, their Argentine-born children enjoyed full rights of citizenship; and they themselves, though noncitizens, enjoyed all civil rights except the vote, plus exemption from military service. Thus the original immigrants lacked incentive to become citizens, because citizenship carried no short-run advantages. Yet the absence of it did carry long-run and severe disadvantages for Argentine development after 1914.

In the meantime, the immigrants assimilated very well culturally. Or, to say it better, because they were such a huge proportion of the population, they dominated the culture, which was hardly true of Italians in the United States.[53] Italians not only were a much larger presence within the Argentine population, but also they built a "multiclass society" with a solid "institutional structure." Some were workers, some shopkeepers, some professionals, whereas Italians in the United States in this period often were day laborers, one among many groups in the ethnic shuffle. The "tiny Argentine elite" considered Italians more civilized than most of the native-born.[54] Even the birds of passage contributed to cultural uplift, as Jefferson pointed out:

> Madam [Adelina] Patti could and did sing in London and Paris in the winter and take steamer in March for Buenos Aires for another season of opera in June and July—the southern winter. . . . So did many a modest Italian company of small-city opera singers, chorus and all; for a South American city of 50,000 people would have felt disgraced if it had to go through the winter without a few weeks of opera. These people by their numbers were far more significant than the celebrities.[55]

Compared with their countrymen in the United States, the Italians in Argentina involved themselves much more in agriculture, especially before the mid-1890s. But they were urbanites as well. They distributed themselves up and down the occupational scale more successfully than did Italians in the United States. By 1914, when 53 percent of the native-born lived in cities, 69 percent of the Italian-born and 78 percent of the Spanish-born did so.[56] With land ownership closed to them, and since Argentina lacked a mining sector, recent immigrants located in cities and engaged in construction, retailing, manufacturing, international trade, and almost all occupations ranging from manual labor to upper-middle-class positions. Perhaps one-third to one-half returned to Europe; some of these came back to Argentina. Before 1914 rural-to-urban migration within Argentina was rarer than new migration from the Mediterranean to Argentina.[57] That suggests a great deal of chain migration as well as kinship and same-village connections to jobs of all kinds.

A small industry has developed to provide comparisons among Argentina,

Canada, Australia, and other "settler societies" and to account for Argentina's relatively slow economic growth since the 1920s despite its extremely promising record before 1914. Tempting though it is to digress along those lines, it is appropriate here only to suggest keeping the Argentinian land situation in mind. It probably affected the rate and sources of immigration. Lord Bryce may have been correct when he concluded that Argentina "is not, like western Canada, a place suitable for British or Scandinavian immigrants of small means, not merely on account of the climate, but because they could not easily get small farms and the means of working them."[58] Solberg, trenchantly and in detail, makes the Canadian-Argentine comparison and comes down to three differences. First, "the prairies were a society primarily of small owner-operators. . . . The pampas, in contrast, were a society of tenants who rented land on short-term contracts and who moved about frequently." Second, prairie people, though mostly immigrants, "quickly became citizens" and had to, to gain clear legal title; Argentine immigrants seldom became citizens. Third, Canadian prairie farmers "formed vigorous and large cooperative movements" with political clout; "pampa farmers remained a marginal group in Argentine society" as cooperatives there "remained small and weak."[59] No one has said it better.

13

BRAZIL

Brazil's migration differed distinctly from Argentina's and North America's in several ways. It was smaller, both in total numbers and in proportion to the receiving population. It included an early phase (1820s through 1870s) when Italians and Germans settled in colonies in Rio Grande do Sul, Santa Catarina, and Parana provinces in the far south. Germans first appeared in 1822 in the valley of Jacui, north of Porto Alegre, and in 1824 established a larger colony nearby at São Leopoldo. Novo Hamburgo and other colonies followed. The imperial government encouraged those settlements, which assured the colonists private ownership of land. From the late 1850s to 1878, a series of new German colonies, beginning with "Picada Glueck-Auf," then Picadas Hermann, Boa Vista, Frank, Catarina, Bismarck, Berlin, Moltke, Koln, Krupp, and others collectively called "Teutonia," opened in Rio Grande do Sul. They too provided settlers with smallholdings privately owned.[1] Their physical arrangement—the "Picada"—was, however, peculiarly drawn from European experience and differed drastically from North American smallholding patterns. As Frederick Luebke describes it:

> The founders of a colony would decree a long straight cut through the forest that could later become a road. Individual settlers would then receive long, narrow plots of land of one or two hundred acres that stretched out at right angles to the road. Farmhouses were built at the side of the road, thereby creating a strung-out rural village similar to the *Waldhufendorf* or *Strassendorf* of central Germany. Several such *Pikaden* would constitute a colony.[2]

This system isolated the German-Brazilians and greatly retarded their assimilation, linguistic and otherwise, and contributed to the often violent hostility they suffered during World War I.[3]

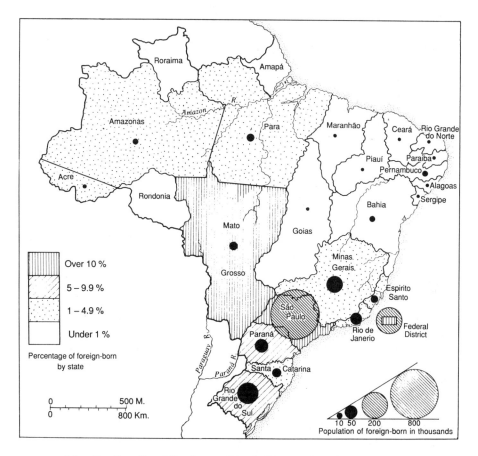

Map 7. Brazil and Its States (*Map by Norman Pounds*)

The bulk of migration after 1889 went to São Paulo state and the three states south of it.

Beginning in 1874, the government brought Italians from the Po Valley to nuclear colonies just north of the Germans in Rio Grande do Sul. By 1890 seven colonies, of which Caxias do Sul was the largest, contained about 80,000 Italians on a 370,000-hectare area provided by the government. Families each received from 25 to 63 hectares, usually in rectangular plots. This Old Italian Colonial Zone, like the German zone, remained endogamous and highly fertile, with a birth rate of 43 (compared with Rio Grande do Sul's average of 26) in 1918–1922.[4] The Germans also increased and multiplied "amazingly," and the colonies remained German or Italian enclaves with peculiar land systems existing in the same *gaucho* state of Rio Grande do Sul with Luso-Brazilian *latifundio* ranches.[5]

Because of their remoteness and generally primitive farming methods, the early colonies never achieved great economic success. Liberal reformers in the 1870s and 1880s, convinced that smallholding and an end to *latifundio* would benefit the country, managed to press for the creation of a few more nuclear colonies in São Paulo.[6] Polish migrants, arriving in the Valley of Iguaçu and other points in Parana after 1887, founded Prudentopolis in 1896. Perhaps 50,000 Poles migrated to Parana in the following decade or so.[7]

By then the second phase of Brazilian migration—the mass phase—was well under way. It was triggered by the collapse of slavery in the late 1880s and by the demands of the politically powerful coffee planters, especially in western São Paulo, that the central and state governments assist Europeans to come to São Paulo as a new labor force to replace the slaves. Heavy Italian immigration continued from then until 1902 when the Italian government, in a rare and early such act, restricted it. During that phase the migration consisted largely of North Italians, from Venezia primarily, who were recruited as families, with their transportation paid by the São Paulo state government. Brazil also received Italians, Portuguese, Spaniards, and smaller groups of other Europeans from the 1870s through the period; these were "spontaneous" (that is, nonassisted) migrants who went to Rio de Janeiro and São Paulo rather than to rural areas. They were usually unattached young men whose migration pattern resembled other South and East Europeans of their age, sex, and rural background who went to Buenos Aires, New York, and other cities of the Americas and Europe.

The subsidized family migration to the coffee plantations (*fazendas*) uniquely characterized Brazilian immigration. Some assisted families went from Italy to Argentina, but they figured much less prominently there than families did in Brazil. Initially, at least, this migration was more labor-seeking than land-seeking, although the labor was on the land rather than in factories, mines, or construction. This mass recruitment of families as an agricultural labor force has much to do with how the "frontier" in Brazil differed from the frontiers of Argentina, Canada, and the United States, and it helps to answer the question of why Brazil (though it certainly qualifies as a major receiver country, unlike, say, Mexico) nonetheless attracted so few Europeans for its large population and immense size.

Most of the country's population growth resulted from natural increase, not from immigration.[8] Total migrants admitted each year ranged from a few hundred to a few thousand from 1820 to the 1870s, most of them Portuguese going to Rio or the sugar-producing northeast, and a smaller number of German or Italian colonists going to agricultural enclaves in the temperate south.[9] About 218,000 migrants entered during 1871–1880, 530,000 in the 1880s, and 1,144,000 in the 1890s; but the number fell back to 695,000 in 1901–1910 and 797,000 in 1911–1920.[10] This pattern ran directly counter to that in the United States, where migration was heavy in the 1880s, slow in the 1890s, and heaviest from 1901 to 1914.[11] The first Brazilian census, in 1872, showed 3.8 percent of the population as foreign-born.[12] From the mid-1870s to 1887, total migration rose slightly, but Italians took a decided lead over Portuguese, with Spaniards and Germans next. In 1887, with the end of slavery imminent and São Paulo already recruiting in North Italy (never in the South), the migrant total rose to 56,000, of whom more than 40,000 were Italians. When all was said and done, about as many Italians went to Brazil as to the United States before 1900, although the total European migration to the United States was five to ten times larger than to Brazil, depending on the year.

In the next ten years, 1888–1897, inmigration passed 100,000 in all but three years and included the all-time peak for Brazil of 216,760 in 1891. The total in those ten years following the abolition of slavery was 1,277,537, of whom 776,394 (60.8 percent) went to São Paulo state, and of whom 750,910 (58.8 percent) were Italian.[13] The proportion of foreign-born in the Brazilian population peaked in the 1900 census at 6.2 percent; immigrant totals never again exceeded one hundred thousand except in 1911–1913 and 1926, 1927, and 1929. In 1927, in step with other New World countries, Brazil passed the first of several laws restricting European immigration.[14]

Of the four-million-plus migrants who came to Brazil between 1888 and 1939, 34 percent were Italian, 29 percent Portuguese, 14 percent Spanish, 4.7 percent Austrian or Russian (these were mostly Jews or Poles), 4.5 percent Japanese (virtually none before 1908), 4.1 percent German, with several other groups under 2 percent.[15] Although the number coming from neighboring countries (Paraguay, Peru, Bolivia, Uruguay, Argentina) will never be known for certain, some thousands appeared in the 1920 census, revealing a considerable unrecorded migration within South America.[16]

Italian immigration fell in the 1898–1907 decade to 273,285, 45.4 percent of the total of 602,528, and another 65,803 arrived from 1908 to 1914. Prior to 1902, the Italians going to Brazil were chiefly Venetians, traveling out of Genoa on prepaid tickets, motivated by grim push factors, and largely ignorant of what awaited them on the *fazendas*. After 1902, they were more often Neapolitans or from elsewhere in the *Mezzogiorno,* of urban rather than peasant background. Return migration reached about 50 percent, a high figure for a migration with much less seasonality than that pertaining to North America or Argentina.[17]

The Italian government's ban on further subsidized transportation—the "Prinetti decree" of March 1902—resulted from Italian consular reports of miserable living conditions on the *fazendas* and the victimizing of one Italian in a murder case. It shut off much, though not all, Italian immigration, and the Spanish government followed suit in 1911 with similar results.[18] Assisted migration stopped; voluntary migration, involving smaller numbers, continued, as did active commerce between Brazil and Italy.[19] The majority of immigrants still went to São Paulo, but about as many Spanish and Portuguese arrived as did Italians.[20] Repatriation figures for Brazil are hard to come by, but do exist for 1899–1907, when they totaled 423,325, or 80.7 percent as many as arrived. Italians provided 58.4 percent of the emigrants, more than their share of arrivals.[21] Nonetheless, in the 1920 census Italians emerged as the largest foreign-born group, and since theirs had been a family migration, their children and grandchildren added substantially to the Italian stock in Brazil by that date.[22] By 1920, 22 percent of the people of São Paulo state were foreign-born, whereas the national percentage had slipped to 5.1 percent.[23]

The Italians assimilated fairly easily, intermarrying more often than did Germans or even Portuguese by the 1930s. They were regarded as "active and well adapted" citizens. More literate than the native population (which was not true of Italians in the United States) and considered (not always correctly) better workers than other groups, they could look forward to upward mobility.[24] Two-thirds lived in São Paulo state and nearly all the rest elsewhere in the southeast and south.[25] Like the Italians, the Spaniards went to the states of São Paulo (two-thirds), Rio de Janeiro, Minas Gerais, or Rio Grande do Sul. In contrast, Portuguese immigrants scattered all over the country, from Recife and Bahia in the northeast to Rio, São Paulo, and elsewhere.[26] As for other groups (all of them together constituting only one-fifth as many people as the Italians, Portuguese, and Spanish), Germans had always headed for the temperate south (Rio Grande do Sul or Santa Catarina) and maintained distinct cultural and linguistic enclaves as late as the 1960s and beyond.[27]

The coffee region of the São Paulo plateau was not the only part of Brazil that attracted people in those years. So did cities. The population of Rio, at 267,000 in the 1872 census, rose to 523,000 in the 1890 census and topped a million by 1920; but the population of São Paulo, only 31,000 in 1872 and 65,000 in 1890, surged to 240,000 in 1900 and 579,000 in 1920.[28] Immigrants accounted for some of this. Italians in São Paulo city worked at almost every skilled trade; their ranks included carpenters, shoemakers, barbers, fruit vendors, teamsters, peddlers, newsstand operators, masons, and others.[29] The immigrant working class comprised one-time coffee pickers from the *fazendas* and the assisted immigrants who avoided going there in the first place. To them were added former Italian factory workers sought after by Brazilian industrialists, and some former slaves.[30] A minority of the Italians were entrepreneurs, members of an immigrant bourgeoisie who held that position as much by virtue of the capital and skills that they brought with them as by upward mobility.

The Italians' early appearance on the scene of São Paulo's expansion helped greatly to make them part of it. Even more was this true of Italians in Buenos Aires, in either case quite in contrast to the experience of Italians in American cities. By 1920, Italians owned half of the noncorporate businesses in São Paulo.[31] The greatest success story, as related by Warren Dean, was Francesco Matarazzo, a Calabrian of "modest middle-class family" who came in 1881, aged twenty-five, with a wife and two children. He took up lard rendering (a business he already knew in Italy) in a town in western São Paulo state, and by 1890 formed an import-export business in São Paulo city. Mill followed on mill, banking connections sprouted, near-monopolies of various consumer products emerged through a strategy of vertical integration, and he became perhaps the most successful Italian immigrant in Brazilian history.[32] Like Amadeo P.

Giannini in San Francisco, Matarazzo was a unique case but not an improbable one.

Immigrants also accounted for part of a statistically amazing shift in race composition. Brazil's population apparently went from 37 percent white in 1872 to 44 percent in 1890 to 63 percent in 1940, while the number of blacks declined from 19 percent (1872) to 15 percent (1940) of the population, and mulattoes from 41 percent (1872) to 21 percent (1940). But as was far from being the case in the United States, one's race in Brazil was pretty much what one told the census taker it was. In 1890, the "inebriamento" following abolition encouraged many mulattoes (*pardos*) to say they were white, and blacks to say they were mulattoes.[33]

Law—regarding slavery, immigration, and land—had serious effects on Brazil's migration patterns. Slavery disappeared in a series of gradual steps; Brazil suffered no conflict remotely like the United States Civil War. Brazil outlawed the African slave trade in 1851, after having absorbed 38 percent of it since 1500. The "Law of the Free Womb" passed in 1871, whereby children of slave mothers were born free. Slaves over the age of sixty were freed in 1885; and by May 1888, when the Princesa Isabel proclaimed the "*Lei Aurea,*" the Golden Law of full abolition, the slave population had shrunk from nearly two million to six or eight hundred thousand.[34] Brazil's large number of free people of color made it possible for many slaves in the 1880s simply to walk off the plantation, and so they did. Slavery was doomed by the mid-1880s; the refusal of banks by 1886 to lend money with slaves as collateral was the final blow.

By then the Paulista planters, more entrepreneurial than the poorer, land-exhausted planters of Rio and Minas Gerais, had fastened on sponsored immigration, particularly of North Italians, as the way to acquire a new labor force to replace the slaves.[35] Abolition in Brazil brought immigration. The planters persuaded the government, especially São Paulo state, to pay for the steamship and rail fares, the hostels, and other costs of their new labor force. The "stunning fact" about post-abolition plantation labor was that the public—everybody—paid for it, including the newly freed slaves themselves. Had that not happened, the large *fazendas* would probably have been broken up, and immigrants might have become fewer in numbers but smallholders more quickly.[36] One estimate puts assisted immigration at 935,000 and nonassisted at 614,000 in the twenty-five years between abolition and 1914. This system probably brought to São Paulo state a larger number of assisted immigrants than Australia, with its much more famous subsidy program, received during that time.[37]

State and federal law continued to sponsor or encourage immigration past the turn of the century. World War I virtually stopped the inflow of Italians and Germans. After 1919, immigration resumed, though in reduced numbers; despite the huge virgin areas of the country, good land accessible to markets had become scarce. In December 1930, the new regime of Getulio Vargas greatly restricted immigration to protect manual workers during the Depression crisis.[38] By then, the migration out of Europe to New World countries had slowed greatly. The heyday of Brazilian immigration preceded 1914 (and for Italians, 1902). Brazil underwent a shift from an "old" to a "new" immigration, a very different shift from that in the United States: before 1885, the typical immigrant was a young Portuguese man bound for the coastal cities from Recife to Rio to find jobs in the sugar industry or in services. After 1885, the typical immigrant was an Italian man or woman arriving as part of a family to take up a *colono* contract on a coffee *fazenda*.[39]

The *fazenda*, the large coffee plantation, rather than the small family farm, was the norm in southeastern Brazil. As the writer Joaquim Nabuco lamented in the Chamber of Deputies in 1880, they were "grandes dominios feudais," owned and run by *latifundistas* with "absolute sovereignty."[40] In colonial times the crown granted *sesmarias* of three or four dozen square miles to its favorites, and other large tracts were simply occupied by squatting planters. Titles to these holdings were confirmed in a law of 1850, which was also supposed to inaugurate a survey-and-sale system for the rest of the crown lands, similar to the system begun in the United States in 1785. It never happened in Brazil. Instead, when the Republic replaced the monarchy in 1889, crown lands reverted to the states; and in São Paulo, where the big planters held great political power, this meant the further concentration of land in the planters' hands. Except for parts of the south, notably the pre-1880 German and Italian colonies, smallholdings were "episodic or occasional" and "did not find a home or . . . characterize the social landscape" in Brazil.[41]

Before the 1880s, the Brazilian coffee industry centered chiefly in the Paraiba Valley west and north of Rio de Janeiro. Soil exhaustion together with railroad development in São Paulo state soon encouraged planters to resettle there. As immigrant Italians replaced slaves, Santos had by 1890 replaced Rio as the leading port of coffee shipments.[42] Lord Bryce observed that

> many of the coffee plantations [in the Paraiba Valley] of forty or even thirty years ago have been abandoned, and their sites are now practically undistinguishable from the rest of the forest. . . . [yet] there is still so much virgin land waiting to be planted that the question is of more importance to the individual owner than to the nation at large.[43]

The *fazendeiros* were often absentee landords living in São Paulo city or Rio. The world's largest *fazenda*, the Dumont plantation 300 miles from São Paulo included 13,000 acres on which were 5 million coffee trees, 2,500 acres of pasture, and 5,000 people in 23 colonies of up to 70 families. But some *fazendas* were small; inheritance was partible, and as slavery crumbled in the 1880s many *fazendeiros* faced ruin for want of a labor force.[44] Slaves had worked the coffee groves, had served as domestics and artisans, and had performed virtually all functions on the *fazendas*. By the mid-1880s, however, slaves were running off, anticipating emancipation. Some attacked their overseers on the way, and police reported themselves "overwhelmed with the task of retrieving runaway slaves" in 1885–1888.[45] The planters desperately needed a new labor force.

The answer, proposed by the parliamentarian Jose Vergueiro in 1870, was discussed and rejected by most planters, then stated again by Louis Couty, a professor at the Rio Politecnico, in a newspaper article of late 1883. The end of slavery is greatly desirable, he argued, but planned immigration had to accompany it; immigrant families should be colonized on small lots along the railroad routes as in the United States, Canada, and Argentina.[46] In Rio and São Paulo, relief was already on the way. The central government established the Bureau of Colonization and Immigration, which began publishing maps and documents in several languages; and in São Paulo, the private but state-supported *Sociedade Promotora de Imigração* began helping to pay transatlantic fares in 1884. A year later, Italians were specifically targeted, and Luis Bianchi Betoldi, a Lombard who had lived in São Paulo since 1872, led the São Paulo effort to recruit Lombards, Venetians, Piedmontese, and Ligurians.

According to a São Paulo provincial law of March 29, 1884, only families were to be subsidized. Single men were welcome, but they had to get to Brazil on their own. (Before long, families already established in Brazil began paying for a brother or cousin, in the usual pattern of chain migration). From mid-1887, the state government paid the *Sociedade* 75 *milreis* for each immigrant over twelve, half that for younger children. This money in turn paid the steamship and railway fares.[47] Many Europeans went to Brazil because of the free passage although they knew little about it and much of that was "lurid reports."[48]

The usual route took them from Genoa to Santos in twenty to thirty days on steamships holding several hundred, though the *Adria*, probably badly overloaded, in 1887 carried about 1,500. From Santos the migrants climbed the three-thousand-foot escarpment "by the railroad that etches the Serra-do-Mar, and which . . . [gave] the passenger the spectacle of a superb panorama of the mountain chain covered by virgin forests," and rode into São Paulo to the large hostel operated by the *Sociedade*. Those whose ship brought them to Rio went to a hostel on the Ilha de Flores. At either hostel, where they received free food and shelter for several days, they agreed to a labor contract.

A minority of the migrants went to "nuclear colonies" (*núcleos coloniais*), while the majority became *colonos* on *fazendas*.[49] In some areas, such as the Paraiba Valley of Rio de Janeiro province and the province of Minas Gerais, sponsored immigration arrived too late; soil erosion or exhaustion had created "denuded, eroded slopes" by the 1880s, after "a ruthless use of natural resources and an equally ruthless exploitation of man."[50] For São Paulo state and its planters, however, as railroads were making possible the transformation of virgin land into endless coffee groves hundreds of miles inland from the city, the arrival of the immigrants-become-*colonos* signaled that the slaves could depart and that the planters would have an even more stable labor supply. "The plantations were not only saved," Dean writes, "they were energized by this massive inflow of labor."[51]

The immigrant family usually had to wait no more than three days at the São Paulo hostel before someone presented them with a contract, often verbal. A free rail trip took them to the *fazenda* to begin their life as *colonos*. They agreed to tend perhaps two thousand coffee trees per adult for a small fixed wage, along with a fixed sum for each liter of coffee berries harvested. They lived rent-free in a "modest dwelling" close by others, all made of "sun-dried mud plastered on a framework of poles."[52] Since coffee trees started producing only three or four years after planting, the family's contract might be for four to six years.[53] Some contracts ran for only one year, but since the idea was to tie the *colono* to the plantation, they usually ran longer. Often the family had the right to grow garden crops around their home or between the coffee trees, and perhaps to keep a cow. For many, this provided not only subsistence but also a surplus that they could sell at local markets. In these ways—wages for tending the trees, wages at harvest, day labor around the plantation, free housing and food, and cash sale of some crops—the *colonos* might manage to save enough to buy a small lot or two, or to begin life in a town or city.[54] Some no doubt did so. Others returned to Italy.

In general, therefore, the immigrants were sharecroppers on a wage, with some ability to produce their own food. Contracts were binding on the *fazendeiro*, but in disputes few immigrants had the time or the money to go to court, if indeed one could be found. Braving the gunslingers that some *fazendeiros* employed was also risky. Supplies usually had to be bought at the plantation store, where high prices, interest, and one-sided accounting could leave the immigrants with nothing at the end of a year—the same situation that often faced sharecroppers at country stores in the American South. Nonetheless, some *colonos*, especially those with able-bodied sons and daughters, accumulated enough savings after years of work to gain their own land.[55]

A minority of Italian migrants to Brazil came on their own, without a travel subsidy, and brought enough money to avoid the *fazendas*. The government provided them with food and lodging for a few days at the hostel, and then free rail transportation to a "colonial nucleus." There they received a plot of land for cultivation. The size and price varied. In São Paulo in the late 1880s, one could get thirty hectares for the equivalent of about $250 cash, or about $300 if one used the maximum credit period of five years (very occasionally ten); in Espírito Santo, the land was a bit cheaper.[56] The planters did not regard the *núcleos* as competition, but rather as a source of temporary manpower.

The São Paulo state government started twenty-five *núcleos* between 1885 and 1911. It bought land from down-at-the-heels or cash-hungry planters; the state surveyed it and staked out plots of ten to forty hectares that it sold to immigrants, including in some cases *colonos* who had saved enough to buy in. The immigrant promised to preserve the lot lines and marks and to put out new ones if the originals were damaged. Six months after arrival, the immigrant had to plant a minimum area and build a small house.[57] The state also provided an "administrator" in the early years, and when the migrants paid their loans, the *núcleo* was simply absorbed into the *município* containing it. Thus the *núcleos* were a device for instant smallholding, but they never played a major role. The Campos Sales colony, for example, contained 32 families (mostly Swiss and German) when it opened in 1897, and by 1905 held 164 families with 925 persons. Pariquera-Açu colony, created later, held 310 families with 1,595 persons in 1907, among them 179 Brazilian families, 55 Italian, 32 Polish, 23 Austrian, 8 German, and a scattering of others.[58] At their peak (1918) they included about 21,000 people out of several hundred thousand workers in the coffee region.[59]

What happened to the former slaves after abolition became complete in 1888? According to a recent account, they either "settled in isolated areas [and] became involved in subsistence agriculture, or [were] relegated on the coffee plantations to the most menial forms of labour not directly linked to production."[60] Some drifted to São Paulo city or Santos and worked on the docks and railroads or in warehouses and factories. Some moved off into the wilderness beyond the plantation region, joining the *caipiras* (roughly, "poor whites") and *caboclos* (roughly, "half-breeds") in subsistence agriculture. In Vassouras, where the plantations were wearing out, many slaves fled when they were emancipated but "slowly flowed back to the plantations" to work the harvest or to become sharecroppers. In São Paulo, some stayed on plantations but worked for wages. Many planters demanded that the government compensate them for the loss of their slaves by abolition. They were not compensated. Neither were the slaves for the work they had done.[61]

Could the immigrant to Brazil, Italian or otherwise, become a small landowner? Was there an agricultural ladder from wage worker or *colono* to tenant to *núcleo* resident to independent owner? Answers vary. Lucy Maffei Hutter is rather sanguine: the Italian *colonos,* men, wives, and children, were "hardworking, always peaceful and happy." This allowed them to adapt to Brazil and prosper, whether as craftworkers in the cities and towns or as agriculturists.[62] Manuel Diegues Junior implies that immigrant families could become landowners if "everybody in the family worked day or night."[63] For Michael M. Hall, the *fazendeiros* "did what they could to make sure that the immmigrants largely remained landless laborers and thus available for their own use on the plantations," and an Italian survey made in 1897 found that *colonos* at that time rarely became landowners.[64] Thomas Holloway, on the other hand, after a careful look at land records, finds that "many first generation immigrants became the owneroperators of small and medium-sized farms. . . . for there was more good land in the São Paulo plateau than anyone at the time knew what to do with. . . . There was misery, isolation, and exploitation, but there were also opportunities." If one could "put together a nest egg, there were few barriers" to owning land. He even sees Turnerian elements in the Brazilian picture, with rural São Paulo's available land serving as a safety valve for Italian and Spanish landless peasants.[65] Holloway cites a 1905 survey of property owners by national origin that shows that immigrants owned 22 percent (Italians alone, 14 percent) of the land in the western São Paulo coffee region and that by 1920 they owned 39 percent (Italians alone, 32 percent—much the most successful group).[66]

But Warren Dean, while agreeing that some immigrants did achieve owner-ship, stresses that "the 'average' immigrant, or 'many' immigrants," did not. In Rio Claro *município* as of 1905, fewer than 12 percent of farm workers owned the land they worked on. They were probably better off than they had been or would have been in Europe, but they were far from well off. The Italian govern-ment apparently agreed when it banned further promotional subsidies in 1902.[67] Silvio Coletti, an Italian official, declared in 1908 that "the colonists would be better off in Italy." Hall concludes that the "story of the first genera-tion of Italian immigrants to São Paulo" is "an almost unrelieved tale of exploita-tion and bitter disappointment."[68] Holloway asserts that the "São Paulo *colono* had an enviable existence" compared with that of slaves, indentured servants, and peons elsewhere in Latin America (or in the American antebellum South), and perhaps the *colono* and his wife and children did.[69] But those are frightful comparisons. Were there glasses half-full, or half-empty? Only if all family mem-bers worked hard for fifteen or twenty years, all the time avoiding disease, accident, and bad judgment, could they climb from *colono* to small farmer.

The far southern states (Parana, Santa Catarina, and especially Rio Grande do Sul) provide some contrast to this problematic picture of São Paulo state. Lord Bryce wrote that Italians in Rio Grande do Sul "have become well-to-do peasant proprietors, living in less comfort than their German neighbours, but working just as steadily." A few years later, Robert Foerster added that Italians in the three states were "so sharply marked off from those of the *fazendas* and the cities, that I am loath to leave them without a word. . . . They are never hired farm hands, but all are proprietors and most are secure in their possessions. . . . Few are rich, few poor. Abject poverty they do not know."[70] Some of these Italians and Germans were probably third- or fourth-generation descendants of colonists who arrived as early as the 1820s. Novo Hamburgo, a German settlement about twenty-five miles north of Porto Alegre, remained unalloyedly Teutonic in lan-guage and culture in 1900, and continued to resist assimilation for decades beyond that. Many *Riograndenses* still spoke German as their first and main language in the 1960s.[71]

Some colonists who were part of the recruited and assisted migration of the 1890s did not proceed inland when they arrived at Santos or Rio. Instead, they transshipped on a five- or six-day voyage to Rio Grande, on the coast, and then to Porto Alegre and inland. A British consul reporting in 1890 on conditions at a new settlement called Marianna Pimentel, not far from Porto Alegre, wrote that Italians and Poles had been coming since 1888 (as had six British families, who lasted only thirty-three days). Each family received a small sum of cash, some tools, and about thirty hectares to live on. The task was daunting, but if Foerster and Bryce were any judges, many succeeded.[72]

Apparently the São Paulo *colono* was not in an enviable position compared with a smallholding immigrant, even an *arrendatario,* in Argentina, or compared with the Italians who made the shorter hop to New York, or Spaniards to Cuba, to become urban wageworkers. Brazil simply did not attract migrants as Argentina and the United States did, in relative or absolute numbers, despite the relatively familiar language and culture of Brazil for Italians, Spaniards, and Portuguese. Conditions of work were just not attractive. Without recruitment and subsidies, the migration would have been much smaller.[73] Return migration from the *fazendas,* or flight to São Paulo city, was frequent. Let Foerster have the last word on Italian migrants:

> The history of the great period of Italian immigration [to Brazil] tells of an abruptly acquired impetus [recruitment and assistance], a long and hectic advance with occasional retreat, then a spectacular collapse and a stagnant aftermath. . . . When the best has been said, the experience of the immigrants on the *fazendas* has been one of broken hopes and vanished dreams. . . . [A] narrow and stunted life, hedged about with worry, has been the reward of the mass of the cultivators.[74]

There are other reasons why Brazilian immigration was relatively low. The demographer Paul Hugon reels off a list: most important, uncertainty of land titles, the different climate, tropical diseases, and (until 1888) competition from slaves; and secondarily, poor agricultural credit, a poor or nonexistent school system (particularly agricultural schools), and rudimentary transportation.[75] Vianna Moog's *Bandeirantes and Pioneers,* with its intriguing comparisons of Brazil and the United States, also mentions the absence of a superior network of interior waterways such as the United States has, the lack of coal, and above all the exploitative *bandeirante* ethos, which he contrasts with that of the less romantic but steadier American pioneers.[76]

In particular, many writers have stressed the difficulty and risk in getting and keeping land. Nathaniel Leff states flatly that if Brazil had had a liberal sale-and-survey policy like the United States', it would probably have run the United States a close race in attracting immigrants. But there was no such policy, nor the social overhead capital for internal improvements; and these "adverse geographical and infrastructure conditions" prevented Brazil's development—including the human capital which migration represents.[77] J. D. Gould explains repatriation from São Paulo state on the grounds that "the dominant class [the planters] made it very difficult for immigrants to acquire land,"[78] whereas T. L. Smith blames government for the lack of land surveys, firm titles, or an effective homestead act or any other cheap and secure land grant.[79] An American visiting Brazil in the 1880s spoke to the point:

> During three centuries the Crown has been making grants of land to various parties, the records of which do not appear to exist in any accessible form, if they exist at all. A man might expend weeks in exploring the wild lands, and, if he should then find a tract he wished to purchase, he would not be sure of a clear title. If he resolved to run his risk and buy of the Government, his first proceeding would be to formally request, in writing, the president of the province in which the land was situated to

cause the tract to be surveyed. The president of the province would designate a surveyor to make the survey and report upon the land, after which the Government would fix the price and conditions for its sale. If a sale should be effected, the purchaser would take the land subject to the claims of other individuals, which, if any were preferred, would, unless amicably adjusted, have to be determined by expensive and dilatory proceedings before a judicial tribunal.[80]

The writer believed it would take fifty years just to clear the existing titles. Conceivably the agricultural depression of 1887–1897 in the United States, together with Brazil's subsidized recruitment program at just that time, diverted European peasants from the United States to Brazil. That is, however, unlikely. North Italians and Spaniards were rarely seekers of American farmland either before 1887 or after 1897. Migration to Brazil ate instead into Argentina's share.[81] South Italians and East Europeans usually chose the United States, with its shorter voyage, higher wages, and (except for 1893–1897) many industrial job opportunities. Migration to a *fazenda* or a *núcleo* also involved a longer commitment of time, maybe a permanent migration. It had to include the whole family, not just a footloose son or brother, and may help to explain why Italians in Brazil, compared with Italians in the United States, sent so little money home.[82]

Thus while migration to the United States simply extended the traditional seasonal migration within Europe, the Brazilian option was a good deal more complicated and, literally, unsettling. Worth remembering also are traditional cultural affinities of Germans, Irish, and British for North America, and the American denigration of Latin Europeans. As for other contrasts between Brazil and the United States, there were many. Brazil's vast interior, most of it never settled, was not functionally available for smallholding yeomen; it was very unlike the creeping American farm frontier. Only in the three states of the south were smallholdings commonplace. Immigrant life in Rio and São Paulo bore some resemblances to life in New York or Buenos Aires, but there were differences too.[83]

The closest American comparison to the São Paulo coffee region is the cotton-growing South. In Brazil the former slave after emancipation in 1888 had no better, perhaps an even worse, time than the American freedpeople after 1865. The imported *colonos,* as wageworkers on contract, if they had an American counterpart, resembled poor whites, in that most of them had to buy at the country/plantation store, all had to defer to the planter/*fazendeiro,* and all had to look out for the sheriff/hired gun who enforced his wishes.[84] Lord Bryce remarked that the *fazendeiro*

> loves his rural life, as did the Virginian planter in North America before the Civil War, and lives on the *fazenda* in a sort of semi-feudal patriarchal way, often with grown-up sons and daughters around him. Estates (except in the extreme south) are extensive; near neighbours are few; families are often large; the plantation is a sort

of little principality, and its owner with his fellow-proprietors is allowed, despite all democratic theory, to direct the politics of the district just as in England, eighty years ago [1832, before the Great Reform Bill], the county families used to control local affairs and guide the choice of representatives in Parliament.[85]

The *fazendeiros* had been accustomed to owning and ruling slaves, and their habits persisted when they dealt with the *colonos*. As a practical matter, considering the cost of lawyers, the distance from courts, the obligations of judges and police to the planters, and the sheer physical risk, *colonos* lacked legal redress.[86] *Latifundio* continued (even strengthened) after the abolition of slavery because, as a Brazilian scholar noted, the great proprietors forced the governments to furnish "help, subventions, conversions, reversions, valorizations, in fact every kind of artifice aimed at perpetuating an economic order which, in truth, should have fallen."[87] So many aspects of the Brazilian scene—above all, low immigration despite great size—differ from the other New World receivers that if any country was "exceptional," it was Brazil, not the United States.

14

CANADA

Canada, the world's second-largest country in area, received fewer Europeans than Argentina or the United States but more than Brazil. Its effective living space for whites in 1871 hugged the Atlantic coast, the St. Lawrence River, and the eastern Great Lakes. By 1914, thanks in large part to immigration from Europe—and from the United States—its immense west was occupied two hundred to three hundred miles north of the forty-ninth-parallel border to the environs of Saskatoon and Edmonton. The Peace River settlements, begun in 1907, leaped a further three hundred miles northwest of Edmonton, on a latitude with Labrador and southern Alaska, the northernmost agricultural communities in North America.

From the mid-nineteenth century to the present, Canada's population grew at about the same rate as the United States', and remained roughly one-tenth the size of the United States' at each census. The rural proportions of the two countries were almost identical; the census in 1871 showed Canada to be 80 percent rural; in 1901, 62.5 percent; and in 1921, 50.5 percent. The comparable American census figures for 1870, 1900, and 1920 were 75, 60, and 51.[1] Migration ebbs and flows were similar—low immigration in the 1870s, high in the 1880s, low in the 1890s, and high from 1901 to 1914, with a lull during World War I, and high again for a time after the war. Total numbers arriving in Canada were one-fifth to one-tenth the U.S. level, with 1883 the peak year (134,000 immigrants) before 1900, and 1913 (401,000) the peak year after 1900. The thinnest year (between the 1860s and the 1930s) was 1896, when only 17,000 arrived.[2]

The major difference from the United States was that Canada, in terms of migrants, was a sieve. From 1861 to 1901, the net migration flow of people from Canada—those born there as well as those born in Europe who lived there

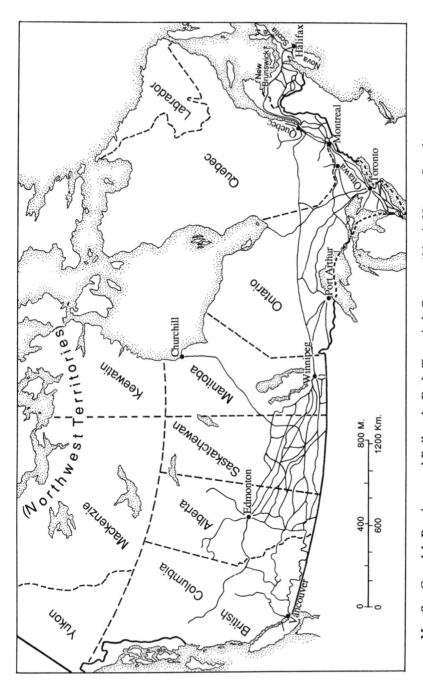

Map 8. Canada's Provinces and Railroads, Early Twentieth Century (*Map by Norman Pounds*)

The "triangle" from Winnipeg to Edmonton south to the United States border received the most thorough railroad development, grain and cattle enterprises, and migrants.

or were "passing through"—was outward, mostly to the United States. Canada slowly gained population in the late nineteenth century—a half-million per decade in the 1880s and 1890s—by retaining some of its natural increase, not from net immigration. By one estimate, two million persons born in Canada left for the United States between 1891 and 1931, but so did six million who had come to Canada from somewhere else.[3] While estimates vary on precise numbers coming and going, all agree that net migration was outward between 1861 and 1901, and inward from 1901 to 1931. The net outflow was greatest in the 1880s, when perhaps 900,000 arrived and 1.1 million departed. The net inflow was highest between 1901 and 1911, perhaps 715,000.[4] In that decade total population rose by 1.9 million, of which net immigration thus accounted for 40 percent.[5]

The reasons for the deficit of the 1880s and the surplus of 1901–1911 seem in both cases to lie in Canada's economic attractiveness compared with that of the United States. In the 1880s, the Canadian prairies were not yet reachable for settlement, while the American Great Plains were. In the 1900s, on the other hand, the Canadian West became the last prairie farm frontier, with new settlers being vigorously recruited by the Ottawa government as well as by the Canadian Pacific Railroad. Farm seekers from abroad looked to Montana's high Plains and other parts of the American Northwest, and even more to Canada's western prairie. But 1901–1910 was very unusual. Only in the 1911–1921 and 1921–1931 decades did Canada also enjoy net immigration, and the balances for those decades were much smaller than for 1901–1911. In fact only because of the inflow of 1901–1911 did Canada have a positive balance at all in the entire century from 1851 through 1950. In the other nine decades, Canada either lost population or (in the 1910s and 1920s) managed only small increases.[6] Canada was a country of immigration in the sense that it always had many foreign-born. But it was not a country of immigration in the sense of gaining greatly from it, as Argentina and the United States did.

Migration to Canada came almost exclusively from England-Wales, Scotland, and Ireland; North and East Europe; and, uniquely, the United States. The exact numbers contributed by each country can never be known, any more than can the gross and net totals given just above. The usual problems of record keeping (failure to record certain groups at certain times, changes in destinations, changes in legal definitions, and so on) were compounded in the Canadian case by the failure for long periods to record who crossed the American-Canadian land border in either direction and by the very sieve-like nature of Canadian migration, which make it impossible to say who was a "true" immigrant and who was a transient. According to the painstaking calculations of Duncan Mc-Dougall, the numbers and sources of immigration to Canada between 1871 and 1915 are as shown here in table 17.

The American contribution evidently remained remarkably stable at two of every seven, with British and Irish contributing four- to six-tenths, and other Europeans the rest. With migration figures of all kinds as uncertain and disputed

TABLE 17

Sources of Canadian Immigration, 1871–1915

Decade	British Isles		Europe		U.S.A.		Total	
1871–80	162	64.0%	20	7.9%	71	28.1%	253	100.0%
1881–90	255	56.9	62	13.8	131	29.2	448	99.9
1891–1900	100	40.0	79	31.6	70	28.0	250	99.6
1901–10	599	53.9	201	18.1	311	28.0	1112	100.0
1911–15	538	51.8	209	20.1	292	28.1	1039	100.0

Duncan M. McDougall, "Immigration into Canada, 1851–1920," *Canadian Journal of Economics and Political Science,* 27 (May 1961), 170. Percentages are my calculations. Americans were not counted in 1892–96. A "true" figure would be higher, but probably not much higher.

as they are, it is not possible to state retention rates. The changing ethnic makeup of the prairie provinces in particular suggest that Europeans and people of British origin who went there stayed there. Americans and that other sizable emigrant group—native-born Canadians—probably made up the bulk of those who left. This was certainly true of French Canadians, who went to the United States in large numbers and who were replaced only by natural increase, not by immigration from France. The Continental European contribution has to be measured from census data on birthplaces rather than from the problematic immigration figures. In 1871, only 292,000 (8.4 percent) of the 3.5 million population were neither British nor French in ethnic origin (counting Americans as British stock); 203,000 were German, 30,000 Dutch, and perhaps 5,000 were from elsewhere in Europe—the rest Indian, Inuit, and black. East and South Europeans began appearing in the 1901 census, and many more in 1911 after a decade when immigration was four or five times greater than in 1891–1901. For the period 1881–1911, residents who were neither British, Irish, nor French were reported in censuses as shown here in table 18.

In the census decade 1911–1921, the number of Germans declined to 295,000, but every other European group listed rose substantially. Spanish and Portuguese never appeared, just as Scandinavians or Ukrainians virtually never appeared in Argentina or Brazil. But Italians, peripatetic as ever, were clearly present, alone among Latin Europeans. Again, the French did not emigrate to French Canada (and never had in great numbers). Judging by the later ethnic makeup of Canada's provinces, prairie farmland attracted Germans, Ukrainians, Poles, Scandinavians, and other Europeans disproportionately (that is, not many stayed in Ontario, Quebec, or the Maritimes). Substantial Jewish communities sprang up in Montreal, Toronto, and Winnipeg.

For the American-born and Canadian-born, the border was hardly an inconvenience as they crossed it, sometimes several times, in search of economic improve-

TABLE 18

Nativity of Canadians, 1881–1911 (000 Omitted)

Group	1881	1901	1911	% Incr. 1901–11
Austrian	0	11	44	400.0
German	254	311	403	29.6
Italian	2	11	46	318.2
Jewish	1	16	76	375.0
Netherlands	30	34	56	64.7
Polish	0	6	34	466.7
Russian	1	20	44	120.0
Scandinavian	5	31	113	264.5
Ukrainian	0	6	75	1150.0

Warren E. Kalbach and Wayne W. McVey, *The Demographic Bases of Canadian Society,* 2d ed. (Toronto: McGraw-Hill Ryerson Ltd., 1971), 198–99, table 8:2. "Austrians" and "Russians" were sometimes Jewish, so the category "Jewish" is an undercount.

ment (or survival) in northeastern cities or on western farms.[7] In the language of economic historians, the usual migrant was a "maximizing individual . . . responsive to interstate income differentials and . . . demand for labor."[8] More concretely, the "international boundary meant as little to the American farmers from the Middle West [between 1902 and 1913] as two decades before it had meant to the Ontario citizens who had moved into the Mississippi Valley."[9] The border was even more permeable than were most European borders, and no Ellis Island (New York) or Ilha da Flores (Rio de Janeiro) stayed the crossings even momentarily. Except for a few years before 1914, the net gain was the United States'. Saying it again, migrants crossing the border between the United States and Canada were usually not counted, and if they had been, having to categorize them as either immigrants or transients would have confounded the records. Censuses on both sides, however, reveal how many persons born in Canada lived in the United States, and how many born in the United States lived in Canada, at the decennial censuses (see table 19).

The censuses also show that roughly 300,000 to 380,000 Canadians arrived in the United States in each decade from 1871 to 1901, while the flow of Americans to Canada was far smaller: 20,000 in the 1870s, 11,000 in the 1880s, 55,000 in the 1890s. In 1881, 16 percent of all living persons born in Canada lived in the United States, and the proportion rose to a peak in 1901 at 20 percent. After 1901, however, the proportion fell because of changing patterns of farm settlement in the American and Canadian Wests. For the whole 1901–1910 decade, the balance still favored the United States (189,000 Americans northbound, 214,000 Canadians southbound), but those figures hide the fact that the flow

Table 19

Canadian-Born in U.S., U.S.-Born in Canada, 1871–1901

(000 Omitted)	1871	1881	1891	1901
Canadian-born living in the U.S.	493	717	981	1,180
U.S.-born living in Canada	65	78	81	128
Net balance in favor of U.S.	428	639	900	1,052

R. M. Coats and M. C. Maclean, *The American-Born in Canada: A Statistical Interpretation* (Toronto: The Ryerson Press, 1943), 24; Leon E. Truesdell, *The Canadian-Born in the United States: An Analysis of the Canadian Element in the Population of the United States 1850 to 1930* (New Haven: Yale University Press, 1943), 9–16.

reversed to favor Canada late in the decade. From 1911 to 1920, the United States received only 13,000 new Canadians, while 101,000 American-born migrated to Canada.[10]

High natural increase together with shrinking amounts of affordable or arable land promoted emigration from Ontario and Quebec, just as they were doing from Italy and East Europe. Marital fertility in rural Anglophone Ontario declined between 1851, when it was still a frontier of settlement, and 1891. But it was still high enough to produce farm children for whom there would be no farms. In much of Quebec it was phenomenal, higher than anywhere in Europe at that time.[11] Young French-Canadians migrated individually or as families to nearby parts of the United States. In 1890, two-thirds of the 302,000 French-Canadians in the United States lived in New England, with another 15 percent in Michigan and about 12 percent in the northern border counties of New York State. All told, about 30 percent of all Canadian migrants to the United States in this period were French speakers.[12] Young French-Canadians traveled southward from Quebec and New Brunswick, first seasonally and later more permanently, to find jobs in brickyards, construction sites, and logging camps, or on railroads and canals. Prince Edward Island, New Brunswick, and Nova Scotia had already begun their chronic depression by 1871, and started contributing young French and English speakers to New England.[13] Ontario farm offspring migrated to nearby Michigan and in the 1880s to settlements along the Red River in Minnesota and Dakota Territory. A brief gold rush pulled fortune hunters from both countries to the Skagit River in Washington Territory and British Columbia.[14]

Canadian migration to the United States varied from the permanent to the temporary to the seasonal. United States consular officers reported that young Canadians were leaving parental farms for Kingston, Ontario, staying a few months, then crossing the St. Lawrence into northern New York. From Montreal, French families went to New York and New England mill towns, Scots to the American Northwest. From Chatham, Ontario, near Detroit, some Canadians left for American industrial towns, but those who could manage it took up farmland in Minnesota or the Dakotas, often encouraged by railroad recruiters.[15]

For farm youngsters in eastern Ontario, however, nonpartible inheritance forced many of them off the land their grandparents had pioneered in the 1830s and 1840s. They sought opportunities in New York State, but "almost 60 percent . . . located within a 40-mile radius of their place of birth"—that is, they did not go far over the border, and when they could, they often went back. The Ontario cities of Kingston and Brockville simply did not provide the entry-level jobs that the New York cities of Watertown, Syracuse, or Ogdensburg did. This migration was labor-seeking, not land-seeking; it included families as well as individuals; and it ranged from seasonal to permanent. In these respects the French and English Canadian migrations to the eastern United States were rather alike, a back-and-forth movement similar to much of the intra-European migration of that and other times. Anglo-Canadian migration to the Canadian prairies after 1900, however, was land-seeking, more familial, and more permanent (in intent as well as in fact). Other migrants to the prairies (Americans, British, and Continental Europeans) shared these characteristics.[16]

Reasons for the Canadian pattern of negative migration during the 1880s and quite positive balances after 1901 include public policy, resultant land availability together with affordable farm prices, and the lay of the Canadian land. Ontario ceased to be a frontier area of cheap, arable land after the 1860s.[17] The same interaction of high birth rates, crowding on ever-dearer land, and then westward migration of the young, which constituted the historic frontier-rural process in the United States, typified Ontario as well. But the westward path for young Ontarians was interdicted, as it was not for young Ohioans or Iowans, by topography: the Great Lakes, and to the east and north of them, the immense Canadian Shield that made farming impossible because of thin or nonexistent soil overlaying granite, or trackless forest often covering muskeg, not to mention an almost momentary growing season. The southern edge of this barrier stretches from near Kingston to lower Georgian Bay, and then northwestward across the northern shores of Lakes Huron and Superior, nearly to Winnipeg, where arable land begins again. In Canada the frontier line of settlement, which could not proceed across the Shield, had to go around it. Thus through the 1870s and much of the 1880s, young Canadians seeking farms went first to Michigan, found it settled, and went on to Kansas, Nebraska, and the Dakotas. When farm depression struck the American Great Plains after 1887, Canadians stopped moving there, and were forced to wait until the Canadian West became accessible. It became so after 1900.

Under the leadership of Prime Minister John A. Macdonald (1867–1873 and 1878–1891), the Canadian government developed the "National Policy" in the 1870s and 1880s with the West very much in mind. Above all, the government

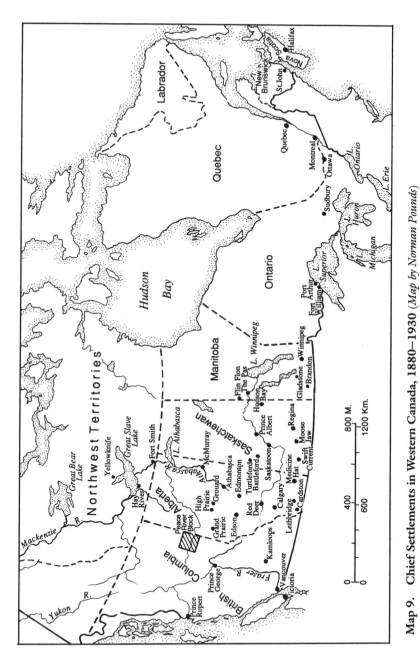

Map 9. Chief Settlements in Western Canada, 1880–1930 (*Map by Norman Pounds*)

Note the Peace River block in British Columbia, Grand Prairie and High Prairie in Alberta, and other settlements well north of Edmonton.

had to keep it Canadian. The object was to avoid "the fate of Oregon," that is, settlers from the United States overwhelming the population and pulling it into American control. The American purchase of Alaska in 1867 contributed to the threat perceived in Ottawa, and the frontier flood into Minnesota and the Dakotas through the 1870s and 1880s inflamed it. To prevent Canada from becoming no more than the region east of the Shield, Macdonald had to retain the prairies. Canada achieved this goal by copying the United States' device for cementing its own West to itself: build a transcontinental railroad.

By 1869, when the first American transcontinental began operating, many thinking Canadians believed that western Canada could never be settled, or even held, without one of their own. Ottawa, in a first step, took over the immense properties of the Hudson's Bay Company, which became the "Dominion Lands," and later the three prairie provinces and the Northwest Territories.[18] Distribution policies closely resembled the American ones.

The Dominion Lands Act of 1872 granted free homesteads of 160 acres to families who would live on and improve them for at least three years. The newly created Canadian Pacific Railway company received 25 million acres, interspersed with the homestead lands. Farm families could homestead 160 acres, preempt an adjoining 160 acres of Canadian Pacific land, and create a farm better suited in size to the semi-arid conditions that began around Brandon, not far west of Winnipeg.[19]

In his comparative history of Canada and Argentina, Carl E. Solberg concludes that while Argentina did not have a national policy of land distribution, Canada did. This basic difference underlay "many of the other contrasts."[20] The Dominion Lands policy together with railroad building not only kept Canada stretching, as its motto reads, *A mari usque ad mare*, but it also accounted for Canada's advance and Argentina's eventual stagnation; Canadian governmental activism and protectionism bore better results than Argentine laissez-faire.[21]

In 1870, Americans pushing northward down the Red River Valley threatened to overwhelm the *métis* settlements north of the border. Macdonald created the Province of Manitoba in order to keep the area Canadian. Settlers poured in, primarily from Ontario and Britain, and also in smaller numbers from Hungary, Iceland, Denmark, Sweden, Belgium, Germany, and even Quebec. But the dominant culture was "Protestant, conservative, and very British" before the 1900s.[22] As early as 1872, advertisements for western land were directed toward the "preferred countries" of Britain and Ireland. Through the 1880s the Dominion government, the railroads, and steamship companies continued to target British tenant farmers and, from the early 1880s, the Irish, who, for the most part, became wage workers on the Canadian Pacific and elsewhere rather than homesteaders.

Tariff, drought, and depression kept migration and settlement low during the 1880s and 1890s, but even then, over a dozen ethnic groups settled in Manitoba. Slovaks had begun to appear in Manitoba and around Lethbridge, Alberta, by 1885, many of them as workers on the Canadian Pacific. Others took coal-mining and steel-mill jobs in eastern Canada, giving the country a Slovak population of perhaps 5,000 in 1900, rising to 40,000 by 1931.[23] Jews appeared after the 1881 pogroms, the first ones coming to Winnipeg in May 1882. By 1900, 114,000 were living in Canada.[24] About 2,000 Icelanders established an enclave on Lake Winnipeg in 1875; Mennonites arrived in Manitoba in the mid-1870s, as they did farther south in Kansas, and established 100 small villages in Saskatchewan by 1900. Ruthenians, later called Ukrainians, appeared in 1894, followed by a group of about 4,000 in 1897, and took up homesteads in all three provinces before the end of settlement in 1930. Their experience in growing wheat on semi-arid steppe lands adapted them unusually well to the Canadian prairies. The Ukrainians remained probably the largest and most visible non-Anglo-Saxon group in the prairie west throughout the twentieth century.

A new advertising policy begun in 1892 reached out for Americans, especially former Canadians. After 1896, when the energetic Clifford Sifton became minister of the interior in the Liberal government of Wilfred Laurier (1896–1911), Canada recruited East Europeans as well. National-origin preference for Anglo-Saxons relaxed in order to bring in enough people to settle the western prairies.

The National Policy ran into severe problems during the 1880s. The Canadian Pacific Railway, a magnificent engineering achievement, was completed in November 1885 and opened the following spring. In the meantime, more than 70,000 settlers had homesteaded in Manitoba, mostly by the Red River route northward from the United States. Macdonald's National Policy had also put a high protective tariff into effect to please Ontario. The tariff on manufactured goods, together with the Canadian Pacific's transportation monopoly, severely hurt Manitoba and discouraged settlement. Canadians kept migrating to the United States, in "an intolerable drain," as one Canadian wrote. The drought and farm depression of 1887–1897 then arrived to stop frontier advances on either side of the border.[25]

After 1900 a much more favorable cycle of rainfall began, and it helped greatly to people the Prairie provinces. With government and the private sector promoting the prairie boom in tandem, settlement became spectacular from 1901 to 1913. The Canadian Pacific lured people to southern Saskatchewan and Alberta (from Moose Jaw to Calgary) after 1900; both areas became provinces in 1905; and Americans as well as British and Europeans poured in, attracted by 320-acre farms for $400, pieced together from government and railroad land. Homesteads and railroad land sales peaked in 1906 and again in 1910–1912, and continued for years afterward. Almost a million new settlers, a great many of them American farmers and farm hands, invaded Saskatchewan and Alberta during 1901–1911, and they never stopped coming until 1930.

The aggressive promotions of Sifton and the railroads, together with the same prosperous world wheat and livestock markets that fueled Argentine and American growth, and the same "excess" of land-hopeful young people in Ontario, the American Middle West, and across North and East Europe, gave Canada its positive migration balance after 1901. Ten thousand German-Russians settled

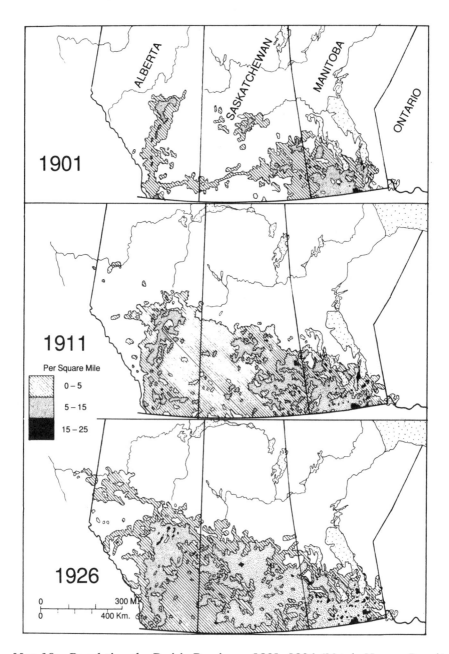

Map 10. Populating the Prairie Provinces, 1901–1926 (*Map by Norman Pounds*)

The working-out of the "Dominions Land policy" is illustrated here. Note in 1901 the thin line connecting Regina and eastern Saskatchewan with the Calgary-Edmonton salient. In 1926 the arid district earlier called "Palliser's Triangle" is represented by the 0–5 person per square mile area in southeastern Alberta and southwestern Saskatchewan.

near Saskatoon in 1903, and others elsewhere; most "Germans" in western Canada were from Russia or Austria-Hungary rather than from the Reich. The Doukhobors, a chiliastic communal sect, left the Russian Caucasus in the late 1890s. Sponsored by English Quakers, they traveled across Canada and formed three colonies in central Saskatchewan. By 1904, 8,000 to 8,500 Doukhobors were living in *Strassendorf*-type villages of about 40 families each, slowly conforming to the Canadian land system. Theirs and others' enclaves persisted in some cases beyond 1940 (almost as long as the German enclaves in southern Brazil), and they retained distinct ethnic identities later than that. Mormons from Utah, bringing their successful irrigation methods to arid southern Alberta, centered in Cardston; by 1905, 6,000 were living there, their numbers rising to upward of 20,000 by 1912, making Cardston part of the Mormon culture area.[26] In 1905–1907, about 200 black Americans from Oklahoma, fleeing new Jim Crow laws that disfranchised them, arrived west of Edmonton; 500 more followed in 1911, causing "some apprehension." Canada, however, proved not to be the "racial utopia the blacks were seeking," and Boards of Trade in the west prompted Ottawa to prevent or "dissuade" black immigration.[27]

Of the many migrants from the United States between 1901 and 1913, perhaps half had been born in Canada, or in the United States of Canadian parents. Between 1907 and 1915, Americans, many of them former Canadians or their children, patented 40 percent of all final homestead entries. Canada received even more British than American migrants after 1900—two and a half times as many in 1911–1913.[28] By 1940, only half of western Canadians were of British stock, the other half consisting of about 20 percent East Europeans, 20 percent West Europeans, and a miscellaneous 10 percent.[29]

The Canadian Pacific Railway, with millions of acres in Alberta, not only recruited homesteaders to the better-watered prairie portions but also surveyed three million acres of arid land in southern Alberta in 1903 and began marketing them two years later. It continued to do so until prosperity halted in 1913. The result was fairly solid settlement all along the Canadian–United States border east of the Rockies. North of it, the settled area of the Canadian West by 1906 resembled a gigantic "U" on the map: on the east, in central Saskatchewan, running from the border north about 300 miles to Prince Albert; in the south, a strip between the Canadian Pacific and the border, extending from Manitoba to the Rockies; and on the west, north along the lee of the Rockies to Edmonton. After 1907, when the Grand Trunk Pacific Railway opened a line from Saskatoon westward to Edmonton, another east-west block filled up—more with Europeans and eastern Canadians than with Americans because the area was more accessible by rail from the east than from the south. Finally the railroad, and settlers, came to the Peace River "agricultural empire" in 1912–1913. At that point, the sudden onset of agricultural recession put the quietus on further immigration and settlement in Canada and the United States.[30]

After World War I, politicians reasserted, briefly, the distinction between "preferred" and "other" immigrants, but Ukrainians and other non-Anglo-

Saxons continued to arrive for several more years.[31] All this while, immigrants were becoming Canadians. The Dominion Land Law required that individuals must be Canadian citizens to gain clear title to their homesteads. Consequently 47 percent of the Canadian foreign-born (55 percent in the prairie provinces) had become naturalized by 1911, a very different story from Argentina's.[32]

For about ten years after World War I, settlement by Ukrainians, Britons, and others resumed on the Canadian prairies. Canada imposed restrictive measures against East Europeans in 1919 and 1920. By 1925, however, pressure from the railroads and other business interests had brought a reversal, allowing the railroads to recruit almost anyone they thought could be "properly assimilated." The government in 1922 opened promotional offices in Paris, Warsaw, Danzig, Lvov, and Bucharest. In the years from 1925 through 1930, more than 730,000 additional immigrants came to Canada.[33]

When Ottawa closed out its Dominion Lands policy in 1930, only about 12 percent of the 1870 area remained undistributed. The National Policy had worked.[34] The settlement of the prairies of Canada was not "easily won or effectually consolidated"; and the free homesteads, only 59 percent of which were successfully patented, involved much "human wastage," indeed "a truly appalling number of casualties," in the judgment of land historian Chester Martin.[35] But that is another story, also with its counterpart in the American Great Plains. The onset of the Great Depression, and the turning over of the remaining Dominion Lands to the provinces, ended the Canadian settlement frontier in 1930. In the United States there was no such reprise. The frontier closed after 1920, and reverse migration depopulated large areas of the High Plains in the 1920s and 1930s. That too is another story.

The Canadian prairies also attracted migrants who were not colonists or farm seekers. The Canadian Pacific needed workers to build the track and then to maintain it, and in the 1880s Irish and Chinese filled the need as they had been doing in the United States since the 1860s. In the years 1908 to 1914, Italians and men from the Balkans arrived in Canada (including the west) in some numbers and, as in the United States, the proportion of unskilled workers from South Europe rose in Canada. Many were seasonal or short-term; "the phenomenon of the 'guest worker' was as well-known in western Canada in the early twentieth century as it is in western Europe today."[36] But their numbers and their impact were much smaller than in the United States in the same period. Western Canada, even eastern, was too remote for most labor seekers, who could much more easily satisfy their migratory urges in New York or Buenos Aires if not in Europe itself.

Canada's migration, into it and out of it, is distinctive most of all because of its sieve-like quality, the numbers who came but then left; because migration was tied to a nation-building policy that worked, at least compared with the Argentine and Brazilian experiences; because it donated so many of its own people, chiefly to the United States and chiefly before 1900, but to some extent afterward; and because it was the final frontier of European land-seeking migrants.

15

UNITED STATES OF AMERICA

The bibliography on migration from Europe to the United States is notoriously vast. Coming first from journalists, essayists, sociologists, and policy makers from the 1890s into the 1920s, who often were frightened by the exotic "new immigration" and wished to restrict it, the stream of writing was enriched by members of immigrant groups themselves, or by their progressive and liberal defenders, who emphasized the contributions the immigrants were making. By the 1930s and 1940s, historians such as Marcus Hansen (*The Atlantic Migration,* 1940) and Oscar Handlin (*Boston's Immigrants,* 1941) had begun to provide scholarly discussions of a high order. In 1951, Handlin's *The Uprooted,* which won the Pulitzer Prize in history, presented a paradigm that guided migration historians for the next generation. The transatlantic crossing, according to Handlin, meant a traumatic cutting-off from one's former culture and a sudden, jarring placement in a new and strange world.

All of that provoked Frank Thistlethwaite's complaint in 1960 that although "recent American scholarship has wonderfully enriched our knowledge of immigrant adjustment . . . there still appears to be a salt-water curtain inhibiting understanding of European origins."[1] Historians responded to this challenge only gradually. In the 1970s and 1980s, however, in a spate of books and essays often dealing with single ethnic groups or specific communities of them, yet occasionally comparative, historians increasingly wrote of European origins as well as of American destinations. A number of important monographs, of which Josef Barton's *Peasants and Strangers* is an early example, revised migration history in several ways: by discussing European origins; by using sources in the languages of the "new immigration," such as Polish, Slovak, Romanian, Yiddish, and Greek; and by questioning with growing explicitness the idea that the migrants were "uprooted."[2] John Bodnar (*The Transplanted: A History of Immi-*

grants in Urban America, 1985) presents a well-documented alternative paradigm, contending that migrants brought with them extensive cultural baggage,
transplanted it, and created new cultures that amalgamated features of their old
and new countries.[3] Although the salt-water curtain still remains to be fully rent
(and this book is intended to do so), the scholarship of the past two decades has
done much to answer Thistlethwaite's challenge.[4]

A full review of the recent scholarship, either as historiography or for its
historical content, would stretch on almost endlessly. For good recent syntheses
of the history of immigration from Europe to the United States, one may
consult Bodnar's *The Transplanted,* Thomas Archdeacon's *Becoming American,*
and Alan Kraut's *The Huddled Masses.*[5] An extremely useful reference work, with
essays on specific migrant groups, United States policy, assimilation, and related
topics, is *The Harvard Encyclopedia of American Ethnic Groups.*[6] Since many comparisons have been made already, only a few points need mentioning to situate
migration to the United States within the comparative context. These include
the size, shape, and timing of American migration; its sex and age structure and
some mention of women as migrants; repatriation and the nativist reaction to it;
and a few final comparisons with other countries.

The most immediately striking feature of the migration to the United States is
its great size, more than six times the number who went to the second-place
receiver, Argentina (see table 20). But the United States throughout the period
was much the largest receiving society to begin with, and the rate of migration
into it was lower than Argentina's, even in the peak decade (for rate, not numbers) of the 1880s and the near-peak decade of 1900–1910. As noted earlier, the
proportion of foreign-born in the Argentine population, at its height (1914),
was more than double the American proportion at its height (1910).[7]

Second, migration to the United States came from more places than did
migration to Argentina, Brazil, or Canada (see table 21). Except for the Spanish

TABLE 20

Net Migration to the United States, by Decade

Decade	*Number in Millions*
1871–1880	2.622
1881–1890	4.966
1891–1900	3.711
1901–1910	6.294
1911–1920	2.484

Richard A. Easterlin, "Immigration: Economic and Social Characteristics," in Stephan Thernstrom,
ed., *Harvard Encyclopedia of American Ethnic Groups* (Cambridge: Belknap Press of Harvard University Press, 1980), 476. Easterlin cites calculations by Conrad and Irene Taeuber (1958) by subtracting natural increase from total increase between censuses to yield net migration.

TABLE 21

Foreign-Born Population in U.S. by Country of Birth, 1870–1920
(000 Omitted)

	1870	1880	1890	1900	1910	1920
Germany	1,691	1,967	2,785	2,663	2,311	1,686
Ireland	1,856	1,855	1,872	1,615	1,352	1,037
Italy	17	44	183	484	1,343	1,610
Russia	5	36	183	424	1,184	1,400
Poland	14	49	147	383	938	1,140
England-Wales	630	747	1,009	934	960	881
Sweden	97	194	478	582	665	626
Austria	71	124	241	433	846	576
Hungary	4	12	62	146	496	397
Norway	114	182	323	336	404	364
Scotland	141	170	242	234	261	255
Denmk-Iceland	30	64	133	154	182	189
Greece	0.4	0.8	2	9	101	176
France	116	107	113	104	117	153
Switzerland	75	89	104	116	125	119
Portugal + Azores	9	16	22	38	77	104
Spain	4	5	6	7	22	50
Canada	493	717	981	1,180	1,205	1,125
Mexico	42	68	78	103	222	486

U.S. Bureau of the Census, *Historical Statistics of the United States, Colonial Times to 1970* (Washington: Government Printing Office, 1975), series C230-C264, I:117.

and Portuguese, very few of whom ventured north of the Caribbean, every group migrating from Europe arrived in some numbers in the United States. Before the creation of the railroad and steamship networks, migrants to the United States came chiefly from the British Isles, Germany, and Scandinavia. Russian-Germans, Czechs, Swiss, and a few other Central Europeans began arriving in the 1870s, most of them in that industrially depressed decade in search of western land. East Europeans, Italians, and various Balkan peoples enriched the mix in the 1880s and 1890s. While Argentina and Brazil took in Mediterraneans for the most part plus small contingents of Germans, Poles, and others, and while Canada (before 1900) took in British and Irish almost exclusively, the United States received everyone. Even Iberia was represented, though in nothing like the numbers farther south; Basques herded sheep in California, Idaho, and Nevada; Cubans of Spanish background, alongside Italians, rolled cigars in Tampa; Portuguese ran fishing boats out of southeastern New England.[8] Eighty-five to 95 percent of the migrant Irish, Germans, and Scandinavians; a smaller majority of Central and East Europeans; a majority of British before 1900 (but not after, when most went to Canada); roughly half the Italians; and a small number of Spanish and Portuguese, came to the United States.

Although land seekers outnumbered seekers of wage-earning jobs before 1880 and wage seekers predominated after 1900, the shift was by no means complete or even that dramatic. The United States received both types. By 1914, however, it had become the principal New World receiver of urban-industrial, labor-seeking migrants. Many of the Irish, German, and Scandinavian "older," pre-1890 immigrants came and stayed as non-farm workers, swelling the small and middle-sized cities as well as the metropolises. Germans were always prominent in such cities as Syracuse, Rochester, Cincinnati, and Chicago; Irish were visible and mobile not only in Boston and New York but also on Great Plains farms, mining towns such as Butte, and all over the West.

In 1900, 72 percent of German-stock employed males worked outside agriculture, as did about 84 percent of the Irish-stock. The Irish-Americans by then "had attained relative occupational parity with native white America,"[9] their upward mobility aided by the many post-Famine Irish women who were filling a range of white-collar jobs. Jews and Italians contributed to San Francisco's distinct flavor; Scandinavians did the same in Chicago, Minneapolis and St. Paul, Seattle, and Tacoma. The "new" immigrants arriving after 1900 located, it is true, in industrial-urban settings: Hungarians in South Bend, Croatians around the refineries of Whiting, Indiana, Poles in the climatically Polish-like belt from Buffalo to Milwaukee, Italians in distinctly un-Italian-like western Massachusetts and northern New York, and so on. These examples are almost stereotypes.

Yet it is less often realized that more homesteads began after 1900 than before. Hundreds of thousands of people poured into the western Great Plains, Washington State, and California, particularly from 1901 to 1913, and many were foreign-born. Montana, for example, rose from 143,000 in 1890 to 376,000 in 1910, mostly from immigration rather than from natural increase, and of those migrants about two-thirds were foreign-born.[10] The northern Great Plains of the United States did not absorb as many people from the Russian Empire as the Canadian prairies did, lacking the Canadians' aggressive recruiting efforts; nor did the migration last into the 1920s, as it did in Canada. The homesteading boom ended with World War I, and Montana actually lost about 2 percent of its population during the 1920s. Earlier, however, Norwegians and Russian-Germans poured into areas where land was available. They dominated North Dakota by 1910; 71 percent of the state's population in 1910 consisted of those two immigrant groups and their children.[11] North Dakota tripled in population between 1890 and 1910, an increase largely attributable to land-seeking immigrants.[12] The point is that, although land seekers outnumbered job seekers before the agricultural depression of 1887–1897 and the industrial depression of 1893–1897, both groups were always present. Moreover, the land seekers were by no means entirely permanent, nor were the job seekers entirely transient and likely to return to Europe. The stereotypes have some validity, but many exceptions existed.[13]

Other general points are well known or have been mentioned already in the context of European out-migration and need only a brief mention here. One is that serial and chain migration played a huge role in directing specific people to specific places. Although the reasons why the first from somewhere in Europe went to a specific place in the United States are usually obscure, once the migrants were located and employed, the flow of information soon after brought brothers, fiancees, and townsmen. Young men from East Europe arrived at Castle Garden or (after 1892) Ellis Island, followed directions inland, met their relatives or friends at boarding houses, were introduced to shop foremen or others in a position to hire, and went to work. Bodnar, writing of Steelton, just south of Harrisburg, Pennsylvania, observed that it gained "large numbers of Croats, Slovenes, Serbs and Bulgarians from specific regions but almost no Slovaks, Ukrainians, Rusins, or Poles."[14] Certain parishes in Pittsburgh, studied by June Alexander, received Slovaks from a band of neighboring villages; and "when firms desperately needed labor, foremen promised jobs to [Slovak] employees' friends or relatives if they would send for them."[15] When these Slovaks became foremen they hired other Slovaks whom they knew or were related to.

Relationships continued outside the workplace. Endogamous in the old country, Slovaks into the second generation in the United States very often married people from the same village or nearby.[16] Jews from Lithuania, the Russian Pale, or Polish Galicia created synagogues whose congregations came from the same areas and founded "a remarkable network of societies called *landsmanshaftn*," expressing "fierce affections for the little places they had lived in, the muddy streets, battered synagogues, remembered fields from which they had fled."[17] Italians were scarcely less renowned for their *campanilismo*, literally their loyalty to the area within the sound of their own church bells, rather than to the recently united abstraction called Italy.

Another point that needs no belaboring is that the economic attractions of the United States were real. Success eluded many, native as well as foreign, but an agricultural ladder did exist, at least in the Midwest and West through World War I. Railroads still had land to sell, and the government had homesteads to give. For the many who lacked the cash and credit to begin as owner-operators, the first rung of the ladder could be tenancy or wage-labor, with the reasonable expectation that, unlike in Europe, one could reach the top of the ladder eventually.

Wages in factories, on railroads, in construction, or in mines surpassed European levels while the cost of living was the same or lower. Wages in Chicago in skilled trades were two to four times higher than in European cities as of 1885; examples could be multiplied.[18] Italians built railroads and other public works all over the Northeast, Midwest, and West. Poles, Slovaks, and other Slavs populated steel mills and coal mines. Jews virtually created the mass-consumption garment industry. Irish men staffed police and fire departments and the post office while Irish women became domestics, then increasingly clerks, office workers, and school teachers. Many intended to accumulate some capital to send or take back to Europe; some of them did return, but for others "the ethnic neighborhood was the final destination . . . spiritually as well as physically."[19] Still others, however, came intending to stay, and did.

European migrants, and soon their offspring as well, appeared in every part of the United States where land or labor was available (see table 22). That meant everywhere except the South, although pockets of immigration existed there too. Within the South as defined by the census, the area stretching from Texas northeastward around the Gulf and Atlantic coasts to Maryland, small groups of Chinese lived in Georgia, Italians in Florida and Louisiana, Irish in New Orleans. In Texas, larger groups of Germans and Poles had been settling farmland

TABLE 22

Foreign-Born and Foreign-Stock in U.S., by Census Region (Numbers in Millions)

	1870 No.	Pct.	1890 No.	Pct.	1910 No.	Pct.
Northeast						
Foreign-born	2.5	20.5	3.9	22.3	6.6	25.7
Foreign-stock	N.A.		4.4	25.0	7.6	29.5
Both	N.A.		8.2	47.1	14.3	55.2
Midwest						
Foreign-born	2.3	18.0	4.1	18.1	4.7	15.7
Foreign-Stock	N.A.		5.6	25.0	8.3	27.8
Both	N.A.		9.7	43.1	13.0	43.5
West						
Foreign-born	0.25	25.2	0.7	21.5	1.3	18.3
Foreign-stock	N.A.		0.7	22.7	1.7	23.6
Both	N.A.		1.4	44.1	3.0	41.9
South						
Foreign-born	0.4	3.2	0.5	2.6	0.7	2.5
Foreign-stock	N.A.		0.8	4.1	1.3	4.3
Both	N.A.		1.4	6.7	2.0	6.8

Calculated from U.S. Bureau of the Census, *Historical Statistics of the United States, Colonial Times to 1970* (Washington: Government Printing Office, 1975), series A172, A190–A192, I:22–23. Foreign-born (immigrants) and foreign-stock (their children) in the West included Asians as well as Europeans, and few Asians lived outside the West in this period. Census figures give 63,701 Asians in 1870 (63,042 of them Chinese); 111,136 in 1890 (106,701 Chinese); 129,164 in 1910 (56,756 Chinese, 67,744 Japanese, 4,664 Indian); ibid., series C273–C275, I:117.

since the 1850s, but their migration had more in common with land seeking in the prairies and plains of the Midwest than with typically southern patterns.[20]

A number of southern states tried to attract foreign-born migrants but without much success. The obvious reason was the presence already of a labor force of several million black people who could fill, or were compelled to fill, such industrial and service jobs as there were, and who if on the land were usually relegated to sharecropping or tenancy. Slavery as it existed in Brazil and slavery in the South of the United States have been compared, but comparative histories of the former slaves and their descendants in the two countries *after* emancipation have yet to be done. Such studies might explain why Brazilian ex-slaves disappeared into cities or into the interior, whereas American ex-slaves usually remained on the land, though often not on the plantation where they had been enslaved; and why the Brazilian coffee planters successfully (at least between the late 1880s and 1902) recruited thousands of Italian families to work for them, whereas American cotton planters did not. The lives of black people in the American South in the era of increasingly tight Jim Crowism was most unenviable, but the lives of Brazilian ex-slaves, supplanted by Italian-born *colonos,* was probably worse.

In any event, Europeans kept to the North and the West. The also kept southern black people from migrating north. As Brinley Thomas has pointed out, blacks did not migrate from the rural South to the urban North and Midwest until European mass migration stopped because of World War I, and more definitively by the restriction laws of 1921 and 1924. Only then did the historic "great exodus" of blacks begin.[21] The Northeast, Midwest, and West, in the meantime, attracted European migrants, shutting out the South almost entirely.

Scholars are only beginning to study the history of women migrants. The assumptions have been that in the "older," presumably family-dominated migration before 1880, in which the sex ratio was nearly balanced, women were present as wives and mothers in nuclear families. In the "newer," reputedly individual wage-seeking migration, women were a smaller minority, as the male-skewed sex ratios indicate—and therefore were not studied.[22] But there were many women migrants. Hasia Diner's *Erin's Daughters in America* (1983) and Donna Gabaccia's "Female Migration and Immigrant Sex Ratios, 1820–1928" (1989) and "Women of the Mass Migrations: From Minority to Majority, 1820–1930" (1990) are welcome and pathbreaking contributions.[23] Diner has made her readers aware of the nearly even sex ratio of Irish emigrants and the fact that so many Irishwomen came to the United States in roles other than that of wife and mother. They were single and very often stayed that way, supporting themselves and sending much of their earnings back home. These points have been made earlier, in considering Irish emigration.

Gabaccia, who analyzes women migrants across the whole range of ethnic groups, has shown that sex ratios vary by group and over time. Of all migrants throughout the 1871–1914 period, the majority were male; after 1916 and to the present, the majority have been female. In the 1870s and in 1900 Irish women outnumbered men, and came close at other times. From that level the proportion of males among the migrants and among the foreign-born who persisted in the American population ranged upward to roughly the 55 to 60 percent level among East European Jews, Scandinavians, Germans, and British; to the 65 to 70 percent level among Poles, Magyars, Slovaks, Lithuanians, and other nationalities from the Russian and Austro-Hungarian empires; to above 70 percent among Italians; and finally to almost 90 percent among Greeks, Serbs, and certain other peoples from the Balkans.[24]

Many were indeed wives and mothers. Thousands of them, however, served also as family wage earners—as laundresses, part-time domestics, dressmakers, keepers of boarders or, more elaborately, operators of boarding houses. Outside the home, domestic service occupied migrant women more than any other kind of job throughout the period, as it did native-born women as well. The needle trades collectively employed the next largest group; clerical work, office jobs, retailing, and teaching provided increasing opportunities as those positions gradually expanded within the American occupational structure from the 1880s onward. As the female segment of the gainfully employed rose from 14.7 percent in 1870 to 21.2 percent in 1910,[25] immigrant women shared in and contributed to the rise. The distinction between in-home and wage-working employment was not always clear, since family and work often overlapped for both men and women.[26]

Women returned to Europe less frequently then men did, which (as noted earlier) allowed immigrant groups in the New World a much more closely balanced sex ratio, thus considerably more marital endogamy than the three-to-one male preponderance among Italian migrants, for example, would suggest. As one might expect, rates of return migration differed among national groups, with the lowest and highest rates for women appearing in the respective groups lowest and highest for men—Jews and Irish, for example, under 10 percent; Bulgarians and Romanians, Cubans and West Indians, over 50 percent for both sexes.[27]

Return and repeat migration deserves some attention, not only for its intrinsic aspects but also because of the hostile native American reaction to "birds of passage." Attempts to count return and repeat migrants confront a statistical morass even deeper then usual. One can safely say that a strong eastbound flow did take place, perhaps a third to half as large as the westbound flow. The rate varied over time and among national groups. As noted earlier, English, Italians, and several Slavic migrants went back frequently (and many made several visits). Returning and repeating were obviously more attractive after steamships replaced sailing vessels and as steamships became larger, faster, and safer. Also, as labor seekers gradually began outnumbering land seekers after 1880, the return and repeat flows increased.

That said, however, the subject becomes very imprecise. Repeaters never were counted as such, and American authorities did not begin to enumerate departing persons until 1908. From 1908 through 1914, according to the figures recorded then, 7,357,935 passengers who were not American citizens arrived, and 3,382,335 left—a net inflow of 3,975,600, or 54 percent of the gross. In those same years, 1,586,393 United States citizens arrived, and 1,735,347 left—a net outflow of 148,954.[28] Some of them were naturalized but foreign-born. The immigration officials did not attempt to differentiate between permanent and temporary migrants, and obviously could not, since the migrants themselves often did not know. These figures are also incomplete in that they include no movements to or from Mexico and Canada.

Steamship companies recorded passenger flows from 1871 through 1907. These records are of some help, although they too exclude Canadian and Mexican flows, do not distinguish temporary from "permanent" migrants, and inconsistently include or leave out cabin-class passengers. Several scholars have attempted to calculate net in-migration, beginning with Richmond Mayo-Smith in 1893 and continuing through Jeremiah Jenks and W. Jett Lauck (1911), Walter F. Willcox (1931, 1940), and, with greatest precision, Simon Kuznets and Ernest Rubin (1954).[29] A reasonable estimate put eastbound departures by sea at 10 percent of westbound arrivals before 1860, 25 percent in the 1870s, 17 percent in the more prosperous 1880s, 45 percent in the depression-ridden 1890s, and (from the official figures given above) 46 percent from 1908 to 1914.[30]

Impressionistic and anecdotal evidence abounds regarding return migration. French- and Anglo-Canadians, someone noted in the 1880s, " 'come in the spring, and just as soon as the woodcock takes his flight, they take theirs backward.' "[31] Umberto Coletti, executive secretary for the Society for Italian Immigrants in New York, dated heavy return migration from 1903. "The Italians started sailing back to their native land in surprising numbers, which increased until the climax of the re-patriation was reached in 1907." Coletti claimed that 38 percent of

the Italian laborers, after they have worked for awhile in this country, return to Italy, where, with their savings, averaging three to four hundred dollars per capita, they look forward to a comfortable future, trading and farming, keeping alive in their mountain villages of Abruzzi, Calabria and Sicily some of the American spirit they acquired in this country. Yet a large majority of the re-patriated sooner or later return to America.[32]

Coletti may have exaggerated, but the return and the repeat migration were common phenomena. Migrants' letters as well as modern scholarship almost universally attest to it.

The "bird of passage" was gravely unsettling to makers of opinion and policy in the United States. Wage-seeking migrant labor had a long history in Europe and, in truth, was hardly unknown in the United States. But the form that it began to take in the 1880s, and very visibly took after 1900—a Mediterranean or East European young man coming for a season, or for a couple of years, saving or sending money to a home he intended to maintain and improve (and very possibly to a family who needed it)—clashed with certain cherished American notions.

Racist ideas about Anglo-Saxon, Aryan, and Teutonic superiority over Slavic and Mediterranean peoples infected the thinking of many native white Americans, some of whom (business leaders and editorialists) feared that migrants would import anticapitalist ideas and conspiracies.[33] Many, though not all, labor leaders shared doubts about the ability of "new" immigrants to assimilate.[34] Richmond Mayo-Smith, a Columbia University professor who became a leading restrictionist, feared that Hungarians, Bohemians, and probably Italians were "of such a character as to endanger our civilization."[35] Francis Amasa Walker, pioneer statistician and director of the census, pleaded in 1896 for a restriction law, since 40 percent of migrants by then were arriving from East and South Europe. "They are beaten men from beaten races," wrote Walker. "They have none of the ideas and aptitudes which fit men to take up readily and easily the problem of self-care and self-government, such as belong to those who are descended from the tribes that met under the oak-trees of old Germany to make laws and choose chieftains."[36] One of the reasons Walker gave for his view was "the complete exhaustion of the free public lands of the United States"—which was an utter mistatement of fact, as were his germ-theory notions about the origin of democracy in German forests. Yet Mayo-Smith and Walker were highly respected authorities, writing in the most respectable of journals.[37]

Biological and cultural racism appear in the 1907 book of John R. Commons, the progressive labor historian and economist at the University of Wisconsin, who distinguished between the "old" and the "new" immigration in a long series of false dichotomies:

> A line drawn across the continent of Europe from northeast to southwest, separating the Scandinavian Peninsula, the British Isles, Germany, and France from Russia, Austria-Hungary, Italy, and Turkey, separates countries not only of distinct races but also of distinct civilizations. It separates Protestant Europe from Catholic Europe; it separates countries of representative institutions and popular government from absolute monarchies; it separates lands where education is universal from lands where illiteracy predominates; it separates manufacturing countries, progressive agriculture, and skilled labor from primitive hand industries, backward agriculture, and unskilled labor; it separates an educated, thrifty peasantry from a peasantry scarcely a single generation removed from serfdom; it separates Teutonic races from Latin, Slav, Semitic, and Mongolian races.[38]

Henry Pratt Fairchild, another "reformer," writing about twenty years later, complained that the new immigrants, with their Mediterranean and occasionally "Alpine germ plasm," diluted the Nordic character of the American population.[39] Examples of "respectable" racism could be multiplied indefinitely.

The birds of passage inflamed opinion in a special way. America was believed to be the haven for Europe's oppressed; immigrants were expected to stay once they arrived. To leave again implied that the migrant came only for money; was too crass to appreciate America as a noble experiment in democracy; and spurned American good will and helping hands. "After 1907," as one historian states, "there was tremendous hostility . . . toward temporary or return migrants. . . . The inference frequently drawn was that [they] considered the United States good enough to plunder but not to adopt. The result was a high degree of antipathy."[40] A speaker in the Quebec Assemblée Législative in 1883 quoted the following as an example of New England attitudes toward Québecois migrants:

> With a few exceptions, the French Canadians are the Chinese of the East. They have no consideration for our civil, political, or educational institutions. They do not come to establish themselves among us and become citizens; their aim is to return to their place of origin when they have made enough money here. They rarely become naturalized. They do not put their children in school if they can help it, but employ them in factories at the tenderest age. . . . The Canadians are a horde of industrial invaders, a sordid people of low level. . . .[41]

The official report of the United States Immigration Commission in 1911 (often called the Dillingham Report after Senator William P. Dillingham of Vermont, who chaired it) stressed that in "the matter of stability or permanence of residence in the United States there is a very wide difference between European immigrants of the old and new classes." The "new" immigrants were to be discouraged from coming, because of their transiency as well as because of their national origins. The commission's position was publicized further in the contemporaneous book by Jeremiah Jenks and Jett Lauck, of the commission's staff, in which transient migrant workers became the number-one target for restriction.[42] The Dillingham Report included a table giving numbers of immigrants admitted in 1907 and numbers who departed in 1908, by nationality, and with some exceptions the old-new distinction did appear (see table 23).

Among respected academic and social-science authorities on immigration, Peter Roberts was one of the few who argued that the "birds of passage" actually "have not left us poorer, but rather richer." He pointed out that the "Hudson Tunnel is an asset to New York City, [for example]; it is an invaluable agency in the production of wealth; and the Italians who dug it, if all of them had returned to Italy with their savings, would have enriched us by their toil."[43] An economic historian's recent assessment agrees for different reasons. With lowered immigration, the labor force would have been smaller and thus production slower; and land would not have been put to the plow as quickly. Finally, "with fewer savers, capital accumulation would have been less," and overall output would not have been as rapid.[44] Emily Balch was another exception. She pointed out that they formed

> an elastic labor supply on a large scale, and this is an inestimable advantage. The bird of passage has been so much, and often so stupidly, inveighed against that it is worth

TABLE 23

**Return Migrants of 1908 as Percentage of Incoming Migrants of 1907
(Larger Groups Only)**

South Italians	61.0
Croatians and Slovenians	59.8
Slovaks	56.1
Hungarians	48.7
North Italians	37.8
Poles	33.9
Finns	23.3
Serbs and Bulgarians	21.9
Germans	15.5
Scandinavians	10.9
English	10.4
Czechs	7.8
Irish	6.3
"Hebrews"	5.1

"Abstracts of Reports of the Immigration Commission," U.S. Senate Document 747, 61st Congress, 3d Session (Washington: Government Printing Office, 1911), I:180, table 14.

while to emphasize this point. While England appoints commissions on the unemployed, starts relief funds and subsidizes emigration of her own flesh and blood, our Slovaks or Sicilians return to their farms, when work is not to be had here, and employ themselves at home—vastly to their advantage and ours. Conversely when new works are to be opened up, there is a reservoir of indefinite capacity to draw from.[45]

More resonant, however, was the "scornful denunciation" of migrants for accumulating American money "for the subsequent consumption of 'porridge, bloaters, maccaroni [sic] and sauerkraut' on the other side of the Atlantic."[46] The newer immigrants, therefore, faced hostility on several counts: their habit of return migration, traditional across Europe but regarded as exotically subversive by American authoritative opinion; their search for wage work rather than farm land—indeed the fact that they kept coming despite what was (falsely) believed to be the exhaustion of free land after 1890; their presence as individual young men rather than as families; their suspected anarchism and socialism; and at root, their very nationality, called "race" or "germ plasm," which supposedly made them unassimilable. American opinion regarded the United States as the exception among nations, the antithesis of Europe, yet the worst of Europe seemed to be pouring through the gates. Another nativist bogey was "race suicide," the notion that the native stock would ultimately vanish because of the immigrant's higher fertility. In truth, "the fears of contemporary observers were misplaced," because the fertility of immigrants as well as their children was well below that of the native-born. But "race suicide" added to the nativist chorus.[47] After repeated efforts by restrictionists, a bill excluding migrants who failed a literacy test became law over President Woodrow Wilson's veto in 1917. Following World War I, Congress passed the Johnson Act of 1921 and the Johnson-Reid Act of 1924, which restricted immigration on the more candid and thorough ground of national-origins quotas.[48]

For Europeans, return and repeat migration was normal and traditional. For the increasingly nativist "thinking people" in the United States, fearfully watching their frontier close, it was an added burden, even insult, to the problematic arrival of millions of Europeans. Pre-1880s immigrants may not have been warmly welcomed, but they did stay. Irish fleeing the Famine did not go back, and Germans and Scandinavians who carved out new farms in the Midwest also remained. But many of the post-1880 migrants came and left. Because they made money in the United States and took (or sent) it home, they appeared guilty of exploiting their hosts. Never mind that Germany and Italy were undergoing much greater losses of human capital.

Americans offended by repatriation, however, should have looked to their own historic frontier and seen how transience had always been part of it. The Jeffersonian ideal of yeoman family farms, civilizing an ever greater area behind the westward-moving line of settlement, diverted their eyes from another frontier reality, that is, constant motion. Frederick Jackson Turner reinforced this perception in his persuasive essay of 1893, which argued that the family-farm frontier had been central to the formation of the national character. But there were other frontiers that Turner did not discuss and that were inherently frontiers of exploitation rather than of settlement—mining camps, cattle towns, forts, and others. Unfortunately, American nativist opinion did not see the transience of European migrants as being at all parallel to the transience of frontier Americans. In truth, however, the historical experience of the American frontier was not normal. In the longer European context, it was peculiar and aberrant, an immense but temporary resource to be exploited, even though it took Anglo-America about three hundred years to occupy and conquer that resource. The agrarian frontier was a historical peculiarity, but the American opponents of immigration saw it as normal. Hence they were unprepared to understand the labor-seeking migrants, many of them birds of passage, who arrived in huge numbers during the 1870–1914 period.

In 1914 the World War put a temporary stop to transatlantic migration, and although it resumed for a few years after the Armistice, the 1920s restriction laws and the 1930s Great Depression ended it permanently. In those circumstances, transient labor-seeking migration in and out of the United States—the transatlantic mass migration—did not continue after 1914. Those members of it who managed to stay in the United States did prove as assimilable as their predecessors of the older immigration, though it often took two generations in America—a quicker process, however, than in Brazil. All of these people—

Italians coming from Trieste and Naples, Irish and English from Liverpool, and the rest—sought improved life chances. They were assimilable because most of them sought revolutions neither at home nor in the new country, though they did seek to change their own lives. They were, as Alexis de Tocqueville described the people he saw in the Ohio Valley in 1831, a people of "scanty fortunes," loving change but hating revolution, trying to keep the little they had, and hoping to magnify it.[49] The European migrants were, in aspiration if not yet in fact, a lower middle class, whether white collar or blue collar. As such they fit into American society very well, since most of the native-born were similarly situated.

16

MODERNIZATION, TRANSITION, AND EXCEPTIONALISM

Another aspect of the changing demographic landscape that was disturbing informed American opinion by the 1880s was the accelerating presence of large cities. As the nesting places for tens of thousands of transient migrants, the cities were doubly objectionable. Although western settlement roared on faster than ever—the number of farms in the United States doubled between 1870 and 1900, adding over half a million in the 1880s alone, and rose steeply by another 1.7 million between 1900 and 1911—urbanization was the newer and more problematic development.[1] Usually, the larger the city, the larger the proportion (as well as numbers) of foreign-born migrants. New York, which did not include Brooklyn as yet, passed the million mark in 1880. Chicago and Philadelphia did so in 1890. Dozens of smaller cities topped 100,000 at each new census.

Again a comparative perspective would have revealed to the fearful that the United States was hardly unique. City engineers and public health experts could have told them that urbanization at unprecedented rates was a transatlantic phenomenon of the age. Chicago's doubling during the single decade of the 1880s, from 503,000 to 1.1 million in population, was unusual but not singular. Toronto, though smaller, grew at about that rate, while in the thirty years from 1870 to 1900, São Paulo and Lódz, each at 827 percent, far outran Chicago's growth rate. Berlin grew roughly as fast as New York (about 130 percent) between 1870 and 1900, while Hamburg and Rio de Janeiro at 195 percent surpassed most American cities.[2] Migration—internal, transnational, transatlantic—fed this remarkable city growth in Europe and both Americas. The United States' experience was not exceptional. By 1914, urban dwellers constituted 80 percent of the British population, 66 percent of the German, and about half of the French and American.[3]

The United States shared with the other three New World receiving countries the fact that migrants sought both land and wage-labor jobs, and that this was true at the early end of the period as well as after 1900. It is not true that land-seeking migration stopped by 1887 or that labor-seeking migration began only in the late 1890s. The shift was gradual and one of emphasis only. The United States did possess the capacity to absorb several times as many migrants as any other receiver possibly could. Despite nativist resistance, its space and immense natural resources ensured that it would. It could no doubt have absorbed more, as Argentina did in proportion to its size.

The United States also had the good fortune of having had a system of land laws, going back to 1785, that permitted smallholder ownership and security of title on a broad scale—a system copied by Canada but absent in Brazil and Argentina. High demand for labor was also normal in the United States. And it possessed high levels, for the time, of literacy; a developing infrastructure; fairly democratic naturalization laws; and widespread political participation, which Argentina woefully lacked. Finally, the United States had—although these institutions were not particularly friendly to workers in that period—an independent judiciary and the rule of law, whose operations though imperfect were improvements on those nearly everywhere else.

Our descriptive synthesis is now complete. The theory of demographic transition, in its commonly understood sequential form, was found wanting in an earlier section. Modernization as a general theory is too vague to be testable. Yet whenever it has been pinned down to a set of propositions, they include the idea that societies proceed from a traditional condition to a modern one, along with the idea that individual people shake off inert and unchanging traditional lifestyles and become self-efficaciously modern. The transatlantic migrants fit neither. "Traditional" societies (in the modernizationists' sense) scarcely existed in the countries of migration by the late nineteenth century, if they ever had; and the migrants themselves proved "efficacious" *ipso facto* by migrating. The migrants may not have been visionaries but they were hardly inert or without ideas for self-advancement.

As for exceptionalism, the United States differed from the other New World receivers, as well as from the European donors, in many small ways, as they all did from each other. In only two great ways, however, did the United States differ: its great size and, therefore, its absorptive capacity; and its possession throughout the period of a large area of cheap, accessible land governed by land laws that encouraged smallholding. Brazil had plenty of land but few ways, legally or logistically, for people to occupy it. The United States had no widespread equivalent of Argentine livestock barons or Paulista *fazendeiros,* who retained title to great acreages and forced small agrarians into various forms of tenancy, as in Argentina, or what amounted to wage labor, as in Brazil.[4]

By 1890, many smallholders in the United States were complaining bitterly about their mortgages, cash shortages, and freight charges. These, however, were problems not of a "traditional" peasantry but of a society with complex market relations. Fewer than half of the gainfully employed Americans were working on farms by 1890, and the economic and demographic future lay, for the most part, in cities and with labor seekers migrating to cities. In this respect the United States, although the largest receiver, did not differ much from the others; and indeed, if we leave aside the public domain, not much from the fastest-growing European society, Germany (which up to about 1887 also had a settlement frontier, but it was mostly inside the United States).

Earlier American history had been distinguished by frontier-rural development, which aside from Ontario's had been unique in the transatlantic region. When land was no longer available and the frontier-rural process ceased, so did the United States' chief claim to exceptionalism from a demographic standpoint. Even so, it was not unique. The Canadian West, after 1900 and until 1930, when the Dominion Lands Policy ended, proved to be a frontier of farm settlement much like the already closed American frontier, and for similar reasons: a consistent land survey and policy, railroads, and political order. Canada also attracted European settlers. Argentina had many fewer Turnerian qualities, and its migrants were shunted to Buenos Aires. Brazil had hardly any, and it enjoyed the least migration among the four receivers.

The United States appears different, but not unique or greatly exceptional, from the other receivers with regard to all three demographic determinants (fertility, mortality, and migration). In none of the three were its rates the highest or lowest. The United States' industrial and urban growth was very rapid, but so was Germany's and some other countries'. Blessed with a temperate climate and enormous resources, and the largest population in the New World, the United States ought to have developed rapidly. It had every advantage and reason to. After World War I, when very little arable public domain was still available, American development continued without systematic or exceptional variations from the other urbanized, industrialized nations in the transatlantic region. It had become, and it remains, one country among several in the very fortunate First World.

NOTES

Preface

1. New York: Harper & Row, 1972.
2. Walter Nugent, "Frontiers and Empires in the Late Nineteenth Century," *Western Historical Quarterly,* 20 (November, 1989), 393–408.

Part I: The Atlantic Region and Its Population

1. What This Book Is About

1. Frank Thistlethwaite, "Migration from Europe Overseas in the Nineteenth and Twentieth Centuries," in Comité International des Sciences Historiques, XIᵉ Congrès International des Sciences Historiques, Stockholm, 21–28 Août 1960, *Rapports: V: Histoire Contemporaine* (Göteborg-Stockholm-Uppsala: Almquist & Wiksell, 1960), 34, 37.
2. The problem has been identified and some phases of it have been discussed brilliantly. See Dirk Hoerder, "Migration and the Atlantic Economies: Regional European Origins and Worldwide Expansion," unpublished paper, Social Science History Association meeting, Chicago, November 1988; and Leslie Page Moch, "Europeans Leave Home: Internal, International, and Transatlantic Migrations in the Nineteenth and Early Twentieth Centuries," unpublished paper, Social Science History Association meeting, Washington, November 1989.
3. For a comparison of the generally permanent European settlements in New World frontier areas with the generally transient European colonies in Africa, Asia, and Oceania, see Nugent, "Frontiers and Empires." The basic point is that the European presence would not stick unless the demographic influx was massive compared with the indigenous population.
4. I hope any Latin American readers will forgive my use of "American" in this context to refer to residents of the United States of North America. Latin Americans have as much right to the term as *Norteamericanos* do. If there were an English equivalent of that word, or of the colloquial Italian *Statunitense,* I would use it here.
5. FitzGerald and Noble are quoted in William G. Robbins, "Western History: A Dialectic on the Modern Condition," *Western Historical Quarterly,* 20 (November 1989), 429–30.
6. Turner wrote: "The existence of an area of free land, its continuous recession, and the advance of American settlement westward, explain American development." In "The Significance of the Frontier in American History," in *Annual Report of the American Historical Association for the Year 1893* (Washington: Government Printing Office, 1894), 199. As I will try to demonstrate below, Turner's frontier idea was deficient as a universal explanation of American (or other nations') development, but still has usefulness as a contingent explanation for a large part of that development and to some extent others'. For a consideration of Turner's perplexity about American history after the frontier ended, see Walter Nugent, *Structures of American Social History* (Bloomington: Indiana University Press, 1981), 12–15, 113–14.
7. Dorothy Ross, "The National Ideology of American Exceptionalism," unpublished paper, Organization of American Historians meeting, St. Louis, April 1989, 2; Walter Nugent, "Tocqueville, Marx, and American Class Structure," *Social Science History,*

12 (Winter 1988), 327–47. Dorothy Ross's *The Origins of American Social Science* (Cambridge: Cambridge University Press, 1991), appeared too late for full use in this book. It is an extended and excellent discussion of exceptionalism in American social thought from the 1860s to about 1930. It is, she says, "a critique of the idea of American uniqueness, not an endorsement" (xviii).

8. Sean Wilentz, "Against Exceptionalism: Class Consciousness and the American Labor Movement," *International Labor and Working Class History*, no. 26 (Fall 1984), 2–3.

9. Ibid., 4; Eric Foner, quoted in Frank A. Warren, review of Jean Heffer and Jeanine Rovet, eds., *Why Is There No Socialism in the United States? Journal of American History*, 76 (June 1989), 231–32.

10. Aristide Zolberg, "Conclusion: How Many Exceptionalisms?" in Ira Katznelson and Aristide Zolberg, *Working-Class Formation* (Princeton: Princeton University Press, 1986), 397–455.

11. Personal communication, Hoerder to author, February 12, 1987.

12. Robert W. Johannsen, *The Frontier, the Union, and Stephen A. Douglas* (Urbana: University of Illinois Press, 1989), 77; see the entire essay (chapter 5), "Stephen A. Douglas and the American Mission," 77–102.

13. Martin Ridge, "Ray Allen Billington, Western History, and American Exceptionalism," *Pacific Historical Review*, 56 (November 1987), 509–10.

14. Stanley Meisler, "Home to a Smug, Scared America," (Paris) *International Herald Tribune*, June 6, 1989.

15. Donald W. White, "History and American Internationalism: The Formulation from the Past after World War II," *Pacific Historical Review*, 58 (May 1989), 160–61; Karen J. Winkler, "Historians Debate the Uniqueness of America," *Chronicle of Higher Education*, April 19, 1989.

16. Richard Maxwell Brown, "The New Regionalism in America, 1970–1981," in William G. Robbins et al., *Regionalism and the Pacific Northwest* (Corvallis: Oregon State University Press, 1983), 63.

17. For a more extended discussion, see Nugent, *Structures of American Social History*, 5–12. I believed then that modernization had "some suggestive or heuristic value for students of American social history" (12), but now even that seems excessive praise.

18. Alex Inkeles and David Smith, *Becoming Modern: Individual Change in Six Developing Countries* (Cambridge: Harvard University Press, 1974), 284–85.

19. The literature on modernization, both favorable and critical, is vast. Three of the best critiques, from which I have benefited greatly, are Dean C. Tipps, "Modernization Theory and the Study of National Societies: A Critical Perspective," *Comparative Studies in Society and History*, 15 (March 1973), 199–226; Raymond Grew, "Modernization and Its Discontents," *American Behavioral Scientist*, 21 (November–December 1977), 289–310; Richard A. Higgott, "From Modernization Theory to Public Policy: Continuity and Change in the Political Science of Political Development," *Studies in Comparative International Development*, 15 (Winter 1980), 26–58.

20. An elaboration of modernization for such purposes is Walt Whitman Rostow, *The Stages of Economic Growth: A Non-Communist Manifesto* (New York: Cambridge University Press, 1959), with its idea of a "take-off" into mature, self-sustaining capitalist growth. Other economists who reviewed the book were often skeptical.

21. A careful, persuasive use of modernization as a way of focusing great amounts of historical detail is Eugen Weber, *Peasants into Frenchmen: The Modernization of Rural France, 1870–1914* (Stanford: Stanford University Press, 1976). For the core-periphery idea, see, for example, Immanuel Wallerstein, *The Modern World-System*, 3 vols. (New York: Academic Press, 1974, 1980, 1989). A dynamic definition of the idea is that core and periphery are "historical categories with ever changing reference. Certain peripheral areas catch up, while certain parts of the core break off and lose their 'central' character.

We thus understand by 'periphery' an area dependent on the 'core'. . . . The relationship is fundamentally an unequal one and benefits the core. It is often destructive of the periphery; but it can also be an inducement to development, serving—under appropriate conditions—to lift the area from its peripheral position" (Ivan T. Berend and György Ranki, *The European Periphery and Industrialization, 1780–1914* [Cambridge: Cambridge University Press, 1982], 9).

22. "Demographic Transition and Fertility Decline: The European Case," in International Union for the Scientific Study of Population [IUSSP], *Contributed Papers: Sydney Conference Australia, 21 to 25 August 1967,* (n.d.), 47–55.

23. See, for example, Dirk J. van de Kaa, "Europe's Second Demographic Transition," *Population Bulletin* 42 (March 1987), 4–5.

24. Ansley J. Coale and Susan Cotts Watkins, eds., *The Decline of Fertility in Europe: The Revised Proceedings of a Conference on the Princeton European Fertility Project* (Princeton: Princeton University Press, 1986), 435–36.

2. The Atlantic Region in the Late Nineteenth Century

1. The period 1873–1896 was once called "The Great Depression," and in some sense it may have been for Britain. Even there, however, the term is misleading, and it quite misstates what was happening in Germany and the Americas. See S. B. Saul, *The Myth of the Great Depression, 1873–1896* (London: Macmillan and Co. Ltd., 1969); and Dan S. White, "Political Loyalties and Economic Depression in Britain, France and Germany, 1873–1896," unpublished paper, American Historical Association meeting, New York, December 1979.

2. A note on census data. Nearly all of these countries took censuses from time to time. They vary in reliability, in the kinds of information they tried to collect, and in frequency. Nevertheless they provide invaluable reference points and they do afford comparisons that are safely made, if one does not push them out to very many decimal places, and if one keeps in mind that numerical data are, like any other data, only as reliable as the methods of those who gathered them. For the record, the United States took a census every ten years in the years ending in zero; so did Germany and Austria-Hungary. Canada, Italy (except 1891), and the United Kingdom (including Ireland) took decennial censuses in the years ending in one. France took them every five years, in the years ending in one and six. Mitchell's sources for the numbers given in table 4 were the censuses or other official documents, except for the demographer Khromov's estimates for Russia.

3. J. D. Gould, "European Inter-Continental Emigration, 1815–1914: Patterns and Causes," *Journal of European Economic History,* 8 (Winter 1979), 606.

4. Brazilian growth lagged badly in the first half to two-thirds of the nineteenth century. In 1800 Brazil and the United States were quite close in population size, in the 4 to 5 million range according to the best estimates. Why Brazil reached only 10 million by about 1870, while the United States reached 40 million, is worth further examination.

3. Fertility and Mortality

1. Italian peasant women who migrated to the United States maintained high fertility rates for a time (John W. Briggs, "Fertility and Cultural Change among Families in Italy and America," *American Historical Review,* 91 [December 1986], 1129–45), but stopped bearing children earlier than in Italy, and their daughters "limited their childbearing on average to levels even below those of other native Americans living in larger urban areas. [They] unquestionably assimilated . . . within the space of one generation" (Ira Rosenwaike, "Two Generations of Italians in America: Their Fertility Experience," *International Migration Review,* 7 [Fall 1973], 280).

2. E. A. Wrigley and R. S. Schofield, *The Population History of England, 1541–1871* (Cambridge: Harvard University Press, 1981), 229.

3. B. R. Mitchell, *European Historical Statistics 1750–1970* (New York: Columbia University Press, 1976), series B6, 108–20; John E. Knodel, *The Decline of Fertility in Germany, 1871–1939* (Princeton: Princeton University Press, 1974), Appendix Table 2:1; Robert R. Kuczynski, *The Balance of Births and Deaths* (Washington: The Brookings Institution, 1931), II:41; W. R. Lee, ed., *European Demography and Economic Growth* (New York: St. Martin's Press, 1979), 35–77, on Austria-Hungary; United States Bureau of the Census, *Historical Statistics of the United States, Colonial Times to 1970* (Washington: Government Printing Office, 1975), series B5, I:49; Nathan Keyfitz, "The Growth of Canadian Population," *Population Studies*, 4 (June 1950), 55; Giorgio Mortara, "Pesquisas sobre Populações Americanas," *Estudos Brasileiros de Demografia, Monografia No. 3,* vol. 1 (Rio de Janeiro: Fundação Getulio Vargas, 1947), 86–90 (also 294, for comparative growth rates of American and European countries, and 337–41, for comparative age and sex structures of national populations); O. Andrew Collver, *Birth Rates in Latin America: New Estimates of Historical Trends and Fluctuations* (Berkeley: Institute of International Studies, University of California, 1965), 60, 67; Ansley J. Coale and Melvin Zelnik, *New Estimates of Fertility and Population in the United States* (Princeton: Princeton University Press, 1963), *passim.* A useful table of several long-term estimates of U.S. birth rates is in Morton Owen Schapiro, *Filling Up America: An Economic-Demographic Model of Population Growth and Distribution in the Nineteenth-Century United States* (Greenwich, CT: JAO Press Inc., 1986), 30.

4. From Population Reference Bureau, *1988 World Population Data Sheet* (Washington: Population Reference Bureau, 1988).

"Birth rate" as used here is what demographers refer to, more precisely, as the "crude birth rate," or CBR. It is "crude" because it takes no account of the age and sex structure of the population it refers to; it simply tabulates the number of births per random 1,000 people in a population each year. If a population contains an abnormally high or low proportion of women in their fertile years, the CBR will be skewed one way or another from a normal distribution. One of the reasons why German and Italian CBRs are much lower than Yemeni or Kenyan ones is that the average age is much higher in Germany and Italy, and hence there are many fewer women of potential childbearing age.

A more refined index is the "fertility rate," usually defined as the number of births per 1,000 women in the 15 to 44 age group, per year; this index corrects for abnormal age and sex distributions. The major problem with it in historical demography is that fertility rates were not kept, or have not been reconstructed, far enough back in time. They rarely exist for the 1870–1914 period or earlier. Thus one must use birth rates even though they are "crude." Similarly for death rates. If there are few older people in a population—as in Qatar—its crude death rate will be very low. Obviously many other factors such as culture and economics affect birth and death rates (more precisely, fertility and mortality), but age and sex distributions also make a difference. Conversely, changes in fertility and mortality—both of which took place in the 1870–1914 period—affect the age structure of a population. For example, people began living longer, which swelled the postfertile age groups, which in turn depressed the birth rate for the whole population.

"Replacement rate" also refers to births: reproducing women need to average 2.1 children if the population of their society is to remain level (2.1 rather than 2.0 to make up for celibates and children who die before reaching reproductive age). By 1989 only Ireland, with a replacement rate of 2.11, had reached that level among countries of the European community; Spain at 1.30 and Italy at 1.29 were lowest. This suggests that migration from southern to northern Europe must slow or cease, and migration from outside Europe to both southern and northern Europe must increase. See Alan Riding's story in the *New York Times*, July 22, 1990. A similar pattern began some years ago in the United States (also at or below replacement rate), where south-to-north migration (ca. 1915–1968) no longer occurs, but migration from Latin America continues strongly.

5. For a description of the frontier-rural mode, see Walter Nugent, *Structures of American Social History* (Bloomington: Indiana University Press, 1981), chapters 1–3.

6. In the summary volume of the Princeton European Fertility Project, Ansley J. Coale and Susan C. Watkins suggest that when a country experiences a permanent fertility drop of at least 10 percent, it has entered its modern phase of transition. They date that 10 percent drop in France at 1827, Germany at 1888, England and Wales at 1892, Austria at 1907, Italy at 1913, and European Russia at 1922 (Coale and Watkins, eds., *The Decline of Fertility in Europe*, 1986, 38). See also Thomas McKeown, R. G. Brown, and R. G. Record, "An Interpretation of the Modern Rise of Population in Europe," *Population Studies*, 26 (November 1972), 347. The birth rate of the white population of the United States started falling at least as early as 1800 and continued to do so fairly steadily until the 1940s; for various time series, see Schapiro, 30.

7. The data's softness contrasts with the firmness with which the sequential theory of demographic transition has often been asserted or taken for fact. Since the theory posits a sequence whereby death rates fall first, and birth rates later, it requires data on both. If only one set of data is firm, the result is like clapping with one hand. Even today, mortality data are too scattered to support the theory very securely, even if they were entirely consistent with it, which they are not.

8. Wrigley and Schofield, 236. They add: "Even in the period 1820–70 [life expectancy from birth] was only about two years higher than in the reigns of Elizabeth and James I."

9. Norman J. G. Pounds, *An Historical Geography of Europe, 1800–1914* (Cambridge: Cambridge University Press, 1985), 70 (emphasis added). Robert William Fogel observed a decline in life expectancy in the United States from 1800 to the 1860s, then a gradual rise ("Nutrition and the Decline in Mortality since 1700: Some Preliminary Findings," in Stanley L. Engerman and Robert E. Gallman, eds., *Long-Term Factors in American Economic Growth* [Chicago: University of Chicago Press, 1986], 532; see also the comment by Peter Lindert, 528–29).

10. Schapiro, 14.

11. Gretchen A. Condran, Henry Williams, and Rose A. Cheney, "The Decline in Mortality in Philadelphia from 1870 to 1930: The Role of Municipal Services," *Pennsylvania Magazine of History and Biography*, 108 (April 1984), 175–76. An earlier and more tentative, but more broadly based, study is Gretchen A. Condran and Eileen Crimmins-Gardner, "Public Health Measures and Mortality in U.S. Cities in the Late Nineteenth Century," *Human Ecology*, 6 (1978), 27–54; see esp. 35–41 on diarrheal diseases, infant cholera, and typhoid, 41–44 on tuberculosis and diphtheria, and 52–53 for the conclusion that "almost 80% of the total change in mortality in these [28] cities is accounted for by these . . . disease categories."

12. Berend and Ranki, *The European Periphery and Industrialization*, 53.

13. Metropolitan Life Insurance Company, "Typhoid fever in relation to filtration and chlorination of municipal water supplies in American cities, 1900 to 1924," *Statistical Bulletin*, 8 (March 1927), 5–12.

14. Phyllis Allen Reynolds, "American Attitudes toward the Germ Theory of Diseases (1860–1880)," *Journal of the History of Medicine*, 9 (1954), 428–54; Howard D. Kramer, "The Germ Theory and the Early Public Health Program in the United States," *Bulletin of the History of Medicine*, 22 (1948), 233–47.

15. May N. Stone, "The Plumbing Paradox: American Attitudes toward Late Nineteenth-Century Domestic Sanitary Arrangements," *Winterthur Portfolio*, 14 (Autumn

1979), 283–309, esp. 288–89. On the history of public health I have benefited greatly from conversations with Suellen Hoy, whose work on the history of cleanliness in American culture is in progress.

16. D. S. Smith, "Differential Mortality in the United States before 1900," *Journal of Interdisciplinary History*, 13 (Spring 1983), 759; Edward Meeker, "The Improving Health of the United States, 1850–1915," *Explorations in Economic History*, 9 (Summer 1972), 353–73; Robert W. Fogel, "Nutrition and the Decline in Mortality since 1700: Some Additional Preliminary Findings," Working Paper No. 1802 (Cambridge, MA: National Bureau of Economic Research, January 1986), 10 [my thanks to Professor Fogel for sending me this unpublished paper]. Also, Pounds, 68–71, for a succinct discussion of European fertility and mortality.

17. Wrigley and Schofield, 229, 236, 484n.

18. Knodel; Peter Marschalck, *Bevölkerungsgeschichte Deutschlands im 19. und 20. Jahrhundert* (Frankfurt: Suhrkamp, 1984), 41, 44; Alan Milward and S. B. Saul, *The Economic Development of Continental Europe* (London: George Allen & Unwin Ltd., 1973), 446–49.

19. Schapiro, 7. Schapiro also connects land availability with high fertility in nineteenth-century American very firmly: "It appears that a model based solely on the availability of land can be used to forecast the crude birth rate for the white population living in rural areas within a group of 23 northern states during the nineteenth century" (32).

20. Giorgio Mortara (introduction to "Sviluppo della Popolazione Italiana," 1965, 8), wrote that in Italy the mortality decline began later than in more developed parts of Europe, where sanitary organization came more quickly. But once sanitary reform took place, Italian mortality fell rapidly. Birth rates followed "somewhat slowly" but then accelerated. The average age rose, partly as a result of emigration, which further helped lower both birth and death rates. Mortara is aware, of course, that mortality decline and sanitation appeared earlier in northern Italy than in the *Mezzogiorno*. Differences among regions or provinces were evident also in the German and Austro-Hungarian empires.

21. Some evidence exists of a decline in mortality in Central and West Europe in an earlier period, namely, about 1795 to 1820. If so, a species of transition theory can survive, because nearly everywhere, even in France (though still not the United States), fertility started dropping later, in the posited "lagged response." This earlier mortality decline, however, precedes urbanization and industrialization, except in England-Wales, which weakens the causal explanation of transition theory. This version, however, may have some strengths; it needs to be explored further. I thank James C. Riley for making me aware of it (personal communication, January 10, 1990). Steve Hochstadt (review of Coale and Watkins's *The Decline of Fertility in Europe*, *American Historical Review*, 95 [February 1990], 152–53) wrote: "Perhaps the most significant finding is that the original theory of the demographic transition, a variant of post–World War II modernization theory, cannot explain differences either in the timing of the [fertility] decline or in levels of fertility"; regarding the relation "of declining fertility to declining mortality, one of the primary causal connections claimed by demographic transition theory [is] rejected in this volume."

22. The role of public health and better living conditions, rather than medical innovations, and certainly rather than some mysterious and unspecified "transition process," has been noted for certain countries. See W. R. Aykroyd and J. P. Kevany, "Mortality in Infancy and Early Childhood in Ireland, Scotland and England and Wales 1870 to 1970," *Ecology of Food and Nutrition*, 2 (1973), 16; W. R. Lee, ed., *European Demography and Economic Growth* (New York: St. Martin's Press, 1979), 34–38, 48–49; and Eduardo Arriaga, *New Life Tables for Latin American Populations in the Nineteenth and Twentieth Centuries* (Berkeley: Population Monograph Series No. 3, 1968), 24, 35.

23. In the United States, urban population was growing faster, but rural population nonetheless rose from 28.7 million in 1870 to 50.0 million in 1910 (U.S. *Hist. Stats.*, series A69, I:11).

4. Migration: General Patterns and Motives

1. At a session at the 1988 meeting of the Social Science History Association (Chicago), several historians suggested the need for a multiauthor work on the lines of the Cambridge histories, this one on world population history, emphasizing migration within and among countries and continents.

2. Thistlethwaite, "Migration from Europe Overseas," 35.

3. Pounds, *An Historical Geography of Europe, 1800–1914,* 71–80, is an excellent summary of intra-European migration before 1914.

4. David I. Kertzer and Dennis P. Hogan, "Household Organization and Migration in Nineteenth-Century Italy," *Social Science History,* 14 (Winter 1990), 484.

5. Ibid., 483, 491, 501.

6. Dirk Hoerder, ed., *"Struggle a Hard Battle": Essays on Working-Class Immigrants* (DeKalb: Northern Illinois University Press, 1986), 3–4.

7. Huw R. Jones, *A Population Geography* (New York: Harper & Row, 1981), 254.

8. Gould, "European Inter-Continental Emigration, 1815–1914," 1979, 615–16.

9. Berend and Ranki, *The European Periphery and Industrialization,* 43.

10. Pounds, 79.

11. Jones, 254.

12. Charles Tilly, "Migration in Modern European History," in William H. McNeill and Ruth S. Adams, eds., *Human Migration* (Bloomington: Indiana University Press, 1978), 58. The figure of 60 percent male is from United Nations, Department of Social Affairs, Population Division, *The Determinants and Consequences of Population Trends* (New York: United Nations, 1953), 102. For such numbers, all researchers into transatlantic migration bear a debt to Imre Ferenczi and Walter F. Willcox, who carried out a massive compilation of migration statistics in the late 1920s, sponsored by the International Labour Organization and published by the National Bureau of Economic Research (*International Migrations:* I, *Statistics,* 1929; II, *Interpretations,* 1931.) They arrived at two totals: "For the years 1820–1924 [immigration statistics of receiving countries are] about 55½ millions, while the total recorded emigration from Europe for 1846–1924 amounts to 50 millions. When one remembers that immigration as a rule is more completely recorded than emigration, these totals indicate that no important series of figures are missing" (I:82). True, but Ferenczi and Willcox themselves, and compilers for specific countries such as Friedrich Burgdörfer for Germany, were confronted by major annoyances such as the nearly universal inconsistencies between emigration and immigration figures. The best one can say is that the official figures (whether compiled by Ferenczi and Willcox, B. R. Mitchell, or others) are good enough to afford comparisons of migrant flows, but they are not absolutely precise. In some critical areas, such as rate of repatriation, figures are very spotty or lacking entirely. Net flows in such cases have to be deduced from censuses and other records. A succinct discussion is Max Lacroix, "Problems of Collection and Comparison of Migration Statistics," in Milbank Memorial Fund, *Problems in the Collection and Comparison of International Statistics* (New York: Milbank Memorial Fund, 1949), 71–105.

13. United Nations, 100.

14. Ibid., 101.

15. Gould, 1979, 606.

16. Ferenczi and Willcox, eds., I:86. A footnote states that at the port of New York, "the proportion of sailing vessels was 96.4 per cent in 1856 and 3.2 per cent in 1873."

17. Kerby A. Miller, *Emigrants and Exiles: Ireland and the Irish Exodus to North America* (New York: Oxford University Press, 1985), 256, 354.

18. Edwin C. Guillet, *The Great Migration: The Atlantic Crossing by Sailing-ship since 1770* (Toronto: Thomas Nelson and Sons, 1937), 17, 124.

19. Ibid., 236, 245.

20. Ships of the Navigazione Generale Italiana, sailing from Naples, Genoa, and Marseilles to New York, Argentina, and Brazil were slightly smaller, in the 2,000 to 3,000 ton range. N. R. P. Bonsor, *North Atlantic Seaway: An Illustrated History of the Passenger Services Linking the Old World with the New* (Prescot, Lancashire: T. Stephenson & Sons Ltd, 1955), 22, 111–13, 170–72, 268–69. Also, Freie und Hansestadt Hamburg, Auswandererbehörde, *Passagierlisten*, 1880–1900, in Hamburg State Archive; also available on microfilm from the Genealogical Society of Utah, Salt Lake City.

21. David Budlong Tyler, *Steam Conquers the Atlantic* (New York: D. Appleton-Century, 1939), 344–46, 359–60.

22. For these and many other details of the entire Hamburg passenger operation, see Birgit Ottmüller-Wetzel, *Auswanderung über Hamburg: Die H.A.P.A.G. und die Auswanderung nach Nordamerika, 1870–1914* (Ph.D. diss. Berlin/Hamburg: Freie Universität Berlin, 1986); information in this paragraph is from pp. 29–32, 54–61.

23. Bonsor, 116–21, 134, 173, 268–69, 374–81. For the Hamburg fleet specifically, see Walter Kresse, *Hamburger Seeschiffe 1889–1914: Seeschiffe-Verzeichnis der Hamburger Reedereien* (Hamburg: Museum für Hamburgische Geschichte, 1974).

24. The best description of the steerage crossing and the interior workings of the passenger ships is in Philip A. M. Taylor, *The Distant Magnet* (New York: Harper & Row, 1971), a work whose extensive written sources are fortified by the author's forty-plus steamship voyages. A description concerned specifically with East European Jews is Pamela S. Nadell, "The Journey to America by Steam: The Jews of Eastern Europe in Transition," *American Jewish History*, 71 (December 1981), 269–84.

25. For a succinct recent survey of port facilities, emigrant agents, and governmental regulation, see Günter Moltmann, "Steamship Transport of Emigrants from Europe to the United States, 1850–1914: Social, Commercial and Legislative Aspects", in Klaus Friedland, ed., *Maritime Aspects of Migration* (Cologne and Vienna: Bohlau Verlag, 1989), 309–20.

26. Richard J. Evans, *Death in Hamburg: Society and Politics in the Cholera Years, 1830–1910* (Oxford: Clarendon Press, 1987), vii, 279–92, 300–1.

27. A good summary of port traffic, covering much more than just Italy, is an Italian government document entitled *Dall'Emigrazione dall'Italia comparata con quella che avviene da altri stati d'Europa*, extract from *Bulletin de l'Institut Internationale de Statistique*, II, 1887 (Rome: Tipografia Eredi Botta, 1887), in *Etudes historiques à l'occasion du XIe Congrès International des Sciences Historiques* (Stockholm, 1960), 25–162.

28. Ferenczi and Willcox, eds., I:81–82.

29. Ibid., 81.

30. An excellent discussion of this is John S. Macdonald and Leatrice D. Macdonald, "Chain Migration, Ethnic Neighborhood Formation, and Social Networks," *Milbank Memorial Fund Quarterly*, 42 (January 1964), 82–97.

31. Pounds (83) says that "the Jewish migration differed from that of other European peoples in that there was no significant return flow. Furthermore, whole families migrated"; and they were usually craftsmen and traders, not peasants. For some exceptions, see Jonathan D. Sarna, "The Myth of No Return: Jewish Return Migration to Eastern Europe, 1881–1914," *American Jewish History*, 71 (December 1981), 256–68. Sarna calculates that perhaps 15 to 20 percent of Jewish emigrants returned at least for visits, and that not until the Kishinev pogrom of 1903 was opinion undivided that emigration was "the best solution for Jewish problems" (262).

32. E. G. Ravenstein, "The Laws of Migration," *Journal of the Royal Statistical Society,* 48 (1885), 167–227, and 52 (1889), 214–301; D. B. Grigg, "E. G. Ravenstein and the 'Laws of Migration,'" *Journal of Historical Geography,* 3 (1977), 41–54. Another affirmation is Caroline F. Ware, "Immigration," in E. R. A. Seligman, *Encyclopedia of the Social Sciences* (New York: Macmillan, 1931), VII:588: "The type of opportunity most generally sought is economic; the number of migrants actuated by other than economic motives is proportionably small."

33. Dirk Hoerder, "Comment and Debate: John Bodnar's *The Transplanted:* A Roundtable," *Social Science History,* 12 (Fall 1988), 256; Caroline Golab, *Immigrant Destinations* (Philadelphia: Temple University Press, 1978), 45–46.

34. Rita James Simon and Caroline B. Brettell, eds., *International Migration: The Female Experience* (Totowa, NJ: Rowman & Allenheld, 1986) is a very useful introduction although most of its essays deal with the very recent past; see especially Brettell and Simon, "Immigrant Women: An Introduction" (3–20) and Andrea Tyree and Katherine Donato, "A Demographic Overview of the International Migration of Women," (21–41). Very good work has already been done on the migration of women from Ireland, Scandinavia, Italy, and a few other places; Iberia, on the other hand, has yet to be explored by historians of women or, to a large extent, by social historians in general.

35. Gould, 1979, 606–11 (the quotation is on 609); U.S. *Hist. Stats.,* series C299, I:119.

36. J. Zubrzycki, "Emigration from Poland in the Nineteenth and Twentieth Centuries," *Population Studies,* 6–7 (March 1953), 252; Golab, 74: "It was rare to find a Polish immigrant who had not migrated to some other part of Europe or within his own country before coming to America."

37. Braudel, *The Mediterranean and the Mediterranean World in the Age of Philip II* (New York: Harper & Row, 1972), I:85–102 (section entitled "Transhumance and Nomadism").

38. See Dirk Hoerder, "Migration in the Atlantic Economies: Regional European Origins and Worldwide Expansion," unpublished paper, Social Science History Association meeting, Chicago, November 1988, part 1, "Rural and Protoindustrial Migrations in Europe."

39. James H. Jackson, Jr., and Leslie Page Moch, "Migration and the Social History of Modern Europe," *Historical Methods,* 22 (Winter 1989), 28.

40. Hamburg passenger lists, Hamburg State Archive; Bonsor, 127.

41. Golab, 1977, ix.

Part II: The European Donors

Introduction

1. The small size of the Dutch migration has one advantage for historians, however: it is manageable. Excellent and painstaking analysis of it has been done in several works by Robert P. Swierenga, among which are "Dutch Immigration in the Nineteenth Century, 1820–1877: A Quantitative Overview," *Indiana Social Studies Quarterly,* 28 (Autumn 1975), 7–34; "Dutch Immigrant Demography, 1820–1880," *Journal of Family History,* 5 (Winter 1980), 390–405; and "Dutch International Migration Statistics, 1820–1880: An Analysis of Linked Multinational Nominal Files," *International Migration Review,* 15 (Fall 1981), 445–68.

2. Friedrich Burgdörfer, "Die Wanderungen über die deutschen Reichsgrenzen im letzten Jahrhundert," *Allgemeinisches Statistisches Archiv* (Jena: Verlag von Gustav Fischer), 20 (1930), 161–96 (which duplicates Ferenczi and Willcox, eds., *International Migrations*), II:383–419, 537–51.

3. As did the Italian demographer Massimo Livi-Bacci in his *L'Immigrazione e L'Assimilazione degli Italiani negli Stati Uniti, secondo le statistiche demografiche Americane* (Milan: Dott. L. Giuffre Editori, 1961).

4. J. D. Gould, "Emigration: The Road Home: Return Migration from the U.S.A.," *Journal of European Economic History*, 9 (Spring 1980), 98.

5. Britain (England-Wales and Scotland)

1. Ferenczi and Willcox, eds., *International Migrations*, I:636, table viii.

2. W. A. Carrothers, *Emigration from the British Isles: With Special Reference to the Development of the Overseas Dominions* (London: Frank Cass & Co. Ltd., 1965 [1929]), 218.

3. For the American figures, see also U.S., *Hist. Stats.*, series C91, C92, I:105–106.

4. Dudley Baines, *Migration in a Mature Economy: Emigration and Internal Migration in England and Wales, 1861–1900* (Cambridge: Cambridge University Press, 1985), 279.

5. Ibid., 59.

6. Ibid., 80.

7. Carrothers, 228–36.

8. Charlotte J. Erickson, "Who Were the English and Scots Immigrants to the United States in the Late Nineteenth Century?" in D. V. Glass and Roger Revelle, eds., *Population and Social Change* (London: Edward Arnold, 1972), 359.

9. N. H. Carrier and J. R. Jeffery, *External Migration: A Study of the Available Statistics, 1815–1950* (London: Her Majesty's Stationary Office, 1953), 359–60.

10. Ibid., 368.

11. Baines, 150–59, 279.

12. Colin Holmes, *John Bull's Island: Immigration and British Society, 1871–1971* (Basingstoke: Macmillan Education Ltd, 1988), 20–26, 36–39, 60–65, 308.

13. Ibid., 60–62.

14. Michael Flinn et al., *Scottish Population History from the 17th Century to the 1930s* (Cambridge: Cambridge University Press, 1977), 449–50, 452–53.

15. Baines, 162–63.

16. Carrothers, 242–44.

17. Holmes, 19, 276.

18. Baines, 282.

19. Charlotte J. Erickson, "Emigration from the British Isles to the U.S.A. in 1841: Part I. Emigration from the British Isles," *Population Studies*, 43 (November 1989), 350.

20. Ibid., 367.

21. Oliver MacDonagh, *Emigration in the Victorian Age: Debates on the Issue from Nineteenth Century Critical Journals* (Westmead, Hants: Gregg International Publishers Ltd, 1973), ii.

22. Baines, 85.

23. Erickson, 1972, 371–73; Baines, 85–88, 128, 282.

24. Baines, 130. He prefaces these figures by saying that "the data do not exist to enable us to calculate the true rate of return migration." No doubt. But there can also be no doubt that it was substantial and belies the notion that Scottish and English migrants were chiefly homesteaders or artisan families.

6. Ireland

1. The conflict between "exile," "escape," and other meanings of emigration for the Irish is one of the main themes of Kerby A. Miller's authoritative *Emigrants and Exiles: Ireland and the Irish Exodus to North America* (New York: Oxford University Press, 1985). For the safety valve idea, see Oliver MacDonagh, *Emigration in the Victorian Age*, ii–iii.

2. (Galway City) *Connacht Tribune,* June 16, 1989, 1, 10.

3. Cormac O'Gráda, "Demographic Adjustment and Seasonal Migration in Nineteenth-Century Ireland," in Louis M. Cullen and François Furet, eds., *Irlande et France XVIIe–XXe Siècles: Pour une Histoire Rurale Comparée. Actes du Premier Colloque Franco-Irlandais d'Histoire Économique et Social—Dublin* (Paris: Éditions de l'École des Hautes Études en Sciences Sociales, 1980), 188.

4. Terry Coleman, *Going to America* (New York: Pantheon Books, 1972), 135–37, 151.

5. Oliver MacDonagh, "Irish Emigration to the United States of America and the British Colonies during the Famine," in R. Dudley Edwards and T. Desmond Williams, eds., *The Great Famine: Studies in Irish History 1845–52* (New York: Russell & Russell, 1976 [1957]), 319, 323–24, 328, 329, 362, 363, 369.

6. Cormac O'Gráda, "A Note on Nineteenth-Century Irish Emigration Statistics," *Population Studies,* 29 (March 1975), 144. O'Gráda examined three sets of statistics on nineteenth-century Irish emigration and decided that even the most inclusive was "a considerable underestimate" (145).

7. S. H. Cousens, "Population Trends in Ireland at the Beginning of the Twentieth Century," *Irish Geography,* 5 (1968), 387, 389, 396; in 1901 only 62.3 percent of the 35–44 age group were married, an "all-time low" (399). David Fitzpatrick, "The Modernisation of the Irish Female," in Patrick O'Flanagan, Paul Ferguson, and Kevin Whelan, eds., *Rural Ireland, 1600–1900: Modernisation and Change* (Cork: Cork University Press, 1987), 171–73.

8. Arnold Schrier, *Ireland and the American Emigration, 1850–1900* (Minneapolis: University of Minnesota Press, 1958), 3–6, 22. The Irish counties were Cork, Galway, Kerry, Limerick, Mayo, and Tipperary. The seven states were Massachusetts, Connecticut, New York, New Jersey, Pennsylvania, Ohio, and Illinois.

9. G. R. C. Keep, "Irish Migration to North America in the Second Half of the Nineteenth Century" (Ph.D. diss., University of Dublin, 1951), 393.

10. Miller, 346–53.

11. Carrier and Jeffery, text, 32; Miller, 355.

12. Schrier, 151. Also, Miller, 353, 356.

13. Robert E. Kennedy, Jr., *The Irish: Emigration, Marriage, and Fertility* (Berkeley: University of California Press, 1971), 78, table 23.

14. Miller, 406.

15. Fitzpatrick, 169, 166, 175–76 (quotes).

16. Joseph Wade (of Crookewood, Mullingar, County Westmeath), interview in Arnold Schrier, "Survey of Returned Migrants," vol. 1408 (1955), 120–21, Archives of Irish Folklore, University College Dublin.

17. Kennedy, 84.

18. For other discussions of Irish female migrants (none of which I disagree with), see Miller, 405–8; Kennedy, 82–85; and Hasia R. Diner, *Erin's Daughters in America: Irish Immigrant Women in the Nineteenth Century* (Baltimore: Johns Hopkins University Press, 1983), especially chapters 1 and 2.

19. Miller, 408.

20. Schrier, 103, 108, 112–20.

21. United States Consular Reports, *Labor in Europe.* House Executive Document 54, Part 1. 48th Congress, 2d Session. (Washington: Government Printing Office, 1885), 105.

22. Cormac O'Gráda, "Some Aspects of Nineteenth-Century Irish Emigration," in L. M. Cullen and T. C. Smout, eds., *Comparative Aspects of Scottish and Irish Economic and Social History, 1600–1900* (Edinburgh: John Donald Publishers Ltd., [1977]), 67–68; Schrier, 15–16; Miller, 403.

23. Miller, 362.
24. Schrier, 130.
25. Ibid., 152.
26. Keep, 399–400.
27. Kerby Miller, with Bruce Boling and David N. Doyle, "Emigrants and Exiles: Irish Cultures and Irish Emigration to North America 1790–1922," *Irish Historical Studies,* 22 (September 1980), 100–1.

7. Scandinavia

1. Kristian Hvidt, *Flight to America: The Social Background of 300,000 Danish Emigrants* (New York: Academic Press, 1975), 109.

2. Jon Gjerde, *From Peasants to Farmers: The Migration from Balestrand, Norway, to the Upper Middle West* (New York: Cambridge University Press, 1985), 8, 55.

3. Robert C. Ostergren, *A Community Transplanted: The Trans-Atlantic Experience of a Swedish Immigrant Settlement in the Upper Middle West, 1835–1915* (Madison: University of Wisconsin Press, 1988), 36, 103.

4. Robert C. Ostergren, "Swedish Migration to North America in Transatlantic Perspective," in Ira Glazier and Luigi De Rosa, eds., *Migration across Time and Nations: Population Mobility in Historical Contexts* (New York: Holmes & Meier, 1986), 129–30.

5. Hvidt, 147, and chapter 12 *passim.*

6. Harald Runblom and Hans Norman, eds., *From Sweden to America: A History of the Migration* (Minneapolis: University of Minnesota Press, and Uppsala: Acta Universitatis Upsaliensis, 1976), 121–25, 129. Ostergren, *Community Transplanted,* 111–15.

7. Hans Norman and Harald Runblom, *Transatlantic Connections: Nordic Migration to the New World after 1800* (Oslo: Norwegian University Press (Universitetsforlaget AS), [1988]), 52, 60, 64–68. These authors also discuss emigration from Iceland, which was high in proportion to population. Except for 1887 and 1888, when 1,978 and 1,089 left, and two other years, it numbered only in the hundreds while the four mainland countries were each sending thousands. The Icelandic migration is unique, however, in that nearly all of it went to Canada rather than to the United States (ibid., 59, 289–90).

8. Runblom and Norman, eds., 133–35.

9. Gjerde, 22.

10. Hvidt, 40–45.

11. Gjerde, 4–5. He notes that in 1910, half of the Norwegians in the United States lived in Minnesota, Wisconsin, and North Dakota.

12. Hvidt, 167. Hvidt points out that in the 1910 Census, Iowa, the state with the most Danes, held only 10.4 percent of them, while 19.6 percent of Swedes and 28.6 percent of Norwegians lived in Minnesota. Danish dispersal and Norwegian concentration existed elsewhere as well.

13. Runblom and Norman, eds., 302, 308–9.

14. Norman and Runblom, 72–73.

15. Runblom and Norman, eds., 132.

16. Norman and Runblom, 134: "In traditional agrarian society people had been very mobile, although most moved short distances. . . . Seasonal labor migrations constituted a special form of population movement with old traditions in the Nordic countries."

17. Hvidt, 192. Berit Brattne, writing on the role of transportation, believes that prepaid tickets were "a substantial pull factor" but not as great as the percentage of users suggests; nevertheless she does not deny their importance (Runblom and Norman, eds., 186).

18. Ingrid Semmingsen, *Norway to America: A History of the Migration* (Minneapolis: University of Minnesota Press, 1978), 119.

19. Gjerde, 135. Hvidt (chapter 15) also stresses the importance of emigrant letters.

20. Brattne, in Runblom and Norman, eds., 177–78, 199; Norman and Runblom, 119–21.

21. Runblom and Norman, eds., 180–81; Norman and Runblom, 116.

22. Hvidt, 73–80.

23. Ibid., 83–87, 154; Norman and Runblom, 88–89.

24. Semmingsen, 113.

25. Runblom and Norman, eds., 131.

26. Ostergren, *Community Transplanted,* 3–8, 118–20, 312–13.

27. Norman and Runblom, 85–86; Hvidt, 93–98.

28. Hvidt, 91–92.

29. Gjerde, 37.

30. See the juxtaposed photographs of women working on an unmechanized Swedish beet farm and an American reaper-binder pulled by a thirty-horse team, in Runblom and Norman, eds., following 176.

31. Ibid., 141–47; Gjerde, 65–67, 80–82.

32. Hvidt, 60, 62.

33. Ibid., 45.

34. Norman and Runblom, 78–79.

35. Hvidt, chapter 10, esp. 116–22.

36. Norman, in Runblom and Norman, eds., 158–64.

37. Ibid., 154; for Baines and Erickson, see above, the section on England-Wales.

38. Runblom and Norman, eds., 209.

39. Semmingsen found 50,000 returned Norwegians between 1880 and 1920, giving an average of 25 percent, but since 30,000 returned between 1911 and 1920, the rate of return for earlier decades must have been miniscule. Semmingsen, 120.

40. Hvidt, 181.

41. Norman and Runblom, 111.

42. Ostergren, in Glazier and De Rosa, eds., 131–32.

8. The German Empire

1. See data on German annual increase in Marschalck, *Bevölkerungsgeschichte Deutschlands im 19. und 20. Jahrhundert,* 146. United States annual estimates appear in U.S., *Hist. Stats.,* series A6.

2. See tables 1, 5, and 9, above.

3. René Gonnard, *L'Émigration Européenne au XIXᵉ Siècle* (Paris: Librairie Armand Colin, 1906), 112. Friedrich Burgdörfer estimated that 86,417 Germans left from French ports between 1871 and 1900 ("Die Wanderungen über die deutschen Reichsgrenzen im letzten Jahrhundert," 1930, in Wolfgang Köllmann and Peter Marschalck, eds., *Bevölkerungsgeschichte* [Cologne: Kiepenheuer & Witsch, 1972]), 310.

4. The first Germans arrived in the future United States in 1683, creating Germantown outside Philadelphia, and thousands more, the so-called Pennsylvania "Dutch," settled in the early eighteenth century. This migration, however, was pre-industrial; it consisted largely of more or less radical Protestant sectarians, and it was not continuous with the economically or politically motivated migration of the nineteenth century.

5. U.S. Bureau of the Census, *Historical Statistics of the United States,* series C95, I:106. The per capita loss in 1852–1855 was 4.38 per thousand, and in 1880–1885, 4.26 per thousand (Burgdörfer, in Ferenczi and Willcox, eds., (q.v.), II:318).

6. Burgdörfer, in Köllmann and Marschalck, eds., 308–10; Burgdörfer, 1930, in Ferenczi and Willcox, eds., II:355–56.

7. Burgdörfer, in Ferenczi and Willcox, eds., II:327–37; David V. Glass, introduction to Glass and Revelle, eds., *Population and Social Change,* 7.

8. J. D. Gould, "European Inter-Continental Emigration: The Road Home: Return Migration from the U.S.A.," 1980, 87–98.

9. Burgdörfer, in Ferenczi and Willcox, eds., II:337.

10. Burgdörfer, in Köllmann and Marschalck, eds., 296.

11. See the annual *Jahrbücher* of the Hamburg Emigration Authority (*Auswandererbehörde*) and the publications of the Reichs Statistiches Hauptamt, esp. *Annalen des deutschen Reiches.*

12. Walter D. Kamphoefner, "Transplanted Westfalians" (Ph.D. diss., University of Missouri, 1978), 50–51; a revised version has appeared as *The Westfalians: From Germany to Missouri* (Princeton: Princeton University Press, 1987).

13. Wilhelm Mönckmeier, *Die deutsche überseeauswanderung* (Jena: Verlag von Gustav Fischer, 1912), 92–112. Despite its age and its lack of statistical sophistication compared with the works of Burgdörfer and later writers on German migration, this book remains in many ways the most thorough treatment.

14. Ibid., 120–24.

15. Ibid., 112–16.

16. Ibid., 124–26.

17. Gerhard A. Ritter and Jurgen Kocka, eds., *Deutsche Sozialgeschichte: Dokumente und Skizzen*, 2, 1870–1914 (Munich: Verlag C. H. Beck, 1974), 46–48.

18. Burgdörfer, in Ferenczi and Willcox, eds., II:352; Dieter Langewiesche, "Wanderungsbewegungen in der Hochindustrialisierungsperiode: Regionale, interstädtische und innerstädtische Mobilität in Deutschland 1880–1914," *Vierteljahrschrift für Sozial- und Wirtschaftsgeschichte*, 64 (1977), 18, 23.

19. Klaus J. Bade, "Labour, Migration, and the State," in Bade, ed., *Population, Labour and Migration in 19th- and 20th-Century Germany* (Leamington Spa, Hamburg, and New York: Berg Publishers, 1987), 63. Some out-migration continued after the 1890s, for example, to farmland in Canada; the "alleged closure of the frontier" in America did not cause the fall-off of German out-migration (Bade, "German Emigration to the United States and Continental Immigration to Germany in the Late Nineteenth and Early Twentieth Centuries," in Dirk Hoerder, ed., *Labor Migration in the Atlantic Economies: The European and North American Working Classes during the Period of Industrialization* [Westport, CT: Greenwood Press, 1985], 130).

20. Alan S. Milward and S. B. Saul, *The Development of the Economies of Continental Europe, 1850–1914* (Cambridge: Harvard University Press, 1977), 22–23.

21. Ibid., 24, 25, 35, 43–44, 53–54.

22. Mönckmeier, 167.

23. Franz Rehbein, *Das Leben eines Landarbeiters* (Jena, 1911), in Ritter and Kocka, eds., 205–09.

24. Otto von Leixner, *Soziale Briefe aus Berlin* (Berlin, 1891), in Ritter and Kocka, eds., 277.

25. Günter Moltmann, "The Pattern of German Emigration to the United States in the Nineteenth Century," in Frank Trommler and Joseph McVeigh, eds., *America and the Germans: An Assessment of a Three-Hundred-Year History* (Philadelphia: University of Pennsylvania Press, 1983), 15, 19.

26. U.S. Consular Reports, *Labor in Europe*, 14.

27. Ibid., 12–13, 23.

28. Ibid., 250, 262, 326, 406, 550.

29. Ibid., 550–52.

30. Burgdörfer, in Ferenczi and Willcox, eds., II:357; Marschalck, 51.

31. Wolfgang Köllmann and Peter Marschalck, "German Emigration to the United States," *Perspectives in American History*, 7 (1973), 532.

32. Mönckmeier, 203.

33. Ibid., 145; Burgdörfer, in Ferenczi and Willcox, eds., II:360; Marschalck, 46.

34. Burgdörfer, in Ferenczi and Willcox, eds., II:361.

35. Mönckmeier, 149.

36. Marschalck, 47.

37. Burgdörfer, in Köllmann and Marschalck, eds., 285; Marschalck, 178.

38. Mönckmeier, 186.

39. Hamburg State Archive, Emigration Affairs Authority (Auswandererwesensbehörde), II-B-I-1, "Gesetze, Verordnungen, u.s.w., betr. die Rückwanderung," two police regulations dated August 5, 1882, and April 4, 1892; also, ibid., II-B-I-2, "Überwachung des Rückwandererverkehrs über Hamburg durch die Behörde für das Auswandererwesen bis zw. den Jahren 1902/03," which includes documents between 1877 and 1903.

9. Austria-Hungary and Russia, Jews and Poles

1. Ewa Morawska, " 'For Bread with Butter': Life-Worlds of Peasant Immigrants from East Central Europe, 1880–1914," *Journal of Social History*, 17 (Spring 1984), 387.

2. June Granatir Alexander, letter to author, February 12, 1982. See also Alexander, "The Immigrant Church and Community: The Formation of Pittsburgh's Slovak Religious Institutions, 1880–1914," (Ph.D. diss., University of Minnesota, 1980). A revised version has appeared as *The Immigrant Church and Community: Pittsburgh's Slovak Catholics and Lutherans* (Pittsburgh: University of Pittsburgh Press, 1987).

3. Berend and Ranki, *East Central Europe in the Nineteenth and Twentieth Centuries,* 1977, 24.

4. Emily Greene Balch, *Our Slavic Fellow Citizens* (New York: Charities Publication Committee, 1910), 135–37. Balch personally observed conditions in Austria-Hungary for about two years, and visited Slavic communities in the United States. Like her friend and co-worker Jane Addams, she later won a Nobel Peace Prize.

5. Celina Bobinska and Andrzej Pilch, eds., *Employment-Seeking Emigrations of the Poles World-Wide XIX and XX C.* ([Kraków]: Panstwowe Wydawnictwo Naukowe, 1975), 85.

6. Boguslaw Drewniak, *Emigracja z Pomorza Zachodniego 1816–1914* (Poznań: Wydawnictwo Poznánskie, 1966), 87–88.

7. Köllmann and Marschalck, 532, 540–46; Mack Walker, *Germany and the Emigration 1816–1885* (Cambridge: Harvard University Press, 1964), 160.

8. Hamburg Staatsarchiv, record group IEI2, Auswanderer-Deputation, *Jahrbuch,* 1879, 11.

9. Hamburg Staatsarchiv, Auswandererwesensbehörde, *Auswandererlisten, Direkt und Indirekt,* 1879–1893.

10. Germany, Kaiserlichen Statistischen Amt, "Bericht über die Thätigkeit des Reichskommissars für das Auswanderungswesen . . . 1881," *Annalen des Deutschen Reiches,* 1883, 194, 196; ibid., 1888, 454.

11. Hamburg Staatsarchiv, Auswanderer-Deputation, *Jahrbuch,* 1881.

12. Hamburg Staatsarchiv, *Auswanderlisten,* January–March 1882.

13. Germany, "Bericht über die Thätigkeit des Reichskommissars für das Auswanderungswesen," *Annalen des deutschen Reiches,* 1888, 460–62.

14. Evans, *Death in Hamburg;* Hamburg Staatsarchiv, Auswanderer-Deputation, *Jahrbuch,* 1887, 1892, 1893; also, ibid., record group IIEI1b, reports of Police Col. Kiliszewski to Senator Dr. Stam, 1891–93, on border conditions especially among Russian Jews.

15. Germany, *Reichsgesetzblatt,* June 9, 1897, 463–72: "Gesetz über das Auswanderungswesen."

16. Milward and Saul, *Development of Economies of Continental Europe,* 292.

17. Ibid., 276–77, 285, 290–91, 367–69, 449.

18. Berend and Ranki, *East Central Europe,* 1977, 34.

19. Ivan T. Berend and György Ranki, *Economic Development in East-Central Europe in the 19th and 20th Centuries* (New York: Columbia University Press, 1974), 20; Berend and Ranki, 1977, 16.

20. Balch, 49–54.

21. Julianna Puśkaś, "Hungarian Migration Patterns, 1880–1930: From Macroanalysis to Microanalysis," in Glazier and De Rosa, eds., (*q.v.*), 233. Also, Julianna Puśkaś, "The Process of Overseas Migration from East-Central Europe: Its Periods, Cycles, and Characteristics: A Comparative Study," in Wladyslaw Miodunka and Andrzej Brozek, eds., *Emigration from Northern, Central, and Southern Europe: Theoretical and Methodological Principles of Research. International Symposium, Kraków, November 9–11, 1981* (Kraków: Nakładem Uniwersytetu Jagiellońskiego, 1984), 47.

22. Morawska, 1984, 390–91.

23. Cited in Puśkaś, 1986, 238.

24. Balch, 81.

25. Eva E. Sandis, "Immigration to the United States from Austria-Hungary 1880–1910: Economic and Nationality Issues," in Jean Cazemajou, ed., *L'Immigration Européenne aux États-Unis (1880–1910)* (Bordeaux: Presses Universitaires de Bordeaux, 1986), 111–22, esp. 112–14. Also, Felix Klezl, "Austria," in Ferenczi and Willcox, eds., (*q.v.*), II:390–410, esp. 399, 403.

26. Geoffrey Drage, *Austria-Hungary,* 1909, reprinted in Erickson, ed. *Emigration from Europe, 1815–1914,* 82.

27. Gustav Thirring, "Hungarian Migration of Modern Times," in Ferenczi and Willcox, II:416–17, 419.

28. Puśkaś, 1984, 49; also, Puśkaś, 1986, 240.

29. Puśkaś, 1986, 242–50.

30. June Granatir Alexander, letter to author, February 12, 1982.

31. Monika Glettner, *Pittsburgh-Wien-Budapest. Programm und Praxis der Nationalitätenpolitik bei der Auswanderung der ungarischen Slowaken nach Amerika um 1900* (Vienna: Verlag der österreichischen Akademie, 1980), 17, 19, 26.

32. Alexander, "The Immigrant Church," 33–35, 38–39, 41, 47, 57.

33. Ibid., 74.

34. Balch, 106–7.

35. Ivan Cizmic, "Emigration from Yugoslavia prior to World War II," in Glazier and de Rosa, eds., 255–63; Balch, 176–83 (the quotation).

36. Ferenczi and Willcox, eds., *International Migrations,* II:529.

37. Liebmann Hersch, "International Migration of the Jews," in ibid., 546.

38. Italy, *Dall'Emigrazione dall'Italia comparata con quella che avviene da altri stati d'Europa,* 121.

39. James W. Long, *From Privileged to Dispossessed: The Volga Germans, 1860–1917* (Lincoln: University of Nebraska Press, 1988), xiv–xv, 35, 119–21, 248, 254.

40. Ewa Morawska, "Labor Migrations of Poles in the Atlantic World-Economy, 1880–1914," *Comparative Studies in Society and History,* 31 (April 1989), 251.

41. The first estimate is by Andrzej Pilch, "Migracja Zarobkowa z Galicji w XIX i XX Wieku (do 1918 roku)," *Przegląd Polonijny,* 1 (1975), 15. The second is by Halina Janowska, "An Introductory Outline of the Mass Polish Emigrations, Their Directions and Problems, 1870–1945," in Bobinska and Pilch, eds., 127. The third and most often cited is from J. Zubrzycki, "Emigration from Poland in the Nineteenth and Twentieth Centuries," 252–58.

42. Caroline Golab, *Immigrant Destinations* (Philadelphia: Temple University Press, 1978), 75. The effects of the end of serfdom on Polish peasants of all levels are best

clarified in Stefan Kieniewicz, *The Emancipation of the Polish Peasantry* (Chicago: University of Chicago Press, 1969).

43. Balch, 140.

44. Adam Galos and Kazimierz Wajda, "Migrations in the Polish Western Territories Annexed by Prussia (1815–1914)," in Bobinska and Pilch, eds., 69–75; also, Zbigniew Stankiewicz, "The Economic Emigration from the Kingdom of Poland Portrayed on the European Background," in ibid., 38.

45. Ferenczi and Willcox, eds., II:536.

46. Ewa Morawska, "Motyw Awansu w Systemie Wartośći Polskich Immigrantów w Stanach Zjednoczonych na Przelomie Wieku," *Przęglad Polonijny,* 4 (1978), 61–62, 149; Krzysztof Groniowski, "Polonia w Stanach Zjednoczonych u Schylku XIX w. Pozycja Spoleczna i Postawy Polityczne," ibid., 2 (1976), 195.

47. Florian Stasik, *Polska Emigracja Zarobkowa w Stanach Zjednoczonych Ameryki 1865–1914* (Warszawa: Państwowe Wydawnictwo Naukowe, 1985), 267.

48. Morawska, 1987, 24; Jozef Okolowicz, *Wychodztwo i Osadnictwo Polski, przed Wojna Swiatowa* (Warszawa: Sklad Głowny w Księgarni Gebethner i Wolff, 1920), 37–43, 178–86; Janowska, 134; Krzysztof Groniowski, "Historia Polskiej Emigracji do Ameryki Lacinskiej (do 1914r.)," in Zbigniew Dobosiewicz and Waldemar Rommel, eds., *Polonia w Ameryce Lacienskiej* (Lublin: Wydawnictwo Lubielski, 1977), 16–21; Izabela Klarner, *Emigracja z Królestwa Polskiego do Brazylii, 1890–1914* (Warszawa: Kriązka i Wiedza, 1975), 47–56.

49. Abraham Barkai, "German-Jewish Migration in the Nineteenth Century, 1830–1910," in Glazier and De Rosa, eds., 205, 207.

50. Hersch, "International Migration of the Jews," in Ferenczi and Willcox, eds., II:542.

51. Maj. W. Evans Gordon, "Report," in *Royal Commission on Alien Immigration,* 1903, in Erickson, *Emigration from Europe 1815–1914: Select Documents,* 108.

52. Jonathan D. Frankel, "The Crisis of 1881–82 as a Turning Point in Modern Jewish History," in David Berger, ed., *The Legacy of Jewish Migration: 1881 and Its Impact* (New York: Social Science Monographs—Brooklyn College Press, 1983), 9.

53. Ibid., 12–14.

54. Jonathan D. Sarna, "The Myth of No Return: Jewish Return Migration to Eastern Europe, 1881–1914," *American Jewish History,* 71 (December 1981), 259, 262.

55. Hersch, 543.

56. Simon Kuznets, "Immigration of Russian Jews to the United States; Background and Structure," *Perspectives in American History,* 9 (1975), 88, 94, 98; Shaul Stampfer, "The Geographic Background of East European Jewish Migration to the United States before World war I," in Glazier and de Rosa, eds., 224.

57. Stampfer, 227–28.

10. Italy

1. See tables 9 and 10, above.

2. Luigi Favero and Graziano Tassello, "Cent'anni di Emigrazione Italiana (1876–1976)," in Gianfausto Rosoli, ed., *Un Secolo di Emigrazione Italiana 1876–1976* (Rome: Centro Studi Emigrazione, 1978), 19, 23, 25.

3. Grazia Dore, "Some Special and Historical Aspects of Italian Emigration to America," *Journal of Social History,* 2 (Winter 1968), 102.

4. Kristin Ruggiero, "Social and Psychological Factors in Migration from Italy to Argentina: From the Waldensian Valleys to San Gustavo," in Glazier and De Rosa, eds., 160–62, 166, 168.

5. Donna R. Gabaccia, *From Sicily to Elizabeth Street: Housing and Social Change*

among Italian Immigrants, 1880–1930 (Albany: State University of New York Press, 1984), 10, 52. Also, Rudolph J. Vecoli, *"Contadini* in Chicago: A Critique of *The Uprooted," Journal of American History,* 51 (December 1964), 407.

6. Donna Gabaccia, *Militants and Migrants: Rural Sicilians Become American Workers* (New Brunswick: Rutgers University Press, 1988), 13, 16, 20, 33–36, 49, 54–55, 66.

7. For a detailed description of economic and social conditions among the peasants and artisans, see Robert F. Foerster, *The Italian Emigration of Our Times* (Cambridge: Harvard University Press, 1924 [1919]), chapters 5–7.

8. Gabaccia, 1988, 29.

9. Gary R. Mormino and George E. Pozzetta, *The Immigrant World of Ybor City: Italians and Their Latin Neighbors in Tampa, 1885–1985* (Urbana: University of Illinois Press, 1987), 31.

10. Anna Maria Martellone, "Italian Mass Emigration to the United States, 1876–1930: A Historical Survey," *Perspectives in American History,* new series, 1 (1984), 390–91.

11. Ibid., 395–96.

12. Zeffiro Ciuffoletti and Maurizio Degl'Innocenti, *L'Emigrazione nella Storia d'Italia 1868–1975: Storia e Documenti* (Florence: Vallecchi Editore, 1978), 153.

13. Italy, Giunta per l'Inchiesta Agraria e sulle Condizioni della Classe Agricola, *Atti,* 22 vols. (Rome: Forzani e C., Tipografi del Senato, 1881–1886). This exhaustive work is very rare, at least in the United States. I found a set in the New York Public Library Annex, but it is so brittle as to be almost unusable.

14. Ciuffoletti and Degl'Innocenti, 110–11, 118, 127.

15. Foerster, chapters 3–6.

16. Rosoli, ed., 152.

17. August Sartorius von Waltershausen, *Die Italienischen Wanderarbeiter* (Leipsig: Verlag von C. L. Hirschfeld, 1903), 27.

18. Gould, "Emigration: The Road Home: Return Migration from the U.S.A.," 1980, 77.

19. The remaining 4.5 percent went to North Africa. Italy, *Dall'Emigrazione dall'Italia comparata con quella che avviene da altri stati d'Europa,* 31. The figures are from Italian departure records. This source (30–32, 67) discusses the differences between Italian numbers and Argentine, Brazilian, and U.S. arrival figures. See also Gould, 89–91. Similar differences have been discussed earlier in connection with British and German figures. Up to 1901, in general, Italian departure figures understated actual departures and were smaller than New World arrival figures. A new emigration act of 1901 changed the method of counting departures, which reduced the differences but did not eliminate them.

20. Dore, 116–20.

21. Ira A. Glazier, "Ships and Passengers in Emigration from Italy to the United States, 1880–1900," in Miodunka and Brozek, eds., *(q.v.),* 245–75; also available in Rosalba Ragosta, ed., *Le Genti del Mare Mediterraneo* (Naples: Lucio Pironti Editore, [1981], 1097–1124.

22. Luigi DiComiti and Ira A. Glazier, "Socio-demographic Characteristics of Italian Emigration to the United States from Ship Passenger Lists: 1880–1914," *Ethnic Forum: Journal of Ethnic Studies and Ethnic Bibliography,* 4 (Spring 1984), 86.

23. Ibid., 79–81.

24. See, for example, Gabaccia, 1988, chapter 5, "Links in the Migration Chain," which discusses a number of specific cases revealing the complexity of migration patterns at the individual and family levels.

25. Glazier, 249.

26. Ibid., 250.

27. Rudolph M. Bell, *Fate and Honor, Family and Village: Demographic and Cultural*

Change in Rural Italy since 1800 (Chicago: University of Chicago Press, 1979), 198. Martellone (407) makes a similar point. See also John W. Briggs, *An Italian Passage: Immigrants to Three American Cities, 1890–1930* (New Haven: Yale University Press, 1978), 14, 16. On Sicilians: Gabaccia, 1988, 173–74.

28. Braudel, *The Mediterranean and the Mediterranean World in the Age of Philip II,* I:85–102.

29. Bell, 190.

30. Rosoli, ed., 16; Martellone, 404.

31. Livi-Bacci, *L'Immigrazione e L'Assimilazione degli Italiani negli Stati Uniti,* 43, was one of the first to make this point; many have made it since.

32. Golab, *Immigrant Destinations,* 57; Martellone, 409–10.

33. Barbara Schmitter, "Sending States and Immigrant Minorities—The Case of Italy," *Comparative Studies in Society and History,* 26 (1984), 329; Luigi di Comiti, "Aspects of Italian Emigration, 1881–1915," 153; Betty Boyd Caroli, *Italian Repatriation from the United States, 1900–1914* (New York: Center for Migration Studies, 1973), 64.

34. Donna Gabaccia, "Female Migration and Immigrant Sex Ratios, 1820–1928," unpublished paper, Social Science History Association meeting, Washington, November 1989, 7–8.

35. United States Consular Reports, *Labor in Europe,* 149–50; Favero and Tassello, 25.

11. Spain and Portugal

1. Spain, Consejo Superior de Emigración, *La Emigración Española Transoceánica 1911–1915* (Madrid: Hijos de T. Minuesa de los Rios, 1916), 96. As with other emigrations, official figures from the sending and receiving countries do not quite match; the Spanish authorities point out that their figures do not include departures from foreign ports such as Bordeaux, Lisbon, and Gibraltar (97–98).

2. Ibid., 102–3.

3. Jordi Nadal, *La Población Española (Siglos XVI a XX)* (Barcelona: Editorial Ariel, Esplugues de Llobregat, 1973), 180–82.

4. Quoted in Vicente Perez Moreda, "Spain's Demographic Modernization, 1800–1930," in Nicolas Sanchez-Albornoz, ed., *The Economic Modernization of Spain, 1830–1930,* trans. Karen Powers and Manuel Sanudo (New York: New York University Press, 1987), 17.

5. This Galicia is not to be confused, of course, with Polish Galicia, around Kraków and Lvov, then under Austrian control.

6. Nadal, 193, 201; the emigration rate he gives is 15.1 per thousand per year in 1885–1886 to Spanish colonies and another 2.9 per thousand to other American countries. The Canaries' birth rate in 1910 was 42.6 per thousand. No other province exceeded 37.1 at that time; Catalonia was lowest at 25.0.

7. Magnus Mörner (with the collaboration of Harold Sims), *Adventurers and Proletarians: The Story of Migrants in Latin America* (Paris: UNESCO, and Pittsburgh: University of Pittsburgh Press, 1985), 37–38.

8. Nadal, 193.

9. Spain, Consejo Superior de Emigración, 75, 83. Figures by province for 1911–1915 inclusive show Coruña leading with 61,560, followed by Pontevedra, 53,106; Orense, 52,745; Lugo, 51,883; Oviedo, 47,652; Almería, 36,722; Canárias, 30,270; and Leon 29,415.

10. Perez Moreda, 29.

11. Jaime Garcia-Lombardero, "Economic Transformations in Galicia in the Nineteenth and Twentieth Centuries," in Sanchez-Albornoz, ed., 224–27.

12. Xose Antonio Lopez Taboada, *Economia e Población en Galicia* (La Coruña: Edicions do Rueiro, 1979), 155–56; Spain, Consejo Superior de Emigración, 80–81.

13. Spain, Consejo Superior de Emigración, 105–7, 118.

14. Perez Moreda, 31.

15. Spain, Consejo Superior de Emigración, 103–4.

16. Ferenczi and Willcox, eds., *International Migrations,* I:851–61, II:132–36.

17. Fernando Emygdio da Silva, *Emigração Portuguesa* (Coimbra: Franca & Armenio, 1917), 128–29, 192.

18. Ibid., 130–32.

19. Ibid., 162.

20. Ibid., 192–95.

21. Ferenczi and Willcox, eds., I:844–45, II:128–29.

22. An excellent study combining historical demography and anthropology is Caroline B. Brettell, *Men Who Migrate, Women Who Wait: Population and History in a Portuguese Parish* (Princeton: Princeton University Press, 1986).

23. Da Silva, 181–84.

24. Joel Serrão, *Emigração Portuguesa: Sondagem Historica* (Lisbon: Livros Horizonte, 1974), 83; Da Silva, 197.

25. Da Silva, 152–59, 331.

26. Serrão, 93.

Part III: The American Receivers

Introduction

1. For population and total immigration for the four receivers, by decade, see above, tables 4 and 8.

12. Argentina

1. Jordi Nadal, *La Población Española* (*Siglos XVI a XX*) (Barcelona: Editorial Ariel, Espluges de Llobregat, 1973), 186.

2. Nicolas Sanchez-Albornoz, "The Population of Latin America, 1850–1930," in Leslie Bethell, ed., *The Cambridge History of Latin America* (Cambridge: Cambridge University Press, 1986), IV:136; David Rock, "Argentina in 1914: The Pampas, The Interior, Buenos Aires," in ibid., V:393.

3. Gino Germani, *Politica y Sociedad en una Epoca de Transición: De la Sociedad Tradicional a la Sociedad de Masas* (Buenos Aires: Editorial Paidos, [1965]), 179. For this and other statistics to be cited from Germani, his sources are the censuses of 1869, 1895, 1914, and 1947. The highest proportion of foreign-born in the United States population appeared in the 1910 census; it was 14.7 percent.

4. Ibid., 187–88.

5. Carl Solberg, *Immigration and Nationalism: Argentina and Chile, 1890–1914* (Austin: University of Texas Press, 1970), 7, 31; Horacio C. Rivarola, *Las Transformaciones de la Sociedad Argentina y sus Consecuencias Institucionales* (*1853 a 1910*) (Buenos Aires: Imprenta de Coni Hermanos, 1911), 129–30.

6. Gould, "European Inter-Continental Emigration," 620.

7. Ezequiel Gallo, "Argentina: Society and Politics, 1880–1916," in Bethell, ed., V:363; see also Nicolas Sanchez-Albornoz and Jose Luis Moreno, *La Población de America Latina: Bosquejo Historico* (Buenos Aires: Paidos [1968]).

8. Gallo, in Bethell, ed., V:364; Gallo, *La Pampa Gringa: La Colonización Agrícola en Santa Fe* (*1870–1895*) (Buenos Aires: Editorial Sudamericana, 1982) 269–70. At 345

percent, Santa Fe expanded faster than any other pampean province between the 1869 and the 1895 censuses. Its growth was not quite so fast as, but in the range of, that of farm settlement on the American Great Plains; North Dakota, for example, went from 37,000 in 1880 to 577,000 in 1910 (*U.S. Historical Statistics,* series A195, I:32).

9. Alejandro Bunge and Carlos Garcia Mata, "Immigration to Argentina," in Ferenczi and Willcox, eds., (*q.v.*), II:150; James R. Scobie, *Revolution on the Pampas: A Social History of Argentine Wheat, 1860–1910* (Austin: University of Texas Press, 1964), 29.

10. James Bryce, *South America: Observations and Impressions* (New York: Macmillan, 1912), 338–39.

11. Carl C. Taylor, *Rural Life in Argentina* (Baton Rouge: Louisiana State University Press, 1948), 91–97.

12. Scobie, *Revolution,* 29, using the Italian emigration figures: during 1876–1900 Argentina got 444,000 from the North, 263,000 from the South (while 523,000 went from the South to the U.S.A.); during 1901–1913 Argentina received 316,000 from the North, 328,000 from the South (while the United States received 347,000 from the North, 1.7 million from the south).

13. Carlos F. Diaz Alejandro, "Argentina, Australia and Brazil before 1929," in D. C. M. Platt and Guido di Tella, eds., *Argentina, Australia, and Canada: Studies in Comparative Development 1870–1965* (New York: St. Martin's Press, 1985), 102.

14. Bryce, 339.

15. Roberto Cortes Conde, *El Progreso Argentino 1880–1915* (Buenos Aires: Editorial Sudamericana, 1979), 193.

16. Gustave Beyhaut et al., *Inmigración y Desarrollo Economico* (Buenos Aires: Seminario Interdisciplinario sobre el Desarrollo Economico y Social de la Argentina, 1961), 13ff.

17. Taylor, 98–99; Germani, 188. It is not clear how many immigrant women stayed because of jobs outside their homes; it seems unlikely that many Spanish and Italian women of the first generation did so, but more research is needed to settle the point.

18. Silvio Zavala, "The Frontiers of Hispanic America," in Walker B. Wyman and Clifton B. Kroeber, *The Frontier in Perspective* (Madison: University of Wisconsin Press, 1957), 39.

19. Roberto Cortes Conde, "La Expansión de la Economia Argentina entre 1800 y 1914 y el Papel de la Immigración," *Cahiers du Monde Hispanique et Luso-brésilien,* 10 (1968), 75.

20. Gustavo Beyhaut, R. Cortes Conde, H. Gorostegui, and S. Torrado, "Los Inmigrantes en el Sistema Ocupacional Argentino," in Torcuato S. DiTella, Gino Germani, Jorge Graciarena, y Colaboradores, *Argentina: Sociedad de Masas* (Buenos Aires: EUDEBA, Editorial Universitaria de Buenos Aires, 1966), 91; Oscar Cornblit, "European Immigrants in Argentine Industry and Politics," in Claudio Veliz, ed., *The Politics of Conformity in Latin America* (London: Oxford University Press, 1967), 222; Cortes Conde, 1968, 77n13.

21. Tim Duncan and John Fogarty, *Australia and Argentina: On Parallel Paths* (Carlton, Victoria: Melbourne University Press, 1984), 14–15, 24.

22. Foerster, *The Italian Emigration of Our Times,* 230–40.

23. Michael Edelstein, *Overseas Investment in the Age of High Imperialism: The United Kingdom, 1850–1914* (New York: Columbia University Press, 1982), 297, on the Baring Crisis and other aspects of British investment in Argentina (the third largest foreign borrower behind the United States and Australia). See also Colin M. Lewis, *British Railways in Argentina, 1857–1914: a Case Study of Foreign Investment* (Athlone: Published for the Institute of Latin American Studies, University of London, 1983).

24. Bryce, 315, 331.

25. Carl E. Solberg, *The Prairies and the Pampas: Agrarian Policy in Canada and Argentina, 1880–1930* (Stanford: Stanford University Press, 1987), 51.

26. Ibid., 19.

27. Taylor, 156–57, 183–90.

28. Solberg, 4, 20.

29. Taylor, 156.

30. Cortes Conde, 1979, 152–62; Carlos F. Diaz Alejandro, *Essays on the Economic History of the Argentine Republic* (New Haven: Yale University Press, 1970), 38–39; Mark Jefferson, *Peopling the Argentine Pampas* (New York: American Geographical Society, 1926), 106–7.

31. Jefferson, 1926, 123–28.

32. Diaz Alejandro, 1985, 101.

33. Scobie, *Revolution*, 36.

34. Gallo, 1972, 80–81, 88–94; Scobie, *Argentina: A City and a Nation* (New York: Oxford University Press, 1964), 117–19; Foerster, 243–46.

35. Jefferson, 168–69.

36. Ibid., 171.

37. Scobie, *Argentina,* 120–21. Also, Roberto Cortes Conde, "The Growth of the Argentine Economy, c. 1870–1914," in Bethell, ed., V:333–34; Ezequiel Gallo, "Los Italianos en los Orígenes de la Agricultura Argentina: Santa Fe (1870–1895)," in Francis Korn, ed., *Los Italianos en La Argentina* (Buenos Aires: Fundación Giovanni Agnelli, 1983), 23.

38. Roberto Cortes Conde, *The First Stages of Modernization in Spanish America* (New York: Harper & Row, 1974), 133, 152.

39. Germani, 1965, 192.

40. Taylor, 169–75.

41. Gallo, in Bethell, ed., V:367.

42. Cortes Conde, 1968, 81.

43. Beyhaut et al., 92, 94.

44. Carl Solberg, "Mass Migrations in Argentina, 1870–1970," in McNeill and Adams, *Human Migrations,* 147–51; Scobie, *Argentina,* 130.

45. Bryce, 320.

46. Theodore H. Moran, "The 'Development' of Argentina and Australia: The Radical Party of Argentina and the Labor Party of Australia in the Process of Economic and Social Development," *Comparative Politics,* 3 (October 1970), 84–85, citing Gino Germani.

47. Germani, 194–95.

48. Cornblit, 227.

49. Foerster, 255.

50. Carter Goodrich, "Argentina as a New Country," *Comparative Studies in Society and History,* 7 (1964), 87–88. Cortes Conde (1968, 81) declares that immigrants had a "dominant role" in industrial development.

51. Solberg, 1987, 28–30; Moran, 73, 78.

52. Germani, 203.

53. On naturalization, see Solberg, 1978, 157; James R. Scobie, *Buenos Aires: Plaza to Suburb, 1870–1910* (New York: Oxford University Press, 1974), 239.

54. Samuel L. Baily, "The Adjustment of Italian Immigrants in Buenos Aires and New York, 1870–1914," *American Historical Review,* 88 (April 1983), 299, 303–4, 323; also, Herbert S. Klein, "The Integration of Italian Immigrants into the United States and Argentina: A Comparative Analysis," *American Historical Review,* 88 (April 1983), 318, 329.

55. Jefferson, 183–84.

56. Cornblit, 223.

57. Diaz Alejandro, 1985, 103.
58. Bryce, 333.
59. Solberg, 1987, 225–26.

13. Brazil

1. Klaus Becker, "A Fundação e os Primeiros 30 Anos de Teutonia," in Faculdade de Filosofia da Universidade Federal do Rio Grande do Sul, *I Coloquio de Estudos Teuto-Brasileiros* (Porto Alegre: Universidade Federal de RGS, 1963), 222.

2. Frederick C. Luebke, *Germans in the New World: Essays in the History of Immigration* (Urbana: University of Illinois Press, 1990), 100–1.

3. Ibid., chapter 8: "The German Ethnic Group in Brazil: The Ordeal of World War I."

4. Stuart Clark Rothwell, *The Old Italian Colonial Zone of Rio Grande do Sul, Brazil* (Porto Alegre: Edições da Faculdade de Filosofia, 1959), 8, 13, 24, 37, 42, 44.

5. Jose Fernando Carneiro, *Imigração e Colonização no Brasil* (Rio de Janeiro: Universidade do Brasil, 1950), 39–42, 52. For the marginalization of poorer German immigrants, and the explosive combination of religious and economic discontent in São Leopoldo, see Janaina Amado, *Conflito Social no Brasil: A Revolta dos 'Mucker,' Rio Grande do Sul 1868–1898* (São Paulo: Edições Simbolo, 1978), *passim,* but esp. 271–76.

6. Michael M. Hall, "The Origins of Mass Immigration in Brazil, 1871–1914" (Ph.D. diss., Columbia University, 1969), 5, 54, 78, 102–3.

7. Carneiro, 26.

8. Nathaniel H. Leff and Herbert S. Klein, "O Crescimento da População não Europeia antes do Inicio do Desenvolvimento no Brasil do Seculo XIX," *Anais de Historia* (Assis), 6 (1974), 56–57; Paul Hugon, *Demografia Brasileira: Ensaio de Demoeconomia Brasileira* (São Paulo: Atlas, Editora da Universidade de São Paulo, 1973), 44.

9. T. Lynn Smith, *Brazil: People and Institutions,* 4th ed. (Baton Rouge: Louisiana State University Press, 1972), 134; Rio Grande do Sul, Universidade Federal, Faculdade de Filosofia, *Primeiro Coloquio de Estudos Teuto-Brasileiros* (Porto Alegre: [1964?]), and Stuart Clark Rothwell, *The Old Colonial Zone of Rio Grande do Sul, Brazil* (Porto Alegre: Edições da Faculdade de Filosofia, 1959).

10. Mitchell, *International Historical Statistics,* series B7, 141–42.

11. Giorgio Mortara, "The Development and Structure of Brazil's Population," in Joseph J. Spengler and Otis Dudley Duncan, eds., *Demographic Analysis: Selected Readings* (Glencoe: Free Press, 1956), 669.

12. São Paulo, Universidade, Centro de Estudos de Dinámicas Populacional, "La Population du Brésil," (São Paulo: CICRED, 1975 [cited hereafter as CICRED]), 67; 388, 459 out of 10,112,061.

13. Ferenczi and Willcox, eds., *International Migrations,* I:550; Smith, 122.

14. Gould, "European Inter-Continental Migration, 1815–1914," 1979, 621.

15. Pedro Calderan Beltrão, *Demografia: Ciencia da População, Analise e Teoria* (Porto Alegre: Livraria Sulina Editora, 1972), 198; Donald Hastings, "Japanese Emigration and Assimilation in Brazil," *International Migration Review,* 3 (Spring 1969), 35; Smith 125; Klarner, *Emigracia z Królestwa Polskiego do Brazylii, 1890–1914* (she says the situation of the first Poles on the coffee plantations was "bardzo trudna"—very difficult), 33–37; Bobinska and Pilch, *Employment-Seeking Emigrations of the Poles World-Wide XIX and XX C,* 19. In the mid-1860s "probably three thousand Americans emigrated from the Southern States . . . but four-fifths of them have returned" (Christopher Columbus Andrews, *Brazil, Its Condition and Prospects,* 3rd ed. [New York: D. Appleton and Company, 1891], 345).

16. T. Lynn Smith, 138. After 1914 Argentina received some numbers of Brazilians

and Uruguayans (Mörner, *Adventurers and Proletarians,* 111). As with other poorly recorded migration flows (such as between Canada and the United States), census reports on places of birth can provide at least some evidence of migration flows.

17. Foerster, *The Italian Emigration of Our Times,* 289–90; Michael M. Hall, "Approaches to Immigration History," in Richard Graham and Peter H. Smith, eds., *New Approaches to Latin American History* (Austin: University of Texas Press, 1974), 180–84.

18. An excellent description of the Italian ban, and of the killing of the planter Diogo Salles, brother of the Brazilian president, by the young Angelo Lungaretti, who was defending his father, may be found in Warren Dean, *Rio Claro: A Brazilian Plantation System, 1820–1920* (Stanford: Stanford University Press, 1976), 181–83. See also Foerster, 295; Hugon, 69n30; and Hall, 134, 169–70.

19. Lucy Maffei Hutter, *Imigração Italiana em São Paulo de 1902 a 1914: O Processo Imigratorio* (São Paulo: Instituto de Estudos Brasileiros, Universidade de São Paulo, 1986), 5, 8–10.

20. Ibid.; also, CICRED, 66–67, and Hugon, 66.

21. Ferenczi and Willcox, eds., I:550, I:555, calculated.

22. Of the 1,566,000 foreign-born in Brazil in 1920, 35.7 percent were Italian, 27.7 percent Portuguese, and 14.0 percent Spanish—a total of 77.4 percent from the three Mediterranean donor nations. The persistence rate for 1890–1919—foreign-born in 1920 divided by recorded immigration—is Italian 53.2 percent, Portuguese 59.1 percent, Spanish 46.9 percent; that is, the rest left Brazil or died there between arrival and the 1920 census. (Calculated from T. Lynn Smith, 137, table 24.)

23. Thomas H. Holloway, "Creating the Reserve Army: The Immigration Program of São Paulo, 1886–1930," *International Migration Review,* 12 (Summer 1978), 188; CICRED, 67.

24. Thomas W. Merrick and Douglas H. Graham, *Population and Economic Development in Brazil, 1800 to the Present* (Baltimore: Johns Hopkins University Press, 1979), 110–11.

25. Hugon, 69–72.

26. Ibid., 77.

27. T. Lynn Smith, 134; Luebke, 100–101.

28. Mitchell, series B4, 106, 108. São Paulo passed Rio in population in the 1950s. See also Maria Yedda Linhares and Barbara Levy, "Aspectos da Historia Demografica e Social do Rio de Janeiro (1808–1889)," in Conseil National de Recherche Scientifique, *Histoire Quantitative du Brésil* (Paris: CNRS, 1973), 131–34.

29. Lucy Maffei Hutter, *Imigração Italiana em São Paulo (1880–1889)* (São Paulo: Publicação do Instituto de Estudos Brasileiros, Universidade de São Paulo, 1972), 115. This revised dissertation supervised by Sergio Buarque de Holanda contains a wealth of concrete detail on the sponsored migration of Italians before 1890.

30. Warren Dean, *The Industrialization of Sao Paulo, 1880–1945* (Austin: University of Texas Press, 1969), 51.

31. Hall, 1974, 186–88; precisely 1,446 of 2,966.

32. Dean, 1969, 61.

33. Brazil, Instituto Brasileiro de Geografia e Estadistica, *Estadisticas Demografias: Côr* (Rio de Janeiro: IBGE, 1950), 25–27, 29.

34. Hugon, 51n19. In contrast, the United States took only 4 percent of the entire African slave trade; see Merrick and Graham, chapter 4, esp. 50, 77.

35. Hall, 1969, 82–89, and Jeffrey D. Needell, *A Tropical Belle Époque: Elite Culture and Society in Turn-of-the-Century Rio de Janeiro* (Cambridge: Cambridge University Press, 1987), 6–7, describe the similarities and differences, economic and political, among various groups of planters. Needell: "Pressed to the wall [by 1887], the *paulistas* abandoned the *fluminense* [Rio] and *mineiro* [Minas Gerais] slavocrats, and turned Aboli-

tionist. . . . Some hoped to retain many of their former slaves by granting manumission *en masse*, others struggled indignantly for abolition with compensation. Most called for State subsidization of immigration."

36. Dean, 1976, 157–58; Holloway, "Creating the Reserve Army," 188; Fernando Bastos de Avila, *L'Immigration au Brésil: Contribution a une Théorie Générale de L'Immigration* (Rio de Janeiro: Libraria Agir Editora, 1956), 62–63; Beltrão, 197; Hutter, 1972, *passim*.

37. Charlotte J. Erickson, ed., *Emigration from Europe, 1815–1914: Select Documents* (London: Adam & Charles Black, 1976), 175–76.

38. The 1934 Constitution required "ethnic integration" and "physical and civic capacity" from immigrants; see Hugon, 52–53.

39. Merrick and Graham, 107.

40. Manuel Diegues Junior, *População e Propriedade da Terra no Brasil* (Washington: União Pan-Americana, 1959), 45.

41. Ibid., 28; Warren Dean, "The Brazilian Economy, 1870–1930," in Bethell, ed., (*q.v.*), V:701–2, and Dean, 1976, 16–23; Thomas H. Holloway, *Immigrants on the Land: Coffee and Society in Sao Paulo, 1886–1934* (Chapel Hill: University of North Carolina Press, 1980), 113; T. Lynn Smith, 252–65, 268–72, 284–92, 322–25.

42. Werner Baer, *The Brazilian Economy: Growth and Development*, 3d ed. (New York: Praeger, 1989), 16–17.

43. Bryce, 390.

44. E. Bradford Burns, *A History of Brazil* (New York: Columbia University Press, 1970), 219; Dean, in Bethell, ed., 704.

45. Robert W. Slenes, "The Demography and Economics of Brazilian Slavery, 1850–1888" (Ph.D. diss., Stanford University, 1976), 36, 262. According to Slenes, the slave population of Brazil peaked in 1873 at 1.5 million; 200,000 were manumitted between 1873 and 1888; others died or ran off. He estimates the slave population in 1887 at 751,000. Also, Eulalia Laymeyer Lobo, "Evolution des Prix et du Côut de la Vie à Rio de Janeiro (1820–1930)," in Conseil National de Recherche Scientifique, 209. The quotation is from Dean, 1976, 139–42.

46. Louis Couty, *Le Brésil en 1884* (Rio de Janeiro: Far & Lino, 1884), 156. On Vergueiro, see Dean, 1976, 156.

47. Andrews, 344; Hutter, 1972, 27–32. Slenes says that the *milreis* was worth about 55 cents American at that time (90).

48. Hall, 1969, 118.

49. Hutter, 1972, chapters 4 and 5. The quotation is from M. F.-J. de Santa-Anna Nery, *Le Brésil en 1889, avec une carte de l'Empire* (Paris: Librairie Charles Delagrave, 1889), 501–2. Baer (17) states that "in the 1860s British capital and engineers" built the Santos-São Paulo railway up the escarpment.

50. Stanley J. Stein, *Vassouras: A Brazilian Coffee County, 1850–1900* (Cambridge: Harvard University Press, 1957), 289. Also, John D. Wirth, *Minas Gerais in the Brazilian Federation, 1889–1937* (Stanford: Stanford University Press, 1977), 9, 15.

51. Dean, 1976, 158.

52. Hutter, 1972, 98; Douglas O. Naylor, "Brazil," in Ferenczi and Willcox, eds., (*q.v.*) II:165.

53. Boris Fausto, "Brazil: The Social and Political Structure of the First Republic, 1889–1930," in Bethell, ed., V:780.

54. Merrick and Graham, 114.

55. Hutter, 1972, 96–98; Dean, 1976, 169; Foerster, 291–98; Fausto, 780; Nery, 501–2; Holloway, 1980, 123.

56. Hutter, 1972, 92; Andrews, 341.

57. Hutter, 1972, 109–10.

58. Hutter, 1986, 123–38.
59. Holloway, 1980, 129–37.
60. Fausto, 781–82; Nathaniel H. Leff, *Underdevelopment and Development in Brazil. I: Economic Structure and Change, 1822–1947* (London: George Allen & Unwin, 1982), 58.
61. Dean, 1976, 142–47; Stein, 257–76; Holloway, 1980, 173; Hall, 111–13.
62. Hutter, 1972, 108–9 ("em geral, laboriosos, sempre pacificos e alegres"), 115–17.
63. Diegues Junior, 28.
64. Hall, 1969, 179–80.
65. Holloway, 1980, xvi–xvii, 173–74.
66. Ibid., 151–55; Fausto's conclusion is similar (781).
67. Dean, 1976, 189–90, 192; Dean, 1986, 705.
68. Hall, 1969, 116, 149.
69. Holloway, 1980, 179–80.
70. Bryce, 406; Foerster, 309–10.
71. Author's personal observation in Rio Grande do Sul, 1967 and 1969.
72. "Report by Consul Hearn on a Visit to some of the Foreign Colonies in the State of Rio Grande do Sul . . . ," *British Parliamentary Papers,* 1890–91, LXXXIII, (C. 6424), 32–40, reprinted in Erickson, ed., 176–84.
73. T. Lynn Smith, 118–19.
74. Foerster, 279, 299.
75. Hugon, 104.
76. Clodomir Vianna Moog, *Bandeirantes and Pioneers* (New York: Basic Books, 1964), 22, 164, and *passim.*
77. Leff, 17–19.
78. Gould, "Emigration: The Road Home: Return Migration from the U.S.A.," 1980, 67.
79. T. Lynn Smith, 119–20.
80. Andrews, 342. Andrews at one time was U.S. Consul General in Rio de Janeiro and at another, Minister to Sweden and Norway.
81. Ferenczi and Willcox, eds., *International Migrations* I:264–71. Except for a few years in the 1890s, Argentina took in more people than Brazil did. The years of successful recruitment of Italian *colonos* was an exception.
82. For estimates of such funds, see Warren Dean, "Remessas de Dinheiro dos Emigrantes Italianos do Brasil, Argentina, Uruguai e Estados Unidos da America (1884–1914)," *Anais de Historia* (Assis), 6 (1974), 231–37.
83. Samuel L. Baily, "The Italians and Organized Labor in the United States and Argentina: 1880–1910," *International Migration Review,* 1 (Summer 1967), 56–66; and Baily, "The Adjustment of Italian Immigrants in Buenos Aires and New York, 1870–1914," 1983, 281–305.
84. Mary Lombardi has written that in the Brazilian south, with its small farms, similarities to the American Turnerian farm frontier did exist ("The Frontier in Brazilian History: An Historiographical Essay," *Pacific Historical Review,* 44 [November 1975], esp. 454). Joyce Riegelhaupt and Shepard Forman argue that Brazilian peasants in coffee or sugar regions were never "traditional," that true feudalism never existed in Brazil, and that the plantation areas were more like the antebellum American South than the Turnerian frontier ("Bodo Was Never Brazilian: Economic Integration and Rural Development among a Contemporary Peasantry," *Journal of Economic History,* 30 (March 1970), 110–16.
85. Bryce, 415–16.
86. Hall, 1969, 123–30.
87. Carneiro, 29.

14. Canada

1. Canada, "The Urban and Rural Composition of Canada's Population," *Census 1971, Profile Studies 2* (Ottawa: Statistics Canada, January 1976), 10; U.S. *Hist. Stats.,* series A2, A69, I:8, I:11.

2. Ferenczi and Willcox, eds., *International Migrations,* I:360–61; Mitchell, *International Historical Statistics,* series B7, 138–39; Duncan M. McDougall, "Immigration into Canada, 1851–1920," *Canadian Journal of Economics and Political Science,* 27 (May 1961), 170.

3. Yolande Lavoie, *L'Émigration des Canadiens aux États-Unis avant 1930: Mésure du Phénomène* (Montreal: Les Presses de L'Université de Montréal, 1972), 77.

4. By the highest estimate for the 1880s, that of Nathan Keyfitz ("The Growth of Canadian Population," *Population Studies,* 4 [June 1950], 62). The lowest estimate for the 1880s has 448,000 arriving and 602,000 departing—still a net outflow of 154,000. For 1901–1911, 715,000 is Keyfitz's figure and is at the low end; the highest estimate puts the net inflow at 810,000 (Warren E. Kalbach and Wayne W. McVey, *The Demographic Bases of Canadian Society,* 2d ed., [Toronto: McGraw-Hill Ryerson Ltd., 1979], 54).

5. Kalbach and McVey, 47, 54; Keyfitz, 62.

6. Keyfitz, 62; McDougall, 172; Kalbach and McVey, 54.

7. Kalbach and McVey, 198–204.

8. R. K. Vedder and L. E. Gallaway, "Settlement Patterns of Canadian Emigrants to the United States, 1850–1960," *The Canadian Journal of Economics/Revue Canadienne d'Économique,* 2 (August 1970), 486.

9. Marcus Lee Hansen and John Bartlet Brebner, *The Mingling of the Canadian and American Peoples* (New Haven: Yale University Press, 1940), 18.

10. R. H. Coats and M. C. Maclean, *The American-Born in Canada: A Statistical Interpretation* (Toronto: The Ryerson Press, 1943), 24; Leon E. Truesdell, *The Canadian Born in the United States: An Analysis of the Statistics of the Canadian Element in the Population of the United States 1850 to 1930* (New Haven: Yale University Press, 1943), 9–16.

11. Marvin McInnis, "Fertility Patterns in Late Nineteenth Century Ontario and Quebec," unpublished paper, Social Science History Association meeting, Chicago, November 1988. The Ontario levels of marital fertility (I_g) were in the .600 to .900 range in 1851, .400 to .700 in 1891. The theoretical maximum—or, rather, the observed maximum of 1.000, as used statistically by the Princeton European Fertility Project—is that of Hutterite communities in western Canada. McInnis found three Quebec counties that actually exceeded 1.000 in 1891 (Deux-Montagnes, Rimouski, Terrebonne).

12. Coats and Maclean, 33; Lavoie, 20, 27.

13. Hansen and Brebner, 160–66.

14. Ibid., 188–202.

15. United States, Department of State, *Labor in Europe, Asia, Africa, Australasia, and Polynesia. Reports from Consuls of the United States . . . ,* House Executive Document 54, part 3. 48th Congress, 2d Session (Washington: Government Printing Office, 1885), 16.

16. Randy William Widdis, "Scale and Context: Approaches to the Study of Canadian Migration Patterns in the Nineteenth Century," *Social Science History,* 12 (Fall 1988), 269–89. Widdis describes a young couple married near Kingston who migrated to Fulton, New York (near Syracuse), for two years and returned (plus two children) to Ontario with enough to start buying a farm. Widdis's is a careful, cogent essay on a migration area previously underresearched, as are Widdis's others, "With Scarcely a Ripple: English Canadians in Northern New York State at the Beginning of the Twentieth Century," *Journal of Historical Geography,* 13 (1987), 169–92, and " 'We Breathe the Same Air': Eastern Ontarian Migration to Watertown, New York," *New York History,* 68 (July 1987), 261–80.

17. R. Marvin McInnis, "Childbearing and Land Availability: Some Evidence from Individual Household Data," in Ronald D. Lee, *Population Patterns in the Past* (New York: Academic Press, 1977), 201–27; David P. Gagan, "Land, Population, and Social Change: The 'Critical Years' in Rural Canada West," *Canadian Historical Review*, 59 (September 1978), 293–318.

18. Chester Martin, *'Dominion Lands' Policy* (Toronto: McClelland and Stewart Ltd., 1973), 28.

19. Ibid., x–xi, xxi, 170–71, 233; Gerald Friesen, *The Canadian Prairies: A History* (Lincoln: University of Nebraska Press, 1984), 125–28, 184.

20. Solberg, *The Prairies and the Pampas: Agrarian Policy in Canada and Argentina, 1880–1930*, 228.

21. Ibid., xi–xii, 2.

22. Friesen, 204.

23. Elena Jakesova, "Emigrants from Slovakia—Immigrants to Canada as an Object of Historical Research," in Comité International des Sciences Historiques, 211–16.

24. "Little Shul on the Prairie," *Jerusalem Post* (International Edition), Dec. 21/27, 1980.

25. Donald F. Warner, *The Idea of Continental Union: Agitation for the Annexation of Canada to the United States, 1849–1893* (Lexington: University of Kentucky Press, 1960), 145–48, 161–64.

26. Hansen and Brebner, 200, 230.

27. Ibid., 233; R. Bruce Shepard, "The Origins of the Oklahoma Black Migration to the Canadian Plains," *Canadian Journal of History/Annales Canadiennes d'Histoire*, 23 (April 1988), 1, 10, 22–23.

28. Carrothers, 246; Hansen and Brebner, 227.

29. Friesen, 259–72; Norman Macdonald, *Canada: Immigration and Colonization 1841–1903* (Aberdeen: Aberdeen University Press, 1966), chapter 11. Also, V. J. Kaye, "The Ruthenians," *Canadian Slavonic Papers/Revue Canadienne des Slavistes*, 10 (1986), 97; Mrs. James McDougald, "Cypress Hills Reminiscences," *Saskatchewan History*, 35 (1982), 30; P. L. McCormick, "The Doukhobors in 1904," *Saskatchewan History*, 35 (1982), 12–16; Alexander Royick, "Ukrainian Settlements in Alberta," *Canadian Slavonic Papers/Revue Canadienne des Slavistes*, 10 (1968), 178–79, 283–87; Keith Foster, "The Barr Colonists: Their Arrival and Impact on the Canadian North-west," *Saskatchewan History*, 35 (1982), 81; Betty Ward, "Trek of the Doukhobors," ibid., 17.

30. Hansen and Brebner, 230–31, 242; Carrothers, 254–55.

31. Macdonald, 107, 129, 136, 139–41, 146–48; Hansen and Brebner, 220–21; Gould, 1979, 621.

32. Solberg, 29–30.

33. William H. Katerberg, "Canadian and American Immigration Policy from World War I to the Depression of the 1930s," unpublished seminar paper, Department of History, University of Notre Dame, May 1990, 7, 16, 19.

34. Martin, 226–27, 231.

35. Ibid., 10, 170–71, 241.

36. Friesen, 252, 272, 293–96.

15. United States of America

1. Thistlethwaite, "Migration from Europe Overseas in the Nineteenth and Twentieth Centuries," 34.

2. Josef J. Barton, *Peasants and Strangers: Italians, Rumanians, and Slovaks in an American City* (Cambridge: Harvard University Press, 1975).

3. Bloomington: Indiana University Press, 1985. See also Bodnar's "Immigration,

Kinship, and the Rise of Working-Class Realism in Industrial America," *Journal of Social History,* 20 (Fall 1980), 45–65, in which he first presented the point that ethnic diversity and the multitude of cultural amalgams worked against the development of a militant proletarian consciousness in the United States and instead fostered *embourgeoisement* (46).

4. Rudolph J. Vecoli organized a conference at the University of Minnesota in November 1986, at which Thistlethwaite was present, that helped demolish the curtain; see Rudolph J. Vecoli and Suzanne M. Sinke, eds., *A Century of European Migrations, 1830–1930* (Urbana: University of Illinois Press, 1991).

5. Thomas J. Archdeacon, *Becoming American: An Ethnic History* (New York: The Free Press, 1983); Alan Kraut, *The Huddled Masses: The Immigrant in American Society, 1880–1921* (Arlington Heights, IL: Harlan Davidson, Inc., 1982).

6. Stephan Thernstrom, ed. *Harvard Encyclopedia of American Ethnic Groups* (Cambridge: Belknap Press of Harvard University Press, 1980).

7. Warren S. Thompson and P. K. Whelpton, *Population Trends in the United States* (New York: McGraw-Hill Book Company, 1933), 303. Peak decade, that is, between 1870 and 1920; the 1850s produced the all-time highest rate.

8. Mormino and Pozzetta, *The Immigrant World of Ybor City.* For several dozen vignettes of the experiences of women migrants to the United States, see Maxine Schwartz Seller, ed., *Immigrant Women* (Philadelphia: Temple University Press, 1981).

9. David N. Doyle, *Irish Americans, Native Rights and National Empires: The Structure, Divisions and Attitudes of the Catholic Minority in the Decade of Expansion, 1890–1901* (New York: Arno Press, 1976), 41, 46.

10. Walter Nugent, "The People of the West since 1890," in Gerald D. Nash and Richard W. Etulain, eds., *The Twentieth-Century West: Historical Interpretations* (Albuquerque: University of New Mexico Press, 1989), 44.

11. James R. Shortridge, "The Heart of the Prairie: Culture Areas in the Central and Northern Great Plains," *Great Plains Quarterly,* 8 (Fall 1988), 212–13.

12. Population in 1890 was 191,000; in 1910, 577,000; in 1920, 647,000. Thereafter it was nearly stable and in some decades negative. U.S. Bureau of the Census, *Historical Statistics of the United States,* series A195, I:32.

13. For detailed information on where Slavic migrants went within the United States and what they did, consult Balch, part II, 206–322.

14. Bodnar, 1977, 25.

15. Alexander, 1980.

16. Ibid., 57, 86, 93, and chapter 3 *passim.*

17. Irving Howe, *World of Our Fathers* (New York: Harcourt Brace Jovanovich, 1976), 183–84.

18. United States Consular Reports, *Labor in Europe,* 178–92; Taylor, *Distant Magnet,* 188.

19. Golab, *Immigrant Destinations,* 166.

20. Transpacific migration is outside the scope of this book, but the great bulk of it before 1914, first Chinese and then Japanese, followed by smaller groups of Filipinos and Punjabis, was a wage-labor migration, with an even more male-skewed sex ratio than was true of any European migrant group. For histories with general treatments, see Roger Daniels, *Asian America: Chinese and Japanese in the United States since 1850* (Seattle: University of Washington Press, 1988); and the more popularly written Tricia Knoll, *Becoming Americans: Asian Sojourners, Immigrants, and Refugees in the Western United States* (Portland, OR: Coast to Coast Books, 1982). On the Chinese, see Shih-shan Henry Tsai, *The Chinese Experience in America* (Bloomington: Indiana University Press, 1986); and Sucheng Chan, *This Bitter-Sweet Soil: The Chinese in California Agriculture, 1860–1910* (Berkeley: University of California Press, 1986). On the Japanese, see Yasuo

Wakatsuki, "Japanese Emigration to the United States, 1866–1924: A Monograph," *Perspectives in American History,* 12 (1979), 387–516, and Yuji Ichioka, *The Issei: The World of the First Generation Japanese Immigrants, 1885–1924* (New York: Free Press, 1988). On the Punjabis, see Joan M. Jensen, *Passage from India: Asian Indian Immigrants in North America* (New Haven: Yale University Press, 1988). On the Filipinos and Koreans, see H. Brett Melendy, *Asians in America: Filipinos, Koreans, and East Indians* (Boston: Twayne Publishers, 1977). The early period of Mexican migration to the United States is best described in Lawrence A. Cardoso, *Mexican Emigration to the United States, 1897–1931* (Tucson: University of Arizona Press, 1980).

21. Brinley Thomas, *Migration and Economic Growth: A Study of Great Britain and the Atlantic Economy,* 2d ed. (Cambridge: Cambridge University Press, 1973). James R. Grossman, *Land of Hope: Chicago, Black Southerners and the Great Migration* (Chicago: University of Chicago Press, 1989), is an excellent recent discussion.

22. In *The Transplanted* Bodnar emphasizes the family as a crucial cementing institution among migrants, but devotes less space to how women functioned within families or as independent wage earners; see Bodnar, 1985, 78–82, 91–92.

23. Donna R. Gabaccia, unpublished papers, parts of work in progress; cited with the author's permission.

The absence of women migrants from the preceding discussion of the other three New World receiving countries is the result, not of a lack of good intentions, but of the lack as yet of extensive monographic work on the subject for this period (more has been done for the colonial and early national periods). Asuncion Lavrin and others have begun the study of women in Latin American history, but studies of the length and depth of Gabaccia's and Diner's do not yet exist for that region. The stimulating collection of essays on women as migrants edited by Rita Simon and Caroline Brettell, cited above in the section on migration, should point researchers in fruitful directions although it contains very little directly on the 1870–1914 period.

24. Gabaccia, "Female Migration and Immigrant Sex Ratios, 1820–1928," 1989, 2; Archdeacon, 135–39; Ferenczi and Willcox, eds., *International Migrations,* tables IXa and X, immigrants by sex and nationality, 1871–1914, I:419–39, and table XIX, emigrants by sex and nationality, 1908–14, I:476–79.

25. U.S. *Hist. Stats.,* series D26, I:129.

26. Gabaccia, 1989, 28.

27. Ibid., table 3, for 1908–28.

28. U.S. *Hist. Stats.,* series C297–298, C300–301, I:119.

29. Simon Kuznets and Ernest Rubin, *Immigration and the Foreign-Born* (New York: National Bureau of Economic Research, 1954).

30. Bernard Axelrod, "Historical Studies of Emigration from the United States," *International Migration Review,* 6 (Spring 1972), 32–49; Gould, "Emigration: The Road Home: Return Migration from the U.S.A.," 49; Neil Larry Shumsky, "The Extent and Significance of Return Migration from the United States," in Cazemajou, ed., *L'Immigration Européenne aux États-Unis (1880–1910),* 60–61.

31. Alex Keyssar, *Out of Work: The First Century of Unemployment in Massachusetts* (New York: Cambridge University Press, 1986), 79.

32. Umberto Coletti, "The Italian Immigrant," *Conference of Charities and Correction: Proceedings,* 1912, 249–50.

33. Morrell Heald, "Business Attitudes toward European Immigration, 1880–1900," *Journal of Economic History,* 13 (Summer 1953), 291–304.

34. Lane, *Solidarity or Survival? American Labor and European Immigrants, 1830–1924,* 69–70, 174, 212–14.

35. Richmond Mayo-Smith, review of three books on immigration, *Political Science Quarterly,* 2 (1887), 521.

36. Francis Amasa Walker, "Restriction of Immigration," *Atlantic Monthly,* 77 (June 1896), 828.

37. Ibid., 826.

38. John R. Commons, *Races and Immigrants in America* (New York: Macmillan, 1920 [1907]), 69.

39. Henry Pratt Fairchild, *The Melting-Pot Mistake* (Boston: Little, Brown and Company, 1926), 213.

40. Shumsky, 63.

41. Normand Lafleur, *Les 'Chinois' de l'Est: ou la Vie Quotidienne des Québecois Émigrés aux États-Unis de 1840 à Nos Jours* (Ottawa: Les Éditions Lemeac, 1981), 35.

42. United States, "Abstracts of Reports of the Immigration Commission," Senate Document 747, 61st Congress, 3d Session (Washington: Government Printing Office, 1911), I:179–81; Jeremiah W. Jenks and W. Jett Lauck, *The Immigration Problem: A Study of American Immigration Conditions and Needs* (New York: Funk & Wagnalls, 1922 [5th ed.; first published 1911]), 17, 37–40, 409.

43. Peter Roberts, *The New Immigration: A Study of the Industrial and Social Life of Southeastern Europeans in America* (New York: The Macmillan Company, 1914), 13.

44. Easterlin, "Immigration: Economic and Social Characteristics," 485.

45. Balch, *Our Slavic Fellow Citizens,* 296.

46. Lane, 33.

47. Miriam King and Steven Ruggles, "American Immigration, Fertility, and Race Suicide at the Turn of the Century," *Journal of Interdisciplinary History,* 20 (Winter 1990), 352.

48. An excellent discussion of United States legislation and policy relating to immigration, including the operation of Castle Garden and Ellis Island, is William S. Bernard, "Immigration: History of U.S. Policy," in Thernstrom, ed., *Harvard Encyclopedia of American Ethnic Groups,* 486–95.

49. Tocqueville, *Democracy in America,* ed. J. P. Mayer, trans. George Lawrence (Garden City, NY: Anchor Books, 1969), II:636–38: part III, chapter 21, "Why Great Revolutions Will Become Rare." See also Nugent, "Tocqueville, Marx, and American Class Structure," 327–47.

16. Modernization, Transition, Exceptionalism

1. U.S. *Hist. Stats.,* series K4, I:457.

2. Mitchell, *International Historical Statistics,* series B4, 97–106; Mitchell, *European Historical Statistics,* series B4, 76–78. On the phenomenal growth of Lodz as a textile center, from a village of 2,000 in 1825 and 16,000 in 1850, to a metropolis of over 500,000 in 1913, see Pounds, *Historical Geography of Europe 1800–1914,* 409–13.

3. Anthony Sutcliffe, *Towards the Planned City: Germany, Britain, the United States and France, 1780–1914* (Oxford: Basil Blackwell, 1981), 1–2.

4. Scobie, *Argentina: A City and a Nation,* 112–13, 118–30; Louis Couty, *Le Brésil en 1884* (Rio de Janeiro: Far & Lino, 1884), 152–54.

LIST OF WORKS CITED AND CONSULTED

Part I: The Atlantic Region and Its Population

Arriaga, Eduardo E. *New Life Tables for Latin American Populations in the Nineteenth and Twentieth Centuries*. Berkeley: University of California Population Monograph Series, No. 3, 1968.

Arriaga, Eduardo E. *Mortality Decline and Its Demographic Effects in Latin America*. Berkeley: Institute of International Studies, University of California, 1970.

Aykroyd, W. R., and J. P. Kevany. "Mortality in Infancy and Early Childhood in Ireland, Scotland and England and Wales 1870 to 1970." *Ecology of Food and Nutrition*, 2 (1973), 11–19.

Beaver, Steven E. *Demographic Transition Theory Reinterpreted: An Application to Recent Natality Trends in Latin America*. Lexington, MA: Lexington Books, D. C. Heath and Company, 1975.

Beltrão, Pedro Calderon. *Demografia: Ciencia da População, Analise e Teoria*. Porto Alegre: Libraria Sulina Editora, 1972.

Berend, Ivan T., and György Ranki. *The European Periphery and Industrialization*. Cambridge: Cambridge University Press, and Paris: Editions de la Maison des Sciences de l'Homme, 1982.

Binder, Leonard. "The Natural History of Development Theory." *Comparative Studies in Society and History*, 28 (January 1986), 3–33.

Bonsor, N. R. P. *North Atlantic Seaway: An Illustrated History of the Passenger Services Linking the Old World with the New*. Prescot, Lancashire: T. Stephenson & Sons Ltd., 1955.

Braudel, Fernand. *The Mediterranean and the Mediterranean World in the Age of Philip II*. 2 vols. New York: Harper & Row, 1972.

Brazil. Directoria Geral de Estatistica. *Relatorio e Trabalhos Estatisticos . . .* [Census of 1872]. Rio de Janeiro: Typographia y Lythographia do Movimento, 1872.

Brazil. Ministerio da Industria, Viação e Obras Publicas. Directoria Geral de Estatistica. *Sexo, Raça, e Estado Civil, Nacionalidade, Filiação, Culto, e Analphabetismo de População Recenseada em 31 de Dezembro 1890*. Rio de Janeiro: Officina da Estatistica, 1898.

Brazil. Directoria Geral de Estatistica. *Recenseamento de 31 de Dezembro de 1900. Quadros do Trabalho Preliminar*. Rio de Janeiro: Officina da Estatistica, 1900.

Brazil. Ministerio da Agricultura, Industria e Commercio. Directoria Geral de Estatistica. *Synopse do Recenseamento Realizado em 1 de Setembro 1920. População do Brasil*. Rio de Janeiro: Typographia da Estatistica, 1926.

Brazil. Instituto Brasileiro de Geografia e Estatistica. *Tabuas de Mortalidade e Sobrevivencia Brasileiras. Distrito Federal e Municipio de São Paulo*. Rio de Janeiro: Serviço Grafico do IBGE, 1946.

Brazil. Instituto Brasileiro de Geografia e Estatistica. "Estudos de Estatistica Teorica e Aplicada." *Estatistica Demografica,* 1, 1948.

Brazil. Instituto Brasileiro de Geografia e Estatistica. "Pesquisas Sobre a Natalidade no Brasil." *Estatistica Demografica,* 10, 1950.

Brazil. Instituto Brasileiro de Geografia e Estatistica. "Estudos sobre a Composição da População do Brasil segunda a Côr." *Estatistica Demografica,* 11, 1950.

Brazil. Instituto Brasileiro de Geografia e Estatistica. "Pesquisas sobre o Desinvolvimento da População do Brasil." *Estatistica Demografica,* 13, 1951.

Brazil. Instituto Brasileiro de Geografia e Estatistica. "Analises Criticas de Resultados dos Censos Demograficos." *Estatistica Demografica,* 1956.

Briggs, John W. "Fertility and Cultural Change among Families in Italy and America." *American Historical Review,* 91 (December 1986), 1129–45.

Brown, Richard Maxwell. "The New Regionalism in America, 1970–1981." In William G. Robbins et al., *Regionalism and the Pacific Northwest.* Corvallis: Oregon State University Press, 1983.

Carr-Saunders, A. M. *Population.* New York: Oxford University Press, 1925.

Coale, Ansley J., and Susan Cotts Watkins, eds. *The Decline of Fertility in Europe: The Revised Proceedings of a Conference on the Princeton European Fertility Project.* Princeton: Princeton University Press, 1986.

Coale, Ansley J., and Melvin Zelnik. *New Estimates of Fertility and Population in the United States.* Princeton: Princeton University Press, 1963.

Collver, O. Andrew. *Birth Rates in Latin America: New Estimates of Historical Trends and Fluctuations.* Berkeley: Institute of International Studies, University of California, 1965.

Condran, Gretchen A., and Eileen Crimmins-Gardner. "Public Health Measures and Mortality in U.S. Cities in the Late Nineteenth Century." *Human Ecology,* 6 (1978), 27–54.

Condran, Gretchen A., Henry Williams, and Rose A. Cheney. "The Decline in Mortality in Philadelphia from 1870 to 1930: The Role of Municipal Services." *Pennsylvania Magazine of History and Biography,* 108 (April 1984), 153–77.

Eisenstadt, S. N. "Studies of Modernization and Sociological Theory." *History and Theory,* 13 (1974), 225–52.

Evans, Richard J. *Death in Hamburg: Society and Politics in the Cholera Years, 1830–1910.* Oxford: Clarendon Press, 1987.

Ferenczi, Imre, and Walter F. Willcox, eds. *International Migrations.* 2 vols. New York: National Bureau of Economic Research, 1929, 1931.

Fogel, Robert William. "Nutrition and the Decline in Mortality since 1700: Some Preliminary Findings." In Stanley L. Engerman and Robert E. Gallman, eds., *Long-Term Factors in American Economic Growth.* Chicago: University of Chicago Press, 1986, 439–555.

Fogel, Robert W. "Nutrition and the Decline in Mortality since 1700: Some Additional Preliminary Findings." Working Paper No. 1802. Cambridge, MA: National Bureau of Economic Research, January 1986.

Glass, D. V., and Roger Revelle, eds. *Population and Social Change.* London: Edward Arnold, 1972.

Goodrich, Carter. "Migratory Labor." In E. R. A. Seligman, ed., *Encyclopedia of the Social Sciences.* New York: Macmillan, 1930–1935, XI:441–45.

Gould, J. D. "European Inter-Continental Emigration, 1815–1914: Patterns and Causes." *Journal of European Economic History,* 8 (Winter 1979), 593–679.

Grew, Raymond. "Modernization and Its Discontents." *American Behavioral Scientist,* 21 (November–December 1977), 289–310.

Grigg, D. B. "E. G. Ravenstein and the 'Laws of Migration.'" *Journal of Historical Geography,* 3 (1977), 41–54.

Guillet, Edwin C. *The Great Migration: The Atlantic Crossing by Sailing-ship since 1770.* Toronto: Thomas Nelson and Sons, 1937.

Haines, Michael R. "The Use of Model Life Tables to Estimate Mortality for the United States in the Late Nineteenth Century." *Demography,* 16 (May 1979), 289–312.

Hamburg. Staatsarchiv. Auswandererwesensbehörde. *Auswandererlisten, Direkt und Indirekt,* 1879–1893.

Higgott, Richard A. "From Modernization Theory to Public Policy: Continuity and Change in the Political Science of Political Development." *Studies in Comparative International Development,* 15 (Winter 1980), 26–58.

Hochstadt, Steve. Review of Coale and Watkins, *Decline of Fertility in Europe. American Historical Review,* 95 (February 1990), 152–53.

Hoerder, Dirk, ed. *"Struggle a Hard Battle": Essays on Working-Class Immigrants.* De Kalb: Northern Illinois University Press, 1986.

Hoerder, Dirk. "Migration and the Atlantic Economies: Regional European Origins and Worldwide Expansion." Unpublished paper, Social Science History Association meeting, Chicago, November 1988.

Hoerder, Dirk. "Comment and Debate: John Bodnar's *The Transplanted:* A Roundtable." *Social Science History,* 12 (Fall 1988), 255–63.

Inkeles, Alex, and David Smith. *Becoming Modern: Individual Change in Six Developing Countries.* Cambridge: Harvard University Press, 1974.

Italy. *Dall'Emigrazione dall'Italia comparata con quella che avviene da altri stati d'Europa.* Extract from *Bulletin de l'Institut Internationale de Statistique,* II, 1887 (Rome: Tipografia Eredi Botta, 1887). In *Études historiques à l'occasion du XIe Congrès International des Sciences Historiques* (Stockholm, 1960), 25–162.

Jackson, James H., Jr., and Leslie Page Moch. "Migration and the Social History of Modern Europe." *Historical Methods,* 22 (Winter 1989), 27–36.

Johannsen, Robert W. *The Frontier, the Union, and Stephen A. Douglas.* Urbana: University of Illinois Press, 1989.

Jones, Huw R. *A Population Geography.* New York: Harper & Row, 1981.

Kaa, Dirk J. van de. "Europe's Second Demographic Transition." *Population Bulletin,* 42 (March 1987), 3–57.

Kalbach, Warren E., and Wayne W. McVey. *The Demographic Bases of Canadian Society.* 2d ed. Toronto: McGraw-Hill Ryerson Ltd., 1979.

Kertzer, David I., and Dennis P. Hogan. "Household Organization and Migration in Nineteenth-Century Italy." *Social Science History,* 14 (Winter 1990), 483–505.

Keyfitz, Nathan. "The Growth of Canadian Population." *Population Studies,* 4 (June 1950), 47–63.

Knodel, John E. *The Decline of Fertility in Germany, 1871–1939.* Princeton: Princeton University Press, 1974.

Kramer, Howard D. "The Germ Theory and the Early Public Health Program in the United States." *Bulletin of the History of Medicine,* 22 (1948), 233–47.

Kresse, Walter. *Seeschiffs-Verzeichnis der Hamburger Reedereien.* 3 vols. Hamburg: Museum für Hamburgische Geschichte, 1969.

Kresse, Walter. *Hamburger Seeschiffe 1889–1914: Seeschiffe-Verzeichnis der Hamburger Reedereien.* Hamburg: Museum für Hamburgische Geschichte, 1974.

Kuczynski, Robert R. *The Balance of Births and Deaths.* 2 vols. Washington: The Brookings Institution, 1931.

Lacroix, Max. "Problems of Collection and Comparison of Migration Statistics." In *Problems in the Collection and Comparison of International Statistics.* New York: Milbank Memorial Fund, 1949, 71–105.

Leasure, William. "Factors Involved in the Decline of Fertility in Spain 1900–1950." *Population Studies,* 16 (March 1963), 271–85.

Lee, W. R., ed. *European Demography and Economic Growth.* New York: St. Martin's Press, 1979.

Lockard, Craig A. "Global History, Modernization and the World-System Approach: A Critique." *The History Teacher,* 14 (August 1981), 489–515.

Lowenstein, Wendy, and Morag Loh. *The Immigrants.* Ringwood, Victoria: Penguin Books, 1977.

Macdonald, John S., and Leatrice D. Macdonald. "Chain Migration, Ethnic Neighborhood Formation, and Social Networks." *Milbank Memorial Fund Quarterly,* 42 (January 1964), 82–97.

Marschalck, Peter. *Bevölkerungsgeschichte Deutschlands im 19. und 20. Jahrhundert.* Frankfurt: Suhrkamp, 1984.

Mazrui, Ali A. "From Social Darwinism to Current Theories of Modernization: A Tradition of Analysis." *World Politics,* 21 (October 1968), 69–83.

McKeown, Thomas. "Fertility, Mortality and Causes of Death: An Examination of Issues Related to the Modern Rise of Population." *Population Studies,* 32 (March 1978), 535–42.

McKeown, Thomas, R. G. Brown, and R. G. Record. "An Interpretation of the Modern Rise of Population in Europe." *Population Studies,* 26 (November 1972), 345–82.

McKeown, Thomas, and R. G. Record. "Reasons for the Decline of Mortality in England and Wales during the Nineteenth Century." *Population Studies,* 16 (November 1962), 94–122.

McKeown, Thomas, R. G. Record, and R. D. Turner. "An Interpretation of the Decline of Mortality in England and Wales during the Twentieth Century." *Population Studies,* 29 (November 1975), 391–422.

Meeker, Edward. "The Improving Health of the United States, 1850–1915." *Explorations in Economic History*, 9 (Summer 1972), 353–73.

Meisler, Stanley. "Home to a Smug, Scared America." (Paris) *International Herald Tribune*, June 6, 1989.

Metropolitan Life Insurance Company. "Typhoid Fever in Relation to Filtration and Chlorination of Municipal Water Supplies in American Cities, 1900 to 1924." *Statistical Bulletin*, 8 (March 1927), 5–12.

Miller, Kerby A. *Emigrants and Exiles: Ireland and the Irish Exodus to North America*. New York: Oxford University Press, 1985.

Milward, Alan, and S. B. Saul. *The Economic Development of Continental Europe*. London: George Allen & Unwin Ltd., 1973.

Mitchell, B. R. *European Historical Statistics 1750–1970*. New York: Columbia University Press, 1976.

Mitchell, B. R. *International Historical Statistics: The Americas and Australasia*. Detroit: Gale Research Company, 1983.

Moch, Leslie Page. "Europeans Leave Home: Internal, International, and Transatlantic Migrations in the Nineteenth and Early Twentieth Centuries." Unpublished paper, Social Science History Association meeting, Washington, November 1989.

Mortara, Giorgio. "Tabuas Brasileiras de Mortalidade e Sobrevivencia." *Estudos Brasileiros de Demografia*. Monografia No. 1. Rio de Janeiro: Fundação Getulio Vargas, 1946.

Mortara, Giorgio. "Pesquisas sobre Populações Americanas." *Estudos Brasileiros de Demografia*. Monografia No. 3. Vol. 1. Rio de Janeiro: Fundação Getulio Vargas, 1947.

Mortara, Giorgio. "The Development and Structure of Brazil's Population." *Population Studies*, 8–9 (November 1954), 121–39.

Mortara, Giorgio. *Les Études Démographiques au Brésil*. Rio de Janeiro: Decimalia, 1959.

Mortara, Giorgio. "L'Italia nella Rivoluzione Demografia 1861–1961." Introduction to "Sviluppo della Popolazione Italiana dal 1861 al 1961," *Annali di Statistica*. Serie VIII, vol. 17. Rome: Istituto Centrale di Statistica, 1965.

Nadell, Pamela S. "The Journey to America by Steam: The Jews of Eastern Europe in Transition," *American Jewish History*, 71 (December 1981), 269–84.

Nugent, Walter. *Structures of American Social History*. Bloomington: Indiana University Press, 1981.

Nugent, Walter. "Tocqueville, Marx, and American Class Structure." *Social Science History*, 12 (Winter 1988), 327–47.

Nugent, Walter. "Frontiers and Empires in the Late Nineteenth Century." *Western Historical Quarterly*, 20 (November 1989), 393–408.

Parkerson, Donald H., and Jo Ann Parkerson. "Unresolved Issues in Migration Research: A Re-Examination of Ravenstein's Laws." Unpublished paper, Social Science History Association meeting, Chicago, November 1986.

Population Reference Bureau. *1988 World Population Data Sheet*. Washington: Population Reference Bureau, 1988.

Pounds, Norman J. G. *An Historical Geography of Europe, 1800–1914*. Cambridge: Cambridge University Press, 1985.

Pye, Lucian W. "Political Modernization: Gaps between Theory and Reality." *The Annals,* 442 (March 1979), 28–37.

Ravenstein, E. G. "The Laws of Migration." *Journal of the Royal Statistical Society,* 48 (1885), 167–227, and 52 (1889), 214–301.

Reynolds, Phyllis Allen. "American Attitudes toward the Germ Theory of Disease (1860–1880)." *Journal of the History of Medicine,* 9 (1954), 428–54.

Richards, Toni. "Fertility Decline in Germany: An Econometric Analysis." *Population Studies,* 31 (November 1977), 537–54.

Ridge, Martin. "Ray Allen Billington, Western History, and American Exceptionalism." *Pacific Historical Review,* 56 (November 1987), 495–511.

Robbins, William G. "Western History: A Dialectic on the Modern Condition." *Western Historical Quarterly,* 20 (November 1989), 429–49.

Ross, Dorothy. "The National Ideology of American Exceptionalism." Unpublished paper, Organization of American Historians meeting, St. Louis, April 1989.

Rostow, Walt Whitman. *The Stages of Economic Growth: A Non-Communist Manifesto.* New York: Cambridge University Press, 1959.

Sarna, Jonathan D. "The Myth of No Return: Jewish Return Migration to Eastern Europe, 1881–1914." *American Jewish History,* 71 (December 1981), 256–68.

Saul, S. B. *The Myth of the Great Depression, 1873–1896.* London: Macmillan and Co. Ltd., 1969.

Schapiro, Morton Owen. *Filling Up America: An Economic-Demographic Model of Population Growth and Distribution in the Nineteenth-Century United States.* Greenwich, CT: JAO Press Inc., 1986.

Simon, Rita James, and Caroline B. Brettell. "Immigrant Women: An Introduction." In Simon and Brettell, eds., *International Migration: The Female Experience.* Totowa, NJ: Rowman & Allenheld, 1986, 3–20.

Smith, D. S. "Differential Mortality in the United States before 1900." *Journal of Interdisciplinary History,* 13 (Spring 1983), 735–60.

Somoza, Jorge L. *Nivel y Diferenciales de la Fecundidad en la Argentina en el Siglo XIX.* Buenos Aires: Publicación de la Serie Población y Sociedad, nr. 45, 1967.

Somoza, Jorge L., and Alfredo E. Lattes. *Muestras de los Dos Primeros Censos Nacionales de Población, 1869 y 1895.* Buenos Aires: Instituto Torcuato de Tella, 1967.

Stolnitz, George J. "A Century of International Mortality Trends: I." *Population Studies,* 9 (July 1955), 24–55.

Stolnitz, George J. "A Century of International Mortality Trends: II." *Population Studies,* 10 (July 1956), 17–42.

Stone, May N. "The Plumbing Paradox: American Attitudes toward Late Nineteenth-Century Domestic Sanitary Arrangements." *Winterthur Portfolio,* 14 (Autumn 1979), 283–309.

Taylor, Philip A. M. *The Distant Magnet.* New York: Harper & Row, 1971.

Teitelbaum, M. S. "Relevance of Demographic Transition Theory for Developing Countries." *Science,* 188 (May 2, 1975), 420–25.

Teitelbaum, Michael S. *The Decline in Fertility in Great Britain*. Cambridge: Cambridge University Press, 1984.

Thistlethwaite, Frank. "Migration from Europe Overseas in the Nineteenth and Twentieth Centuries." In Comité International des Sciences Historiques, XIᵉ Congrès International des Sciences Historiques, Stockholm, 21–28 Août 1960, *Rapports: V: Histoire Contemporaine*. Göteborg-Stockholm-Uppsala: Almquist & Wiksell, 1960, 32–60.

Tilly, Charles. "Migration in Modern European History." In William H. McNeill and Ruth S. Adams, eds., *Human Migration*. Bloomington: Indiana University Press, 1978, 48–72.

Tilly, Charles. *As Sociology Meets History*. New York: Academic Press, 1981.

Tipps, Dean C. "Modernization Theory and the Study of National Societies: A Critical Perspective." *Comparative Studies in Society and History*, 15 (March 1973), 199–226.

Tizzano, Antonio. "Mortalità Generale." Chapter 7 in "Sviluppo della Populazione Italiana, dal 1861 al 1961," *Annali di Statistica*. Serie VIII, vol. 17. Rome: Istituto Centrale di Statistica, 1965.

Turner, Frederick Jackson. "The Significance of the Frontier in American History." In *Annual Report of the American Historical Association for the Year 1893*. Washington: Government Printing Office, 1894, 197–227.

Tyler, David Budlong. *Steam Conquers the Atlantic*. New York: D. Appleton-Century, 1939.

Tyree, Andrea, and Katherine Donato. "A Demographic Overview of the International Migration of Women." In Simon and Brettell, eds., (*q.v.*), 21–41.

United Nations. Department of Social Affairs, Population Division. *The Determinants and Consequences of Population Trends*. New York: United Nations, 1953.

United States. Bureau of the Census. *Historical Statistics of the United States, Colonial Times to 1970*. 2 vols. Washington: Government Printing Office, 1975.

Van Nort, Leighton, and Bertram P. Karon. "Demographic Transition Re-examined." *American Sociological Review*, 20 (October 1955), 523–27.

Walle, Etienne van de, and John Knodel. "Demographic Transition and Fertility Decline: The European Case." In International Union for the Scientific Study of Population [IUSSP], *Contributed Papers: Sydney Conference Australia, 21 to 25 August 1967*, n.d., 47–55.

Wallerstein, Immanuel. "The Rise and Future Demise of the World Capitalist System: Concepts for Comparative Analysis." *Comparative Studies in Society and History*, 20 (September 1974), 387–415.

Wallerstein, Immanuel. *The Modern World-System*. 3 vols. New York: Academic Press, 1974, 1980, 1989.

Ware, Caroline F. "Emigration." In E. R. A. Seligman, *Encyclopedia of the Social Sciences*. New York: Macmillan, 1931, V:488–92.

Ware, Caroline F. "Immigration." In E. R. A. Seligman, *Encyclopedia of the Social Sciences*. New York: Macmillan, 1931, VII:587–94.

Warren, Frank A. Review of Jean Heffer and Jeanine Rovet, eds., *Why Is There No Socialism in the United States? Journal of American History,* 76 (June 1989), 231–32.

Weber, Eugen. *Peasants into Frenchmen: The Modernization of Rural France, 1870–1914.* Stanford: Stanford University Press, 1976.

White, Dan S. "Political Loyalties and Economic Depression in Britain, France and Germany, 1873–1896," unpublished paper, American Historical Association meeting, New York, December 1979.

White, Donald W. "History and American Internationalism: The Formulation from the Past after World War II." *Pacific Historical Review,* 58 (May 1989), 145–72.

Wilentz, Sean. "Against Exceptionalism: Class Consciousness and the American Labor Movement." *International Labor and Working Class History,* no. 26 (Fall 1984), 1–24.

Winkler, Karen J. "Historians Debate the Uniqueness of America." *Chronicle of Higher Education,* April 19, 1989.

Wrigley, E. A., and R. S. Schofield. *The Population History of England, 1541–1971.* Cambridge: Harvard University Press, 1981.

Zelinsky, Wilbur. "The Hypothesis of the Mobility Transition." *Geographical Review,* 61 (April 1971), 219–49.

Zolberg, Aristide. "Conclusion: How Many Exceptionalisms?" In Ira Katznelson and Aristide Zolberg, *Working-Class Formation.* Princeton: Princeton University Press, 1986, 397–455.

Zubrzycki, J. "Emigration from Poland in the Nineteenth and Twentieth Centuries." *Population Studies,* 6–7 (March 1953), 248–72.

Part II: The European Donors

Abel, Wilhelm. *Agricultural Fluctuations in Europe, from the Thirteenth to the Twentieth Centuries.* Trans. Olive Ordish. Foreword and bibliography by Joan Thirsk. New York: St. Martin's Press, (1966).

Alexander, June Granatir. "The Immigrant Church and Community: The Formation of Pittsburgh's Slovak Religious Institutions, 1880–1914." Ph.D. diss., University of Minnesota, 1980.

Alexander, June Granatir. *The Immigrant Church and Community: Pittsburgh's Slovak Catholics and Lutherans.* Pittsburgh: University of Pittsburgh Press, 1987.

Bade, Klaus J. "German Emigration to the United States and Continental Immigration to Germany in the Late 19th and Early 20th Centuries." *Central European History,* 13 (1980), 348–77.

Bade, Klaus J. *Vom Auswanderungsland zum Einwanderungsland? Deutschland 1880–1980.* Berlin: Colloquium, 1983.

Bade, Klaus J. "Labour, Migration, and the State." In Bade, ed., *Population, Labour and Migration in 19th- and 20th-Century Germany.* Leamington Spa, Hamburg, and New York: Berg Publishers, 1987.

Baines, Dudley. *Migration in a Mature Economy: Emigration and Internal Migration in England and Wales, 1861–1900.* Cambridge: Cambridge University Press, 1985.

Balch, Emily Greene. *Our Slavic Fellow Citizens*. New York: Charities Publication Committee, 1910.

Barkai, Abraham. "German-Jewish Migration in the Nineteenth Century, 1830–1910." In Glazier and De Rosa, eds., (*q.v.*), 202–19.

Bell, Rudolph M. *Fate and Honor, Family and Village: Demographic and Cultural Change in Rural Italy since 1800*. Chicago: University of Chicago Press, 1979.

Berend, Ivan T., and György Ranki. *Economic Development in East-Central Europe in the 19th and 20th Centuries*. New York: Columbia University Press, 1974.

Berend, Ivan T., and György Ranki. *East Central Europe in the Nineteenth and Twentieth Centuries*. Budapest: Akademiai Kiado, 1977.

Bobinska, Celina, and Andrzej Pilch, eds. *Employment-Seeking Emigrations of the Poles World-Wide XIX and XX C.* (Kraków): Panstwowe Wydawnictwo Naukowe, 1975.

Bowman, Shearer Davis. "Antebellum Planters and *Vormärz* Junkers in Comparative Perspective." *American Historical Review*, 85 (October 1980), 779–808.

Brettell, Caroline B. *Men Who Migrate, Women Who Wait: Population and History in a Portuguese Parish*. Princeton: Princeton University Press, 1986.

Briani, Vittorio. *L'Emigrazione Italiana Ieri e Oggi*. Detroit: Blaine Ethridge Books, 1979 (Rome, 1967).

Briggs, John W. *An Italian Passage: Immigrants to Three American Cities, 1890–1930*. New Haven: Yale University Press, 1978.

Burgdörfer, Friedrich. "Die Wanderungen über die deutschen Reichsgrenzen im letzten Jahrhundert." *Allgemeinisches Statistisches Archiv*. Jena: Verlag von Gustav Fischer, 20 (1930), 161–96, 383–419, 537–51.

Caroli, Betty Boyd. *Italian Repatriation from the United States, 1900–1914*. New York: Center for Migration Studies, 1973.

Carrier, N. H., and J. R. Jeffery. *External Migration: A Study of the Available Statistics, 1815–1950*. London: Her Majesty's Stationery Office, 1953.

Carrothers, W. A. *Emigration from the British Isles: With Special Reference to the Development of the Overseas Dominions*. London: Frank Cass & Co. Ltd., 1965 (1929).

Cazemajou, Jean, ed. *L'Immigration Européenne aux États-Unis (1880–1910)*. Bordeaux: Presses Universitaires de Bordeaux, 1986.

Cinel, Dino. *From Italy to San Francisco*. Stanford: Stanford University Press, 1982.

Cinel, Dino. "The Social Background of the Southern Italian Families at the Time of Mass Emigration." Unpublished paper, Stanford University, June 1985.

Ciuffoletti, Zeffiro, and Maurizio Degl'Innocenti. *L'Emigrazione nella Storia d'Italia 1868–1975: Storia e Documenti*. Florence: Vellecchi Editore, 1978.

Cizmic, Ivan. "Emigration from Yugoslavia prior to World War II." In Glazier and De Rosa, eds., (*q.v.*), 255–63.

Coleman, Terry. *Going to America*. New York: Pantheon Books, 1972.

Conrad, Robert. *The Destruction of Brazilian Slavery, 1850–1888*. Berkeley: University of California Press, 1972.

Cousens, S. H. "Population Trends in Ireland at the Beginning of the Twentieth Century." *Irish Geography,* 5 (1968), 387–401.

DiComiti, Luigi. "Aspects of Italian Emigration, 1881–1915." In Glazier and De Rosa, eds., (*q.v.*).

DiComiti, Luigi, and Ira A. Glazier. "Socio-demographic Characteristics of Italian Emigration to the United States from Ship Passenger Lists: 1880–1914." *Ethnic Forum: Journal of Ethnic Studies and Ethnic Bibliography,* 4 (Spring 1984), 78–90.

Diner, Hasia. *Erin's Daughters in America: Irish Immigrant Women in the Nineteenth Century.* Baltimore: Johns Hopkins University Press, 1983.

Dore, Grazia. "Some Social and Historical Aspects of Italian Emigration to America." *Journal of Social History,* 2 (Winter 1968), 95–122.

Drage, Geoffrey. *Austria-Hungary,* 1909. In Erickson, ed., (*q.v.*), 81–89.

Drewniak, Boguslaw. *Emigracja z Pomorza Zachodniego 1816–1914.* Poznań: Wydawnictwo Poznańskie, 1966.

Erickson, Charlotte J. "Who Were the English and Scots Immigrants to the United States in the Late Nineteenth Century?" In Glass and Revelle, eds., (*q.v.*).

Erickson, Charlotte J. "Emigration from the British Isles to the U.S.A. in 1841: Part I. Emigration from the British Isles." *Population Studies,* 43 (November 1989), 347–67.

Erickson, Charlotte J., ed. *Emigration from Europe, 1815–1914: Select Documents.* London: Adam & Charles Black, 1976.

Favero, Luigi, and Graziano Tassello, "Cent'anni di Emigrazione Italiana (1876–1976)." In Gianfausto Rosoli, ed., *Un Secolo di Emigrazione Italiana 1876–1976.* Rome: Centro Studi Emigrazione, 1978, 9–64.

Fitzpatrick, David. "The Modernisation of the Irish Female." In Patrick O'Flanagan, Paul Ferguson, and Kevin Whelan, eds., *Rural Ireland, 1600–1900: Modernisation and Change.* Cork: Cork University Press, 1987, 162–80.

Flinn, Michael, Judith Gillespie, Nancy Hill, Ailsa Maxwell, Rosalind Mitchison, and Christopher Smout, *Scottish Population History from the 17th Century to the 1930s.* Cambridge: Cambridge University Press, 1977.

Foerster, Robert F. *The Italian Emigration of Our Times.* Cambridge: Harvard University Press, 1924 (1919).

Frankel, Jonathan D. "The Crisis of 1881–82 as a Turning Point in Modern Jewish History." In David Berger, ed., *The Legacy of Jewish Migration: 1881 and Its Impact.* New York: Social Science Monographs—Brooklyn College Press, 1983, 9–22.

Gabaccia, Donna R. *From Sicily to Elizabeth Street: Housing and Social Change among Italian Immigrants, 1880–1930.* Albany: State University of New York Press, 1984.

Gabaccia, Donna R. *Militants and Migrants: Rural Sicilians Become American Workers.* New Brunswick: Rutgers University Press, 1988.

Gabaccia, Donna R. "Female Migration and Immigrant Sex Ratios, 1820–1928." Unpublished paper, Social Science History Association meeting, Washington, November 1989.

Galos, Adam, and Kazimierz Wajda, "Migrations in the Polish Western Territories Annexed by Prussia (1815–1914)." In Bobinska and Pilch, eds., (*q.v.*), 53–76.

Galway City, Ireland. *Connacht Tribune,* June 16, 1989.

Garcia-Lombardero, Jaime. "Economic Transformations in Galicia in the Nineteenth and Twentieth Centuries." In Sanchez-Albornoz, ed., (*q.v.*), 223–39.

Germany. Kaiserlichen Statistischen Amt. *Annalen des Deutschen Reiches,* 1883–1888.

Germany. Kaiserlichen Statistischen Amt. *Handbuch für das Deutsche Reich.* Berlin: Carl Heymanns Verlag, 1882, 1883.

Germany. Kaiserlichen Statistischen Amt. *Monatschefte zur Statistik des deutschen Reichs,* 1885.

Germany. Kaiserlichen Statistischen Amt. *Statistik des deutschen Reiches: Stand und Bewegung der Bevölkerung des deutschen Reichs und fremder Staaten in den Jahren 1841 bis 1886.* Berlin: Puttkammer und Muhlbrecht, 1892.

Germany. *Reichsgesetzblatt.* Berlin: Kaiserlichen Post-Zeitungs-Amt, 1878–1897.

Gjerde, Jon. *From Peasants to Farmers: The Migration from Balestrand, Norway, to the Upper Middle West.* New York: Cambridge University Press, 1985.

Glazier, Ira A. "Ships and Passengers in Emigration from Italy to the United States, 1880–1900." In Miodunka and Brozek, eds., (*q.v.*), 245–75. Also in Ragosta, ed., (*q.v.*), 1097–1124.

Glazier, Ira, and Luigi De Rosa, eds. *Migration across Time and Nations: Population Mobility in Historical Contexts.* New York: Holmes & Meier, 1986.

Glettner, Monika. *Pittsburgh-Wien-Budapest. Programm und Praxis der Nationalitätenpolitik bei der Auswanderung der ungarischen Slowaken nach Amerika um 1900.* Vienna: Verlag der österreichischen Akademie, 1980.

Golab, Caroline. *Immigrant Destinations.* Philadelphia: Temple University Press, 1978.

Gonnard, René. *L'Émigration Européenne au XIXᵉ Siècle.* Paris: Librairie Armand Colin, 1906.

Gordon, Maj. W. Evans. "Report." In *Royal Commission on Alien Immigration,* 1903. In Erickson, ed., (*q.v.*), 108.

Gould, J. D. "European Inter-Continental Emigration: The Road Home: Return Migration from the U.S.A." *Journal of European Economic History,* 9 (Spring 1980), 41–112.

Groniowski, Krzysztof. *Polska Emigracja Zarobkowa w Brazylii, 1871–1914.* Wroclaw: Ossolineum, 1972.

Groniowski, Krzysztof. "Polonia w Stanach Zjednoczonych u Schylku XIX w. Pozycja Spoleczna i Postawy Polityczne." *Przeglad Polonijny,* 2 (1976), 5–20.

Groniowski, Krzysztof. "Historia Polskiej Emigracji do Ameryki Lacinskiej (do 1914r.)." In Zbigniew Dobosiewicz and Waldemar Rommel, eds., *Polonia w Ameryca Lacienskiej* (Lublin: Wydawnictwo Lubielski, 1977), 16–21.

Hamburg. Staatsarchiv. Auswandererwesensbehörde. "Gesetze, Verordnungen u.s.w., betr. die Rückwanderung"; "Überwachung des Rückwanderervekehrs über Hamburg durch die Behörde für das Auswandererwesen bis zw. den Jahren 1902/03."

Hamburg. Staatsarchiv. Auswanderer-Deputation. *Jahrbuch.* 1878–1893.

Haufe, Helmut. *Die Bevölkerung Europas: Stadt und Land im 19. und 20. Jahrhundert.* Berlin: Junker und Dunnhaupt Verlag, 1936.

Hersch, Liebmann. "International Migration of the Jews." In Ferenczi and Willcox, eds., (*q.v.*), II:471–520.

Hochstadt, Steve. "Migration and Industrialization in Germany, 1815–1977." *Social Science History,* 5 (Fall 1981), 445–68.

Hoerder, Dirk, ed. *Plutokraten und Sozialisten: Berichte deutscher Diplomaten und Agenten über die amerikanische Arbeiterbewegung 1878–1917.* Munich: Sauer, 1981.

Hoerder, Dirk, ed. *Labor Migration in the Atlantic Economies: The European and North American Working Classes during the Period of Industrialization.* Westport, CT: Greenwood Press, 1985.

Holmes, Colin. *John Bull's Island: Immigration and British Society, 1871–1971.* Basingstoke: Macmillan Education Ltd, 1988.

Holmes, Douglas R., and Jean H. Quataert. "An Approach to Modern Labor: Worker Peasantries in Historic Saxony and the Friuli Region over Three Centuries." *Comparative Studies in Society and History,* 28 (1986), 191–216.

Hvidt, Kristian. *Flight to America: The Social Background of 300,000 Danish Emigrants.* New York: Academic Press, 1975.

Italy. Giunta per l'Inchiesta Agraria e sulle Condizioni della Classe Agricola. *Atti.* 22 vols. Rome: Forzani e C., Tipografi del Senato, 1881–1886.

Janowska, Halina. "An Introductory Outline of the Mass Polish Emigrations, Their Directions and Problems, 1870–1945." In Bobinska and Pilch, eds., (*q.v.*), 121–44.

Kamphoefner, Walter D. "Transplanted Westfalians." Ph.D. diss., University of Missouri, 1978.

Kamphoefner, Walter D. *The Westfalians: From Germany to Missouri.* Princeton: Princeton University Press, 1987.

Keep, G. R. C. "Irish Migration to North America in the Second Half of the Nineteenth Century." Ph.D. diss., University of Dublin, 1951.

Kennedy, Robert E., Jr. *The Irish: Emigration, Marriage, and Fertility.* Berkeley: University of California Press, 1971.

Kertzer, David. *Family Life in Central Italy 1880–1910: Sharecropping, Wage Labor, and Coresidence.* New Brunswick: Rutgers University Press, 1984.

Kieniewicz, Stefan. *The Emancipation of the Polish Peasantry.* Chicago: University of Chicago Press, 1969.

Klarner, Izabela. *Emigracja z Królestwa Polskiego do Brazylii, 1890–1914.* Warsaw: Książka i Wiedza, 1975.

Klezl, Felix. "Austria." In Ferenczi and Willcox, eds., (*q.v.*), II:390–410.

Köllmann, Wolfgang, and Peter Marschalck, eds. *Bevölkerungsgeschichte.* Cologne: Kiepenheuer & Witsch, 1972.

Köllmann, Wolfgang, and Peter Marschalck. "German Emigration to the United States." *Perspectives in American History,* 7 (1973), 499–554.

Kuczynski, Robert. *Der Zug nach der Stadt. Statistiche Studien über Vorgange der*

Bevölkerungsbewegung in Deutschen Reiche. Stuttgart: Verlag der J. G. Cotta'schen Buchhandlung, 1897.

Kuznets, Simon. "Immigration of Russian Jews to the United States: Background and Structure." *Perspectives in American History*, 9 (1975), 35–124.

Langewiesche, Dieter. "Wanderungsbewegungen in der Hochindustrialisierungsperiode: Regionale, interstädtische und innerstädtische Mobilität in Deutschland 1880–1914." *Vierteljahrschrift für Sozial- und Wirtschaftsgeschichte*, 64 (1977), 1–40.

Lee, W. R. *European Demography and Economic Growth*. New York: St. Martin's Press, 1979.

Lees, Andrew. "Debates about the Big City in Germany, 1890–1914." *Societas*, 5 (1975), 31–47.

Leixner, Otto von. *Soziale Briefe aus Berlin* (Berlin, 1891). In Ritter and Kocka, eds., (*q.v.*), 276–78.

Livi-Bacci, Massimo. *L'Immigrazione e L'Assimilazione degli Italiani negli Stati Uniti, secondo le statistiche demografiche Americane*. Milan: Dott. L. Giuffre Editori, 1961.

Livi-Bacci, Massimo. *A History of Italian Fertility during the Last Two Centuries*. Princeton: Princeton University Press, 1977.

Long, James W. *From Privileged to Dispossessed: The Volga Germans, 1860–1917*. Lincoln: University of Nebraska Press, 1988.

Lopez Taboada, Xose Antonio. *Economia e Población en Galicia*. La Coruña: Edicions do Rueiro, 1979.

MacDonagh, Oliver. *Emigration in the Victorian Age: Debates on the Issue from Nineteenth Century Critical Journals*. Westmead, Hants: Gregg International Publishers Ltd., 1973.

MacDonagh, Oliver. "Irish Emigration to the United States of America and the British Colonies during the Famine." In R. Dudley Edwards and T. Desmond Williams, eds., *The Great Famine: Studies in Irish History 1845–52*. New York: Russell & Russell, 1976 (1957), 319–88.

Martellone, Anna Maria. "Italian Mass Emigration to the United States, 1876–1930: A Historical Survey." *Perspectives in American History*, new series, 1 (1984), 379–423.

Miller, Kerby, with Bruce Boling and David N. Doyle. "Emigrants and Exiles: Irish Cultures and Irish Emigration to North America 1790–1922." *Irish Historical Studies*, 22 (September 1980), 97–125.

Milward, Alan S., and S. B. Saul. *The Development of the Economies of Continental Europe, 1850–1914*. Cambridge: Harvard University Press, 1977.

Miodunka, Wladyslaw, and Andrzej Brozek, eds. *Emigration from Northern, Central, and Southern Europe: Theoretical and Methodological Principles of Research. International Symposium, Kraków, November 9–11, 1981*. Kraków: Nakładem Uniwersytetu Jagiellońskiego, 1984.

Moltmann, Günter. "American-German Return Migration in the Nineteenth and Early Twentieth Centuries." *Central European History*, 13 (1980), 278–392.

Moltmann, Günter. "The Pattern of German Emigration to the United States in the Nineteenth Century." In Frank Trommler and Joseph McVeigh, eds., *America and the*

Germans: An Assessment of a Three-Hundred-Year History. Philadelphia: University of Pennsylvania Press, 1983, 14–24.

Moltmann, Günter. "Steamship Transport of Emigrants from Europe to the United States, 1850–1914: Social, Commercial and Legislative Aspects." In Klaus Friedland, ed., *Maritime Aspects of Migration*. Cologne and Vienna: Bohlau Verlag, 1989, 309–20.

Mönckmeier, Wilhelm. *Die deutsche Überseeauswanderung*. Jena: Verlag von Gustav Fischer, 1912.

Moore, Wilbert E. *Economic Demography of Eastern and Southern Europe*. Geneva: League of Nations, 1945.

Morawska, Ewa. "Motyw Awansu w Systemie Wartości Polskich Imigrantów w Stanach Zjednoczonych na Przelomie Wieku." *Przegląd Polonijny*, 4 (1978), 55–70.

Moraskwa, Ewa. " 'For Bread with Butter': Life-Worlds of Peasant Immigrants from East Central Europe, 1880–1914." *Journal of Social History*, 17 (Spring 1984), 387–404.

Morawska, Ewa. "Labor Migrations of Poles in the Atlantic World-Economy, 1880–1914." *Comparative Studies in Society and History*, 31 (April 1989), 237–72.

Mormino, Gary R., and George E. Pozzetta. *The Immigrant World of Ybor City: Italians and Their Latin Neighbors in Tampa, 1885–1985*. Urbana: University of Illinois Press, 1987.

Mörner, Magnus (with the collaboration of Harold Sims). *Adventurers and Proletarians: The Story of Migrants in Latin America*. Paris: UNESCO, and Pittsburgh: University of Pittsburgh Press, 1985.

Nadal, Jordi. *La Población Española (Siglos XVI a XX)*. Barcelona: Editorial Ariel, Esplugues de Llobregat, 1973.

Neal, Larry, and Paul Uselding. "Immigration, a Neglected Source of American Economic Growth, 1790–1912." *Oxford Economic Papers*, 24 (March 1972), 68–88.

Norman, Hans, and Harald Runblom. *Transatlantic Connections: Nordic Migration to the New World after 1800*. Oslo: Norwegian University Press (Universitetsforlaget AS), (1988).

O'Gráda, Cormac. "A Note on Nineteenth-Century Irish Emigration Statistics." *Population Studies*, 29 (March 1975), 143–49.

O'Gráda, Cormac. "Some Aspects of Nineteenth-Century Irish Emigration." In L. M. Cullen and T. C. Smout, eds., *Comparative Aspects of Scottish and Irish Economic and Social History, 1600–1900*. Edinburgh: John Donald Publishers, Ltd., (1977), 65–73.

O'Gráda, Cormac. "Demographic Adjustment and Seasonal Migration in Nineteenth-Century Ireland." In Louis M. Cullen and François Furet, eds., *Irlande et France XVIIe–XXe Siècles: Pour une Histoire Rurale Comparée. Actes du Premier Colloque Franco-Irlandais d'Histoire Économique et Social—Dublin*. Paris: Éditions de l'École des Hautes Études en Sciences Sociales, 1980, 181–93.

Okolowicz, Jozef. *Wychodztwo i Osadnictwo Polski, przed Wojna Swiatowa*. Warsaw: Sklad Głowny w Księgarni Gebethner i Wolff, 1920.

Ostergren, Robert C. "Swedish Migration to North America in Transatlantic Perspective." In Glazier and De Rosa, eds., (*q.v.*), 125–47.

Ostergren, Robert C. *A Community Transplanted: The Trans-Atlantic Experience of a Swedish Immigrant Settlement in the Upper Middle West, 1835–1915.* Madison: University of Wisconsin Press, 1988.

Ottmüller-Wetzel, Birgit. *Auswanderung über Hamburg: Die H.A.P.A.G. und die Auswanderung nach Nordamerika, 1870–1914.* Ph.D. diss. Freie Universität Berlin, 1986.

Perez Moreda, Vicente. "Spain's Demographic Modernization, 1800–1930." In Sanchez-Albornoz, ed., (*q.v.*), 13–41.

Philippovich, Eugen von. "Auswanderung und Auswanderungspolitik in Deutschland." *Schriften des Vereins fur Socialpolitik,* 52 (1892).

Pilch, Andrzej. "Migracja Zarobkowa z Galicji w XIX i XX Wieku (do 1918 roku)." *Przeglad Polonijny,* 1 (1975), 5–15.

Puśkaś, Julianna. "The Process of Overseas Migration from East-Central Europe: Its Periods, Cycles, and Characteristics: A Comparative Study." In Miodunka and Brozek, eds., (*q.v.*), 33–53.

Puśkaś, Julianna. "Hungarian Migration Patterns, 1880–1930: From Macroanalysis to Microanalysis." In Glazier and De Rosa, eds., (*q.v.*), 231–54.

Ragosta, Rosalba, ed. *Le Genti del Mare Mediterraneo.* Naples: Lucio Pironti Editore, (1981).

Rehbein, Franz. *Das Leben eines Landarbeiters* (Jena, 1911). In Ritter and Kocka, eds., (*q.v.*), 212–15.

Ritter, Gerhard A., and Jurgen Kocka, eds. *Deutsche Sozialgeschichte: Dokumente und Skizzen.* Vol. 2, 1870–1914. Munich: Verlag C. H. Beck, 1974.

Rogmann, H. *Die Bevölkerungsentwicklung im Preussischen Osten in den Letzen Hundert Jahren.* Berlin, 1937.

Rosoli, Gianfausto, ed. *Un Secolo di Emigrazione Italiana 1876–1976.* Rome: Centro Studi Emigrazione, 1978.

Ruggiero, Kristin. "Social and Psychological Factors in Migration from Italy to Argentina: From the Waldensian Valleys to San Gustavo." In Glazier and De Rosa, eds., (*q.v.*), 160–73.

Runblom, Harald, and Hans Norman, eds. *From Sweden to America: A History of the Migration.* Minneapolis: University of Minnesota Press, and Uppsala: Acta Universitatis Upsaliensis, 1976.

Sanchez-Albornoz, Nicolas, ed. *The Economic Modernization of Spain, 1830–1930.* Trans. Karen Powers and Manuel Sanudo. New York: New York University Press, 1987.

Sandis, Eva E. "Immigration to the United States from Austria-Hungary 1880–1910: Economic and Nationality Issues." In Jean Cazemajou, ed., (*q.v.*), 111–22.

Sartorius von Waltershausen, August. *Die Italienischen Wanderarbeiter.* Leipsig: Verlag von C. L. Hirschfeld, 1903.

Schmitter, Barbara. "Sending States and Immigrant Minorities—The Case of Italy." *Comparative Studies in Society and History,* 26 (1984), 325–34.

Schofer, Lawrence. *The Formation of a Modern Labor Force: Upper Silesia, 1865–1914.* Berkeley: University of California Press, 1975.

Schrier, Arnold. *Ireland and the American Emigration, 1850–1900*. Minneapolis: University of Minnesota Press, 1958.

Semmingsen, Ingrid. *Norway to America: A History of the Migration*. Minneapolis: University of Minnesota Press, 1978.

Serrão, Joel. *Emigração Portuguesa: Sondagem Historica*. Lisbon: Livros Horizonte, 1974

Silva, Fernando Emygdio da. *Emigração Portuguesa*. Coimbra: Franca & Armenio; 1917

Sklar, June L. "The Role of Marriage Behaviour in the Demographic Transition: Th Case of Eastern Europe around 1900." *Population Studies,* 28 (July 1974), 231–47.

Spain. Consejo Superior de Emigración. *La Emigración Española Transoceánica 1911 1915*. Madrid: Hijos de T. Minuesa de los Rios, 1916.

Stampfer, Shaul. "The Geographic Background of East European Jewish Migration to the United States before World War I." In Glazier and De Rosa, eds., (*q.v.*), 220–30.

Stankiewicz, Zbigniew. "The Economic Emigration from the Kingdom of Poland Portrayed on the European Background." In Bobinska and Pilch, eds., (*q.v.*).

Stasik, Florian. *Polska Emigracja Zarobkowa w Stanach Zjednoczonych Ameryki 1865–1914*. Warsaw: Państwowe Wydawnictwo Naukowe, 1985.

Swierenga, Robert P. "Dutch Immigration in the Nineteenth Century, 1820–1877: A Quantitative Overview." *Indiana Social Studies Quarterly,* 28 (Autumn 1975), 7–34.

Swierenga, Robert P. "Dutch Immigrant Demography, 1820–1880." *Journal of Family History,* 5 (Winter 1980), 390–405.

Swierenga, Robert P. "Dutch International Migration Statistics, 1820–1880: An Analysis of Linked Multinational Nominal Files." *International Migration Review,* 15 (Fall 1981), 445–68.

Tartakower, Arie. *Emigracja Żydówska z Polski*. Warsaw: Instytut Badan Spraw Narodow-Ośćiowych, 1939.

Thirring, Gustav. "Hungarian Migration of Modern Times." In Ferenczi and Willcox, eds., (*q.v.*), II:411–39.

United States. Consular Reports. *Labor in Europe*. House Executive Document 54, Parts 1 and 3. 48th Congress, 2d Session. Washington: Government Printing Office, 1885.

United States. Consular Reports. *Emigration and Immigration*. House Executive Document 157. 49th Congress, 2d Session. Washington: Government Printing Office, 1887.

Van de Walle, Etienne. *The Female Population of France in the Nineteenth Century*. Princeton: Princeton University Press, 1974.

Vaughan, W. E., and A. J. Fitzpatrick. *Irish Historical Statistics: Population, 1821–1971*. Dublin: Royal Irish Academy, 1978.

Vecoli, Rudolph J. "*Contadini* in Chicago: A Critique of *The Uprooted*." *Journal of American History,* 51 (December 1964), 404–17.

Wade, Joseph. Interview in Arnold Schrier, "Survey of Returned Migrants." Vol. 1408 (1955). Archives of Irish Folklore, University College Dublin.

Walker, Mack. *Germany and the Emigration 1816–1885*. Cambridge: Harvard University Press, 1964.

Weber, Max. *Die Verhältnisse der Landarbeiter im ostelbischen Deutschland*. Berlin: Duncker & Humblot, 1892.

Part III: The American Receivers

Amado, Janaina. *Conflito Social no Brasil: A Revolta dos 'Mucker,' Rio Grande do Sul 1868–1898*. São Paulo: Edições Simbolo, 1978.

Andrews, Christopher Columbus. *Brazil, Its Condition and Prospects*. 3d ed. New York: D. Appleton and Company, 1891.

Archdeacon, Thomas J. *Becoming American: An Ethnic History*. New York: The Free Press, 1983.

Archetti, Eduardo. "Rural Families and Demographic Behaviour: Some Latin American Analogies." *Comparative Studies in Society and History*, 26 (1984), 251–79.

Axelrod, Bernard. "Historical Studies of Emigration from the United States." *International Migration Review*, 6 (Spring 1972), 32–49.

Baer, Werner. *The Brazilian Economy: Growth and Development*. 3d ed. New York: Praeger, 1989.

Baily, Samuel L. "The Italians and Organized Labor in the United States and Argentina: 1880–1910." *International Migration Review*, 1 (Summer 1967), 56–66.

Baily, Samuel L. "The Adjustment of Italian Immigrants in Buenos Aires and New York, 1870–1914," *American Historical Review*, 88 (April 1983), 281–305.

Barton, Josef J. *Peasants and Strangers: Italians, Rumanians, and Slovaks in an American City*. Cambridge: Harvard University Press, 1975.

Bastos de Avila, Fernando. *L'Immigration au Brésil: Contribution a une Théorie Générale de L'Immigration*. Rio de Janeiro: Libraria Agir Editora, 1956.

Becker, Klaus. "A Fundação e os Primeiros 30 Anos de Teutonia." In Faculdade de Filosofia da Universidade do Rio Grande do Sul, *Primeiro Coloquio de Estudos Teuto-Brasileiros*. Porto Alegre: Universidade Federal de RGS, 1963.

Bernard, William S. "Immigration: History of U.S. Policy." In Thernstrom, ed., *Harvard Encyclopedia of American Ethnic Groups*, (q.v.), 486–95.

Bethell, Leslie, ed. *Cambridge History of Latin America*. Vols. 4 and 5. Cambridge: Cambridge University Press, 1986.

Beyhaut, Gustave, et al. *Inmigración y Desarrollo Economico*. Buenos Aires: Seminario Interdisciplinario sobre el Desarrollo Economico y Social de la Argentina, 1961.

Beyhaut, Gustavo, R. Cortes Conde, H. Gorostegui, and S. Torrado. "Los Inmigrantes en el Sistema Ocupacional Argentina." In Torcuato S. DiTella, Gino Germani, Jorge Graciarena, y Colaboradores, *Argentina: Sociedad de Masas*. Buenos Aires: EUDEBA, Editorial Universitaria de Buenos Aires, 1966.

Bodnar, John. "Immigration, Kinship, and the Rise of Working-Class Realism in Industrial America." *Journal of Social History*, 20 (Fall 1980), 45–65.

Bodnar, John. *The Transplanted: A History of Immigrants in Urban America*. Bloomington: Indiana University Press, 1985.

Borges Pereira, João Baptista. *Italianos no Mundo Rural Paulista*. São Paulo: Livraria Pioneira Editora, Instituto de Estudos Brasileiros—USP, 1974.

Brazil. Instituto Brasileiro de Geografia e Estadistica. *Estadisticas Demografias: Côr.* Rio de Janeiro: IBGE, 1950.

Briggs, John W. "Fertility and Cultural Change among Families in Italy and America." *American Historical Review,* 91 (December 1986), 1129–45.

Britain. Parliamentary Papers, 1890–91, LXXXIII (C. 6424), 32–40. "Report by Consul Hearn on a Visit to Some of the Foreign Colonies in the State of Rio Grande do Sul. . . ." Reprinted in Erickson, ed., (*q.v.*), 176–84.

Bryce, James. *South America: Observations and Impressions.* New York: Macmillan, 1912.

Bunge, Alejandro, and Carlos Garcia Mata, "Immigration to Argentina." In Ferenczi and Willcox, (*q.v.*), II:143–60.

Burns, E. Bradford. *A History of Brazil.* New York: Columbia University Press, 1970.

Burns, E. Bradford. *The Poverty of Progress: Latin America in the Nineteenth Century.* Berkeley: University of California Press, 1980.

Canada. "The Urban and Rural Composition of Canada's Population." *Census 1971, Profile Studies 2.* Ottawa: Statistics Canada, January 1976.

Cardoso, Lawrence A. *Mexican Emigration to the United States, 1897–1931.* Tucson: University of Arizona Press, 1980.

Carneiro, Jose Fernando. *Imigração e Colonização no Brasil.* Rio de Janeiro: Universidade do Brasil, 1950.

Carvalho de Mello, Pedro. "Aspectos Economicos da Organização do Trabalho da Economia Cafeeira do Rio de Janeiro, 1850–1888." *Revista Brasileiro de Economia,* 32 (Jan.–March 1978), 19–68.

Chan, Sucheng. *This Bitter-Sweet Soil: The Chinese in California Agriculture, 1860–1910.* Berkeley: University of California Press, 1986.

Coats, R. H., and M. C. Maclean. *The American-Born in Canada: A Statistical Interpretation.* Toronto: The Ryerson Press, 1943.

Coletti, Umberto. "The Italian Immigrant." In Conference of Charities and Corrections, *Proceedings,* 1912, 249–54.

Commons, John R. *Races and Immigrants in America.* New York: Macmillan, 1920 (1907).

Conseil National de Recherche Scientifique. *Histoire Quantitative de Brésil.* Paris: CNRS, 1973.

Cornblit, Oscar. "European Immigrants in Argentine Industry and Politics." In Claudio Veliz, ed., *The Politics of Conformity in Latin America.* London: Oxford University Press, 1967.

Cortes Conde, Roberto. "La Expansión de la Economia Argentina entre 1800 y 1914 y el Papel de la Inmigración." *Cahiers du Monde Hispanique et Luso-brésilien,* 10 (1968), 67–88.

Cortes Conde, Roberto. *The First Stages of Modernization in Spanish America.* New York: Harper & Row, 1974.

Cortes Conde, Roberto. *El Progreso Argentina 1880–1915.* Buenos Aires: Editorial Sudamericana, 1979.

Cortes Conde, Roberto. "The Growth of the Argentine Economy, c. 1870–1914." In Bethell, ed., (*q.v.*), V:327–57.

Couty, Louis. *Le Brésil en 1884*. Rio de Janeiro: Far & Lino, 1884.

Daniels, Roger. *Asian America: Chinese and Japanese in the United States since 1850*. Seattle: University of Washington Press, 1988.

Dean, Warren. *The Industrialization of São Paulo, 1880–1945*. Austin: University of Texas Press, 1969.

Dean, Warren. "Remessas de Dinheiro dos Emigrantes Italianos do Brasil, Argentina, Uruguai e Estados Unidos de America (1884–1914)." *Anais de Historia* (Assis), 6 (1974), 231–37.

Dean, Warren. *Rio Claro: A Brazilian Plantation System, 1820–1920*. Stanford: Stanford University Press, 1976.

Dean, Warren. "The Brazilian Economy, 1870–1930." In Bethell, ed., (*q.v.*), V:685–724.

Denoon, Donald. *Settler Capitalism: The Dynamics of Dependent Development in the Southern Hemisphere*. Oxford: Clarendon Press, 1983.

Diaz Alejandro, Carlos F. *Essays on the Economic History of the Argentine Republic*. New Haven: Yale University Press, 1970.

Diaz Alejandro, Carlos F. "Argentina, Australia and Brazil before 1929." In Platt and Di Tella, eds., (*q.v.*), 95–109.

Diegues Junior, Manuel. *População e Propriedade da Terra no Brasil*. Washington: União Pan-Americana, 1959.

Doyle, David N. *Irish Americans, Native Rights and National Empires: The Structure, Divisions and Attitudes of the Catholic Minority in the Decade of Expansion, 1890–1901*. New York: Arno Press, 1976.

Duncan, Tim, and John Fogarty. *Australia and Argentina: On Parallel Paths*. Carlton, Victoria: Melbourne University Press, 1984.

Easterlin, Richard A. "Immigration: Economic and Social Characteristics." In Thernstrom, ed., (*q.v.*), 476–86.

Edelstein, Michael. *Overseas Investment in the Age of High Imperialism: The United Kingdom, 1850–1914*. New York: Columbia University Press, 1982.

Elliott, Bruce S. *Irish Migrants in the Canadas: A New Approach*. Kingston and Montreal: McGill-Queen's University Press, 1988.

Fausto, Boris. "Brazil: The Social and Political Structure of the First Republic, 1889–1930." In Bethell, ed., (*q.v.*), 779–830.

Fairchild, Henry Pratt. *The Melting-Pot Mistake*. Boston: Little, Brown and Company, 1926.

Foster, Keith. "The Barr Colonists: Their Arrival and Impact on the Canadian North-West." *Saskatchewan History*, 35 (1982), 81–100.

Friesen, Gerald. *The Canadian Prairies: A History*. Lincoln: University of Nebraska Press, 1984.

Gagan, David P. "Land, Population, and Social Change: The 'Critical Years' in Rural Canada West." *Canadian Historical Review*, 59 (September 1978), 293–318.

Gallo, Ezequiel. *La Pampa Gringa: La Colonización Agrícola en Santa Fe (1870–1895)*. Buenos Aires: Editorial Sudamericana, 1892.

Gallo, Ezequiel. "Los Italianos en los Origines de la Agricultura Argentina: Santa Fe (1870–1895)." In Francis Korn, ed., *Los Italianos en La Argentina*. Buenos Aires: Fundación Giovanni Agnelli, 1983.

Gallo, Ezequiel. "Argentina: Society and Politics, 1880–1916." in Bethell, ed., (*q.v.*), V:359–91.

Germani, Gino. *Politica y Sociedad en una Epoca de Transición: De la Sociedad Tradicional a la Sociedad de Masas*. Buenos Aires: Editorial Paidos, 1965.

Gilkey, George R. "The United States and Italy: Migration and Repatriation." *Journal of Developing Areas*, 2 (October 1967), 23–36.

Goodrich, Carter. "Argentina as a New Country." *Comparative Studies in Society and History*, 7 (1964), 70–88.

Grossman, James R. *Land of Hope: Chicago, Black Southerners, and the Great Migration*. Chicago: University of Chicago Press, 1989.

Hall, Michael M. "The Origins of Mass Immigration in Brazil, 1871–1914." Ph.D. diss., Columbia University, 1969.

Hall, Michael M. "Approaches to Immigration History." In Richard Graham and Peter H. Smith, eds., *New Approaches to Latin American History* (Austin: University of Texas Press, 1974), 180–84.

Hansen, Marcus Lee, and John Bartlet Brebner. *The Mingling of the Canadian and American Peoples*. New Haven: Yale University Press, 1940.

Hastings, Donald. "Japanese Emigration and Assimilation in Brazil." *International Migration Review*, 3 (Spring 1969), 32–53.

Heald, Morrell. "Business Attitudes toward European Immigration, 1880–1900." *Journal of Economic History*, 13 (Summer 1953), 291–304.

Heller, Jeffrey. "Little Shul on the Prairie." *Jerusalem Post* (International Edition), December 21–27, 1980.

Holloway, Thomas H. "Creating the Reserve Army: The Immigration Program of São Paulo, 1886–1930." *International Migration Review*, 12 (Summer 1978), 187–209.

Holloway, Thomas H. *Immigrants on the Land: Coffee and Society in São Paulo, 1886–1934*. Chapel Hill: University of North Carolina Press, 1980.

Howe, Irving. *World of Our Fathers*. New York: Harcourt Brace Jovanovich, 1976.

Hugon, Paul. *Demografia Brasileira: Ensaio de Demoeconomia Brasileira*. São Paulo: Atlas, Editora da Universidade de São Paulo, 1973.

Hutter, Lucy Maffei. *Imigração Italiana em São Paulo (1880–1889)*. São Paulo: Publicação do Instituto de Estudos Brasileiros, Universidade de São Paulo, 1972.

Hutter, Lucy Maffei. *Imigração Italiana em São Paulo de 1902 a 1914. O Processo Imigratorio*. São Paulo: Instituto de Estudos Brasileiros, Universidade de São Paulo, 1986.

Ichioka, Yuji. *The Issei: The World of the First Generation Japanese Immigrants, 1885–1924*. New York: Free Press, 1988.

Iwata, Masakazu. "The Japanese Immigrants in California Agriculture." *Agricultural History*, 36 (January 1962), 25–37.

Jakesova, Elena. "Emigrants from Slovakia—Immigrants to Canada as an Object of Historical Research." In Comité International des Sciences Historiques, (*q.v.*), 211–16.

Jefferson, Mark. *Peopling the Argentine Pampas*. New York: American Geographical Society, 1926.

Jenks, Jeremiah, and W. Jett Lauck. *The Immigration Problem: A Study of American Immigration Conditions and Needs*. 5th ed. New York: Funk & Wagnalls, 1922 (1911).

Jensen, Joan M. *Passage from India: Asian Indian Immigrants in North America*. New Haven: Yale University Press, 1988.

Katerberg, William H. "Canadian and American Immigration Policy from World War I to the Depression of the 1930s." Unpublished seminar paper, Department of History, University of Notre Dame, May 1990.

Katzman, Martin T. "The Brazilian Frontier in Comparative Perspective." *Comparative Studies in Society and History*, 17 (July 1975), 266–85.

Kaye, V. J. "The Ruthenians." *Canadian Slavonic Papers/Revue Canadienne des Slavistes*, 10 (1968).

Keyssar, Alex. *Out of Work: The First Century of Unemployment in Massachusetts*. New York: Cambridge University Press, 1986.

King, Miriam, and Steven Ruggles. "American Immigration, Fertility, and Race Suicide at the Turn of the Century." *Journal of Interdisciplinary History*, 20 (Winter 1990), 347–69.

Klein, Herbert S. "The Integration of Italian Immigrants into the United States and Argentina: A Comparative Analysis." *American Historical Review*, 88 (April 1983), 306–29.

Knoll, Tricia. *Becoming Americans: Asian Sojourners, Immigrants, and Refugees in the Western United States*. Portland, OR: Coast to Coast Books, 1982.

Kraut, Alan. *The Huddled Masses: The Immigrant in American Society, 1880–1921*. Arlington Heights, IL: Harlan Davidson, Inc., 1982.

Kuznets, Simon, and Ernest Rubin. *Immigration and the Foreign-Born*. New York: National Bureau of Economic Research, 1954.

Lafleur, Normand. *Les 'Chinois' de l'Est: ou la Vie Quotidienne des Québecois Émigrés aux États-Unis de 1840 à Nos Jours*. Ottawa: Les Éditions Lemeac, 1981.

Lane, A. T. *Solidarity or Survival? American Labor and European Immigrants, 1830–1924*. Westport, CT: Greenwood Press, 1987.

Langman, R. C. *Patterns of Setttlement in Southern Ontario: Three Studies*. Toronto: McClelland and Stewart Ltd., 1971.

Lavoie, Yolande. *L'Émigration des Canadiens aux États-Unis avant 1930: Mésure du Phénomène*. Montreal: Les Presses de l'Université de Montréal, 1972.

Leff, Nathaniel H. *Underdevelopment and Development in Brazil. I: Economic Structure and Change, 1822–1947*. London: George Allen & Unwin, 1982.

Leff, Nathaniel H., and Herbert S. Klein. "O Crescimento da População não Europeia antes do Inicio do Desenvolvimento no Brasil do Seculo XIX." *Anais de Historia* (Assis), 6 (1974), 51–70.

Lewis, Colin M. *British Railways in Argentina, 1857–1914: A Case Study of Foreign Investment.* Athlone: Published for the Institute of Latin American Studies, University of London, 1983.

Linhares, Maria Yedda, and Barbara Levy, "Aspectos da Historia Demografica e Social do Rio de Janeiro (1808–1889)." In Conseil National de Recherche Scientifique, (*q.v.*), 123–38.

Lisanti, Louis. "Problèmes de l'Histoire Quantitative au Brésil: Métrologie et Démographie." In Conseil National de Recherche Scientifique, (*q.v.*), 29–37.

Lobo, Eulalia Laymayer. "Evolution des Prix et du Côut de la Vie à Rio de Janeiro (1820–1930)." In Conseil National de Recherche Scientifique, (*q.v.*), 203–17.

Lombardi, Mary. "The Frontier in Brazilian History: An Historiographical Essay." *Pacific Historical Review,* 44 (November 1975), 437–58.

Luebke, Frederick C. *Germans in the New World: Essays in the History of Immigration.* Urbana: University of Illinois Press, 1990.

Lynch, Katherine A., Geraldine P. Mineau, and Douglas L. Anderton. "Estimates of Infant Mortality on the Western Frontier: The Use of Genealogical Data." *Historical Methods,* 18 (Fall 1985), 155–64.

Macdonald, Norman. *Canada: Immigration and Colonization 1841–1903.* Aberdeen: Aberdeen University Press, 1966.

Marcilio, Maria Luiza. "Accroissement de la Population. Évolution Historique de la Population Brésilienne jusqu'en 1872." In Universidade de São Paulo, *La Population du Brésil.* Paris: CICRED, 1974.

Martin, Chester. *'Dominion Lands' Policy.* Toronto: McClelland and Stewart Ltd., 1973.

Martinez, Alberto B. *El Brasil y la Argentina: Sus Respectivos Crecimientos.* Buenos Aires: Talleres Graficos Argentinos, 1922.

Mayo-Smith, Richmond. Review of three books on immigration. *Political Science Quarterly,* 2 (1887), 520–22.

McCormick, P. L. "The Doukhobors in 1904." *Saskatchewan History,* 35 (1982), 12–19.

McDougald, Mrs. James. "Cypress Hills Reminiscences." *Saskatchewan History,* 35 (1982).

McDougall, Duncan M. "Immigration into Canada, 1851–1920." *Canadian Journal of Economics and Political Science,* 27 (May 1961), 162–75.

McInnis, R. Marvin. "Childbearing and Land Availability: Some Evidence from Individual Household Data." In Ronald D. Lee, *Population Patterns in the Past.* New York: Academic Press, 1977, 201–27.

McInnis, Marvin. "Fertility Patterns in Late Nineteenth Century Ontario and Quebec." Unpublished paper, Social Science History Association meeting, Chicago, November 1988.

Melendy, H. Brett. *Asians in America: Filipinos, Koreans, and East Indians.* Boston: Twayne Publishers, 1977.

Merrick, Thomas W., and Douglas H. Graham. *Population and Economic Development in Brazil, 1800 to the Present*. Baltimore: Johns Hopkins University Press, 1979.

Meyerowitz, Joanne. "Women and Migration: Autonomous Female Migrants to Chicago, 1880–1930." *Journal of Urban History*, 13 (February 1987), 147–68.

Moran, Theodore H. "The 'Development' of Argentina and Australia: The Radical Party of Argentina and the Labor Party of Australia in the Process of Economic and Social Development." *Comparative Politics*, 3 (October 1970), 71–92.

Mortara, Giorgio. "The Development and Structure of Brazil's Population." In Joseph J. Spengler and Otis Dudley Duncan, eds., *Demographic Analysis: Selected Readings* (Glencoe: Free Press, 1956), 652–70.

Naylor, Douglas O. "Brazil." In Ferenczi and Willcox, eds., (*q.v.*), II:161–68.

Needell, Jeffrey D. *A Tropical Belle Epoque: Elite Culture and Society in Turn-of-the-Century Brazil*. Cambridge: Cambridge University Press, 1987.

Nery, M. F.-J. de Santa-Anna. *Le Brésil en 1889, avec une carte de l'Empire*. Paris: Librairie Charles Delagrave, 1889.

Nugent, Walter. "The People of the West since 1890." In Gerald D. Nash and Richard W. Etulain, eds., *The Twentieth-Century West: Historical Interpretations*. Albuquerque: University of New Mexico Press, 1989, 35–70.

Panebianco, Angelo. *Le Crisi della Modernizzazione. L'Esperienza del Brasile e dell'Argentina*. Naples, 1973.

Platt, D. C. M., and Guido di Tella, eds. *Argentina, Australia, and Canada: Studies in Comparative Development 1870–1965*. New York: St. Martin's Press, 1985.

Ramirez, Bruno. "The Emigration from Quebec to the USA, 1870–1915: Questions of Courses, Method, and Conceptualization." Working Paper, *Rapport No. 1*, Université de Montréal, February 1988.

Riegelhaupt, Joyce, and Shepard Forman. "Bodo Was Never Brazilian: Economic Integration and Rural Development among a Contemporary Peasantry." *Journal of Economic History*, 30 (March 1970), 100–116.

Rivarola, Horacio C. *Las Transformaciones de la Sociedad Argentina y sus Consecuencias Institucionales (1853 a 1910)*. Buenos Aires: Imprenta de Coni Hermanos, 1911.

Roberts, Peter. *The New Immigration: A Study of the Industrial and Social Life of Southeastern Europeans in America*. New York: The Macmillan Company, 1914.

Rock, David. "Argentina in 1914: The Pampas, The Interior, Buenos Aires." In Bethell, ed., (*q.v.*), V:393–418.

Rosenwaike, Ira. "Two Generations of Italians in America: Their Fertility Experience." *International Migration Review*, 7 (Fall 1973), 271–80.

Rothwell, Stuart Clark. *The Old Italian Colonial Zone of Rio Grande do Sul, Brazil*. Porto Alegre: Edições da Faculdade de Filosofia, 1959.

Royick, Alexander. "Ukrainian Settlements in Alberta." *Canadian Slavonic Papers/Revue Canadienne des Slavistes*, 10 (1968).

Sanchez-Albornoz, Nicolas. "The Population of Latin America, 1850–1930." In Bethell, ed., (*q.v.*), IV:121–54.

Sanchez-Albornoz, Nicolas, and Jose Luis Moreno. *La Población de America Latina: Bosquejo Historico*. Buenos Aires: Paidoes, 1968.

São Paulo. Universidade. Centro de Estudos de Dinámicas Populacional. "La Population du Brésil." São Paulo: CICRED, 1975.

Schultheiss, Herman J. *Report on European Immigration to the United States of America, and the Causes which Incite the Same; with Recommendations for the Further Restriction of Undesirable Immigration*. Washington: Government Printing Office, 1893.

Scobie, James R. *Argentina: A City and a Nation*. New York: Oxford University Press, 1964.

Scobie, James R. *Revolution on the Pampas: A Social History of Argentine Wheat, 1860–1910*. Austin: University of Texas Press, 1964.

Scobie, James R. *Buenos Aires: Plaza to Suburb, 1870–1910*. New York: Oxford University Press, 1974.

Seller, Maxine Schwartz, ed. *Immigrant Women*. Philadelphia: Temple University Press, 1981.

Shepard, R. Bruce. "The Origins of the Oklahoma Black Migration to the Canadian Plains." *Canadian Journal of History/Annales Canadiennes d'Histoire*, 23 (April 1988), 1–23.

Shortridge, James R. "The Heart of the Prairie: Culture Areas in the Central and Northern Great Plains." *Great Plains Quarterly*, 8 (Fall 1988), 206–21.

Shumsky, Neil Larry. "The Extent and Significance of Return Migration from the United States." In Cazemajou, ed., (*q.v.*), 57–68.

Slenes, Robert W. "The Demography and Economics of Brazilian Slavery, 1850–1888." Ph.D. diss., Stanford University, 1976.

Smith, T. Lynn. *Brazil: People and Institutions*. 4th ed. Baton Rouge: Louisiana State University Press, 1972.

Solberg, Carl. *Immigration and Nationalism: Argentina and Chile, 1890–1914*. Austin: University of Texas Press, 1970.

Solberg, Carl. "Mass Migrations in Argentina, 1870–1970." In McNeill and Adams, eds., (*q.v.*), 146–70.

Solberg, Carl E. *The Prairies and the Pampas: Agrarian Policy in Canada and Argentina, 1880–1930*. Stanford: Stanford University Press, 1987.

Solomon, Barbara Miller. *Ancestors and Immigrants: A Changing New England Tradition*. Cambridge: Harvard University Press, 1956.

Stein, Stanley J. *Vassouras: A Brazilian Coffee County, 1850–1900*. Cambridge: Harvard University Press, 1957.

Stolarik, M. Mark. "From Field to Factory: The Historiography of Slovak Immigration to the United States." *International Migration Review*, 10 (Spring 1976), 81–102.

Sutcliffe, Anthony. *Towards the Planned City: Germany, Britain, the United States and France, 1780–1914*. Oxford: Basil Blackwell, 1981.

Taylor, Carl C. *Rural Life in Argentina*. Baton Rouge: Louisiana State University Press, 1948.

Thernstrom, Stephan, ed. *Harvard Encyclopedia of American Ethnic Groups*. Cambridge: Belknap Press of Harvard University Press, 1980.

Thomas, Brinley. *Migration and Economic Growth: A Study of Great Britain and the Atlantic Economy*. 2d ed. Cambridge: Cambridge University Press, 1973.

Thompson, Warren S., and P. K. Whelpton. *Population Trends in the United States*. New York: McGraw-Hill Book Company, 1933.

Tocqueville, Alexis de *Democracy in America*. 2 vols. Ed. J. P. Mayer. Trans. George Lawrence. Garden City, NY: Anchor Books, 1969.

Topik, Steven. "Recent Studies on the Economic History of Brazil." *Latin American Research Review*, 23 (1988), 175–95.

Truesdell, Leon E. *The Canadian Born in the United States: An Analysis of the Statistics of the Canadian Element in the Population of the United States 1850 to 1930*. New Haven: Yale University Press, 1943.

Tsai, Shih-shan Henry. *The Chinese Experience in America*. Bloomington: Indiana University Press, 1986.

United States. "Abstracts of Reports of the Immigration Commission." Senate Document 747. 61st Congress, 3d Session. Washington: Government Printing Office, 1911.

Vangelista, Chiara. "Immigrazione, Struttura Produttiva e Mercato del Lavoro in Argentina e in Brasile (1876–1914)." *Annali della Fondazione Luigi Einaudi* (Turin), 9 (1975), 197–216.

Vecoli, Rudolph J., and Suzanne M. Sinke, eds. *A Century of European Migrations, 1830–1930*. Urbana: University of Illinois Press, 1991.

Vedder, R. K., and L. E. Gallaway. "Settlement Patterns of Canadian Emigrants to the United States, 1850–1960." *The Canadian Journal of Economics/Revue Canadienne d'Économique*, 2 (August 1970), 00–00.

Vianna Moog, Clodomir. *Bandeirantes and Pioneers*. New York: Basic Books, 1964.

Viotti da Costa, Emilia. "Brazil: The Age of Reform, 1870–1889." In Bethell, ed., (*q.v.*), V:725–78.

Wakatsuki, Yasuo. "Japanese Emigration to the United States, 1866–1924: A Monograph." *Perspectives in American History*, 12 (1979), 387–516.

Walker, Francis Amasa. "Restriction of Immigration." *Atlantic Monthly*, 77 (June 1896), 822–29.

Ward, Betty. "Trek of the Doukhobors." *Saskatchewan History*, 35 (1982), 17–24.

Warner, Donald F. *The Idea of Continental Union: Agitation for the Annexation of Canada to the United States, 1849–1893*. Lexington: University of Kentucky Press, 1960.

Widdis, Randy William. "With Scarcely a Ripple: English Canadians in Northern New York State at the Beginning of the Twentieth Century." *Journal of Historical Geography*, 13 (1987), 169–92.

Widdis, Randy William. " 'We Breathe the Same Air': Eastern Ontarian Migration to Watertown, New York." *New York History*, 68 (July 1987), 261–80.

Widdis, Randy William. "Scale and Context: Approaches to the Study of Canadian Migration Patterns in the Nineteenth Century." *Social Science History*, 12 (Fall 1988), 269–89.

Wilcox, Jerry, and Hilda H. Golden. "Prolific Immigrants and Dwindling Natives? Fertility Patterns in Western Massachusetts, 1850 and 1880." *Journal of Family History*, 7 (Fall 1982), 265–88.

Wirth, John D. *Minas Gerais in the Brazilian Federation, 1889–1937*. Stanford: Stanford University Press, 1977.

Zaslow, Morris. *The Opening of the Canadian North, 1870–1914*. Toronto/Montreal: McClelland and Stewart Ltd., 1971.

Zavala, Silvio. "The Frontiers of Hispanic America." In Walker D. Wyman and Clifton B. Kroeber, *The Frontier in Perspective*. Madison: University of Wisconsin Press, 1957, 35–58.

INDEX

WALTER NUGENT is Andrew V. Tackes Professor of History at the University of Notre Dame and author of *Structures of American Social History*.